AFRICAN ISSUES

**Losing
your Land**

AFRICAN ISSUES

AFRICAN ISSUES

**Losing
your Land**

Edited by
An Ansoms
& Thea Hilhorst

Dispossession
in the Great Lakes

JC JAMES CURREY

James Currey
an imprint of
Boydell & Brewer Ltd
PO Box 9, Woodbridge
Suffolk IP12 3DF (GB)
www.jamescurrey.com
and of
Boydell & Brewer Inc.
668 Mt Hope Avenue
Rochester, NY 14620-2731 USA
www.boydellandbrewer.corn

© Contributors 2014
First published 2014

British Library Cataloguing in Publication Data
A catologue record for this book is available on request from the British Library

ISBN 978-1-84701-105-3 (James Currey paper)

The publisher has no responsibility for the continued existence or accuracy of URLs for
external or third-party internet websites referred to in this book, and does not guarantee
that any content on such websites is, or will remain, accurate or appropriate.

This publication is printed on acid-free paper

Typeset in 9/11 Melior with Optima display
by Kate Kirkwood

CONTENTS

LIST OF ILLUSTRATIONS

NOTES ON CONTRIBUTORS

An Ansoms is assistant professor in development studies at the Université catholique de Louvain (Belgium). She is involved in research on rural development in land-scarce (post-) conflict environments, and particularly focuses on the Great Lakes Region in Africa. She recently co-edited two books, *Natural Resources and Local Livelihoods in the Great Lakes Region: A Political Economy Perspective* (Palgrave, 2011) and *Emotional and Ethical Challenges for Field Research in Africa: The Story Behind the Findings* (Palgrave, 2013).

Giuseppe Cioffo is a PhD candidate at the Université catholique de Louvain (Belgium) where he studies processes of agrarian modernization in Rwanda. He is interested in the social and environmental dynamics linked to green revolution models and peasant family farming in developing countries.

Klara Claessens is a PhD candidate in development studies at the Institute of Development Policy and Management (IOB) at the University of Antwerp (Belgium). Her research focuses on changing land access and distribution patterns in South Kivu, Eastern DRC.

Dan Fahey is working for the United Nations in the Democratic Republic of the Congo. He has a PhD from UC Berkeley and a master's degree from Tufts University. His research focuses on conflict, natural resources, and development in the Great Lakes Region of Africa.

Sara Geenen is a post-doctoral researcher in development studies at the Institute of Development Policy and Management (IOB) at the University of Antwerp (Belgium). Her research focuses on the political economy of access to gold mining in South Kivu, DR Congo, and particularly on the articulation between industrial and artisanal gold mining.

Linda Haartsen is a consultant in Natural Resources Management. During 2011-2012 she lived in Uganda, and participated in field research on tenure insecurity, land disputes and land governance reform.

Thea Hilhorst is a senior advisor at the Royal Tropical Institute in Amsterdam. Her research focuses on land governance, local institutions, natural resource management, all in relation to livelihoods – mostly in sub-Saharan Africa. She also works on these issues in programmes and projects with national and international organizations, both governmental and non-governmental. Since 2006, she has been working on land and other governance issues in Burundi.

Jana Hönke is a lecturer in international relations at the University of Edinburgh and senior research associate at the research centre Governance in Areas of Limited Statehood, Freie Universität Berlin. Her research revolves around governance with and beyond the State, transnational business, security and policing, international political sociology and post-colonial theory.

Chris Huggins specializes in the political economy of land tenure, natural resources rights, and agricultural reform, particularly in post-conflict contexts. His fieldwork focuses on the Great Lakes Region. He is co-author (with Scott Leckie) of *Conflict and Housing, Land, and Property Rights: A Handbook on Issues, Frameworks, and Solutions* (Oxford University Press, 2011).

Doreen Kobusingye is a PhD candidate at the African Studies Centre at Leiden University (the Netherlands). From the end of 2011 to early 2013 she was based in Gulu, researching land conflicts and decentralized land governance in Northern Uganda, as part of the NWO-Wotro funded 'Grounding Land Governance' research programme.

Vincent Manirakiza is a PhD candidate at the Université catholique de Louvain (Belgium). He is involved in research on urbanization issues with a focus on socio-environmental impacts of the modernization process of Kigali City (Rwanda).

Charles Muchunguzi is a lecturer at the faculty of Development Studies, at Mbarara University of Science and Technology (Uganda). Over the last decade he has conducted research on the dynamics of landownership in the Uganda cattle corridor.

Emery Mudinga is a PhD candidate at the Université catholique de Louvain (Belgium). He is involved in sociopolitical land-conflicts analysis, conflict transformation and State-building in the DRC.

Jude Murison is a Senior Research Fellow in Governance and Regulation at the University of Edinburgh. Her research focuses on examining the laws governing human rights, forced migration, health and agricultural production, their interplay into national policies, and their implementation on the ground.

Aymar Nyenyezi Bisoka is a PhD candidate in Political and Social Sciences at the Université catholique de Louvain (Belgium). For several years he worked in the field of development assistance in the Great Lakes Region. He is currently pursuing his doctoral research on land grabbing in Burundi.

Jean-Philippe Peemans is Professor Emeritus at Université catholique de Louvain (Belgium) where he has been President of the Institute of Development Studies. His topics of teaching, research and publications are mainly in the fields of development theory and policies, comparative development history, and in African and Asian studies.

Claudia Piacenza has completed the Erasmus Mundus MSc programme in Rural Development, defending her thesis at Wageningen University (the Netherlands) in 2012. As part of this, she conducted three months of research on the gendered impact of large land acquisitions on the Kalangala islands.

Mathijs van Leeuwen is Assistant Professor at the Centre for International Conflict Analysis and Management (CICAM), Institute of Management Reseach (IMR), at the Radboud University Nijmegen; and researcher at the African Studies Centre at Leiden University (the Netherlands). At the latter, he coordinates the NWO-Wotro funded research programme 'Grounding Land Governance'. His research interests include land conflict and local governance reform, post-conflict peacebuilding and development, and civil society.

Ilse Zeemeijer completed her MA programme in International Development Studies at Utrecht University (the Netherlands) in 2012. In 2011, she did research on new corporate land acquisitions and the impact on local development. She conducted fieldwork on six contested commercial acquisitions in collaboration with the Uganda Land Alliance, a consortium of Ugandan NGOs.

ACKNOWLEDGEMENTS

The editors and authors of this volume would like first and foremost to express their gratitude to the reviewers of this book. Their input and recommendations were constructive and very important in sharpening our arguments. We furthermore thank the Institute for the Analysis of Change in Contemporary and Historical Societies (IACCHOS) of the Université catholique de Louvain, and its administrative assistant, Marie-Charlotte Declève, for her meticulous work in preparing the final version of the volume for publication. Our gratitude also goes to Jaqueline Mitchell of James Currey for her enthusiasm and follow-up on this project. And finally, we would like to thank everyone who participated in the research that lies at the basis of the various chapters in the book. Their involvement allowed the authors of this volume to reflect on the complex dynamics on the ground.

LIST OF ABBREVIATIONS & ACRONYMS

ADEPED	Action pour le développement des peuples en détresse
ADMR	Action pour le développement des milieux ruraux
AFDL	Alliance des forces démocratiques pour la libération du Congo
AGTER	Améliorer la gouvernance de la terre, de l'eau et des ressources naturelles
APC	Action pour la paix et la concorde
APCLS	Alliance patriote du Congo libre et souverain
APEF	Action pour la promotion des enfants et de la femme
ARLPI	Acholi Religious Leaders Peace Initiative
AVEGA	Association des veuves du génocide Agahozo
CARG	Conseils agricoles et ruraux de gestion
CDM	Comité de dialogue et de médiation
CEGEMI	Centre d'expertise en gestion minière
CMDK	Coopérative minière pour le développement de Kalehe
CNDD-FDD	Conseil national pour la défense de la démocratie-Forces de défense de la démocratie
CNDP	Congrès national pour la défense du peuple
CNKi	Comité national du Kivu
CNTB	Commission nationale des terres et autres biens
CODELU	Comité de développement de Luhwindja
COMBECKA	Coopérative minière pour le bien-être communautaire de Kalehe
COMIKA	Coopérative minière de Kalimbi
CONAPAC	Confédération nationale des producteurs agricoles du Congo
CRG	Conflict Research Group
CSR	Corporate Social Responsibility
DFID	Department for International Development (UK)
DRC	Democratic Republic of Congo
DSCRP	Document de stratégie de croissance et de réduction de la pauvreté
EDPRS	Economic Development & Poverty Reduction Strategy

EIC	État indépendant du Congo
FAO	Food and Agriculture Organization (of the United Nations)
FARDC	Forces armées de la République démocratique du Congo
FARG	Fonds d'assistance aux rescapés du génocide
FEC	Federation of Congolese Enterprises
FFM	Farmer Model of Modernization
FDLR	Forces démocratiques de libération du Rwanda
FNL	Forces nationales de libération
FRODEBU	Front démocratique burundais
FRPI	Forces de résistance patriotique d'Ituri
GOR	Government of Rwanda
GOU	Government of Uganda
ICC	International Criminal Court
ICG	International Crisis Group
IDP	Internally Displaced Persons
IFC	International Financial Corporation
ILC	International Land Coalition
IMF	International Monetary Fund
IPDP	Integrated Pastoral Development Project
LAV	Laissez l'Afrique vivre
LDGL	Ligue des droits de la personne dans la région des Grands Lacs
LEMU	Land and Equity Movement of Uganda
LORI	Libération des opprimés et rejetés de l'Ituri
LRA	Lord's Resistance Army
M23	March 23 Movement
MAPE	Ministère de l'agriculture, de la pêche et de l'élevage
MINAGRI	Ministry of Agriculture and Animal Resources
MINECOFIN	Ministry of Finance and Economic Planning
MININFRA	Ministry of Infrastructure
MINIREISO	Ministry of Rehabilitation and Social Integration
MINITERE	Ministry of Lands, Environment, Forestry, Water and Mines
MLHUD	Ministry of Lands, Housing and Urban Development
MONUC	Mission de l'Organisation des Nations unies en République démocratique du Congo
NEPAD	New Partnership for Africa's Development
NGO	Non-governmental Organization
NLTRP	National Land Tenure Reform Programme
NRM	National Resistance Movement
NURC	National Unity and Reconciliation Commission
OAG	Observatoire de l'action gouvernementale
OGP	Observatoire gouvernance et paix
OLL	Organic Land Law
PAP	Plan d'actions prioritaires

PARECO	Patriotes résistants congolais
PDDAA	Programme détaillé de développement de l'agriculture africaine
PVK	Préfecture de la ville de Kigali
PWC	Price Waterhouse Coopers
RCD	Rassemblement congolais pour la démocratie
RCD-ML	Rassemblement congolais pour la démocratie-Mouvement de Libération
RCN	Réseau citoyens-Citizens Network
RISD	Rwanda Initiative for Sustainable Development
RPA	Radio publique africaine
RPF	Rwandan Patriotic Front
RTR	Radio-télévision Renaissance
RwF	Rwandan Francs
SAP	Structural Adjustment Programme
SEASSCAM	Service d'assistance et d'encadrement du *Small-Scale Mining*
SEREMI	Société d'études, de recherche et d'exploitation minière
SMDG	Société minière de Goma
SNIP	Service national d'intelligence et de protection
SPAT	Strategic Plan for the Transformation of Agriculture
TTP	Tent Temporary Permanent
UJCC	Union des jeunes Congolais pour le changement
UNDP	United Nations Development Programme
UNDSS	United Nations Department of Safety and Security
UNHCR	United Nations High Commissioner for Refugees
UNSC	United Nations Security Council
UPDF	Ugandan People's Defence Force
UPRONA	Union pour le progrès national
USGS	United States Geological Survey
UWA	Uganda Wildlife Authority
VLIR	Vlaamse Interuniversitaire Raad
WFP	World Food Programme

1

Introduction

Causes & Risks of Dispossession & Land Grabbing in the Great Lakes Region

AN ANSOMS
& THEA HILHORST

Contemporary contestations in the land arena in Africa's Great Lakes Region are often embedded in long-term historical trajectories in which struggles over land are closely associated with strife and violence. Indeed, the region has for decades been torn by local and regional conflict, war and instability. Today's peace in central Africa is brittle and further conflict never seems far away. Yet however fragile the current situation, new and old underexploited opportunities appear to rebound to the surface, including within the land arena.

In fact, the struggles over land taking place today in the Great Lakes Region tie in with a broader trend of growing competition over land across Africa. In a context of globalization and liberalization, the continent is experiencing a rush to commercialize its natural resources. Land, over the past decade or so, has increasingly become a commodity and a source of fierce competition between internal and external forces. Since 2000, the rate of land transfers has been picking up speed, from the highest national to the lowest local level. These transfers are not always voluntary or transparent. They commonly take place without the consent of local actors or their full understanding of what the transfer implies in terms of present and future land rights. In many cases, local farmers' interests are not (fully) taken into account or even bluntly ignored. To many individuals, loss of land implies a loss of livelihood, particularly given their lack of access to income-generating alternatives. Moreover, land is not just an economic asset; it is also a social, cultural and political space with great relevance to the social, psychological and emotional wellbeing of local populations. Hence the consequences of losing one's land rights extend beyond the economic realm: the rush for land may also be framed in terms of 'soul and identity grabbing'.

Non-transparent and non-voluntary land transactions are increasingly referred to as 'land grabbing', a term now also widely used by NGOs, policymakers and academics. As a notion, it is firmly in the global spotlight. However, 'land grabbing' is a value-loaded term and its definition is not straightforward. What makes a land transaction an instance of land grabbing? The International Land Coalition (ILC) – an alliance of inter-governmental organizations (e.g. World Bank and the Food and Agriculture Organization of the United Nations [FAO]) and civil society organizations (e.g. Oxfam) – has defined land grabbing as acquisitions and concessions that share one or several of the following characteristics:

(i)   in violation of human rights, particularly the equal rights of women;

(ii) not based on free, prior and informed consent of the affected land users;

(iii) not based on a thorough assessment, or in disregard of social, economic and environmental impacts, including the way they are gendered;

(iv) not based on transparent contracts that specify clear and binding commitments about activities, employment and benefits sharing, and;

(v)   not based on effective democratic planning, independent oversight and meaningful participation (extract from the *Tirana Declaration of the International Land Coalition*).[1]

'Grabbing', according to this definition, has connotations of an involuntary transaction, stealth, deceit, displacement and cheating. Still, the definition does not take into account that even the apparent legality and formalization of a land transfer or land use change can cover up a de facto land grab, particularly in contexts where the legal and formal institutions have been instrumentalized by powerful actors for private or political gain. Hence, an apparently 'legal' land transaction may nonetheless be vividly resented locally if not perceived as legitimate by those losing their land rights.

Respect for principles such as the transparency of a land transaction process, in accordance with agreed procedures and involving consultation and broad consent of the local population, may distinguish a transfer from a grab. Still, what is framed by some as local-level consultation and consent is not necessarily perceived as such by all local actors involved. Moreover, the true impact of land deals on local living conditions often only becomes clear after years or even decades, when it may turn out to be far less beneficial to local actors than anticipated at the outset. The authors of this book therefore apply a more comprehensive definition of land grabbing that also takes into consideration 'what is being grabbed, by whom, from whom, for what, and with what effects, and [that] draws attention to injustice and elite capture of resources' (Hall, 2011: 207).[2]

---

[1]   This is an extract from the Tirana Declaration of the International Land Coalition. Source: International Land Coalition, 2011. *Tirana Declaration*. International Global Assembly 2011, Tirana (Albania). Online at: http://www.landcoalition.org/sites/default/files/aom11/Tirana_Declaration_ILC_2011_ENG.pdf (date of last access: 17 October 2013).

[2]   According to Hall, if 'land grabbing' is approached in this manner, it becomes a relevant analytical tool. Source: Hall, R., 2011. 'Land grabbing in Southern Africa: the many faces of the investor rush'. Review of African Political Economy, vol. 38, no. 128, pp. 193-214.

Land grabbing is approached here within a broader context of unfolding global agrarian transformations whereby the bargaining position of smallholder farmers is weakening. We refer not only to the importance of land in securing people's economic livelihoods, but also to the social and symbolic value of land, to the way in which it is embedded in smallholders' 'way of life', and how it constitutes a crucial element to their identities. Furthermore, we consider the various forms of land grabbing in their specific historical and societal contexts, often characterized by extreme conflictuality and highly unequal power relations.

Clearly, involuntary and non-transparent land transfers are a topical issue in the Central African Great Lakes Region. Contested land transfers occur at all levels – within families, between neighbours and in communities – and may involve official and customary authorities, armed groups, and outside actors. Indeed, as this region is one of the most densely populated rural areas in Africa, land is scarce. Increased competition over land may contribute to already existing tensions; and recurrent conflicts over land may hinder a return to local-level peace and stability, while feeding animosities between competing groups. More specifically, land concentration in the hands of local elites and land acquisitions by external actors in these highly populated regions can have an immense impact on local living conditions, and may feed local-level frustration.

This book discusses local instances of 'land grabbing' in the Great Lakes Region on the basis of case studies in Eastern Democratic Republic of Congo, Southwest Uganda, Burundi and Rwanda. These four countries are connected politically and culturally, as well as in the struggle for control of natural resources and minerals. Political alliances and rivalries extend across the national borders. Violence in one country has the potential to spill over to the neighbouring States. All four settings are characterized by intense land scarcity, while smallholder agriculture is the main livelihood strategy for a majority of the population. However, despite strong historical, cultural and economic similarities, land governance and its institutions vary widely across the region. An in-depth analysis of land right conflicts will allow us to draw parallels between the forces involved in competition over land in the different settings. It will furthermore enable us to specify under which conditions land transactions may be labelled as involuntary or non-transparent. Moreover, even if there are no overt violations to be observed in this respect, we will reflect upon the longer-term consequences of legally accepted forms of land concentration. In addition, we will focus on how local populations exert agency and organize local resistance against the threat of loss of land rights.

The chapter by Jean-Philippe Peemans ('Land Grabbing and Development History: The Congolese Experience') emphasizes the importance of adopting a historical perspective on the issue of land grabbing. Peemans considers the case of the Democratic Republic of Congo. The chapter identifies five previous waves of land grabbing, and frames the current sixth wave as another episode in a long history of policies aiming to 'capture' the peasantry. The chapter furthermore illustrates how – throughout the six waves of land grabbing – rural communities have always exerted agency, through their resilience in holding on to land and their capacity to confront the anti-peasant bias of policymakers. Whereas in the past, resistance often occurred underground, the sixth wave of land grabbing is met with more public forms of opposition. Peemans describes how peasant organizations affected the wording of the agricultural code, and how the position of rural communities and smallholder farmers has become a theme in national policy debates.

The subsequent chapter by Dan Fahey ('This Land is my Land: Land Grabbing in Ituri') focuses on the Ituri region in Eastern Congo. This detailed case study covers a period of over a hundred years. It analyses the negotiated nature of the Congolese State, described by Fahey as 'a pluralistic configuration of interests, each struggling for its own legitimacy and power'. Profound shifts in the configuration of power within those state structures have, throughout history, been instrumentalized by more powerful actors as a means of legitimizing their own land claims and obtaining some form of official documentation issued by whoever happens to hold power at a given moment. Such actions provoke counter-claims over land, which are commonly formalized by the next strongman. The ethnic dimension is highly significant, although intra-ethnic competition over land also occurs. All this results in a complex set of overlapping claims, often formalized at some point in time. Consequently, efforts to reach definitive solutions through the implementation of a formal legislative framework stand little chance of success. However, coming to a resolution that is acceptable to all conflicting parties is crucial to the viability of the peace process, as smouldering land disputes 'contain the seeds of future violence'.

Sara Geenen and Jana Hönke in Chapter 4 ('Land Grabbing by Mining Companies: Local Contentions and State Reconfiguration in South Kivu') discuss an instance of land transfer in the context of mining in Eastern DRC. Competition over valuable mineral resources in the underground is closely associated with land grabbing. This chapter provides further evidence of Peemans's assertion that the ambition of the State authorities to gain control of the hinterlands is an important element in understanding ongoing land struggles. Indeed, Geenen and Hönke argue that the Congolese government is deploying a strategy to (re)centralize control over mining rents. Hence it prefers to transfer mining concessions to multinational players, with whom authorities are able to deal more easily than with a multitude of artisanal miners or local enterprises. Part of the international community applauds this strategy, assuming that it enhances the prospects of tangible developmental effects, given that multinational mining companies must conform to global standards of corporate social responsibility. However, as Geenen and Hönke demonstrate, mining rents may nonetheless be captured by local elites in an effort to reinforce their own power positions. The chapter vividly describes the power play among local elites: while some have tried to consolidate their authority through coalition building with the mining company involved, others have committed to organizing opposition against the concern. The end result is that, despite some improvements in operational standards on the mining sites, most people's living conditions have barely improved or may even have deteriorated.

In Chapter 5 Klara Claessens, Emery Mudinga and An Ansoms ('Competition over Soil and Subsoil: Land Grabbing by Local Elites in Eastern DRC') also deal with land struggles in Eastern Congo. The cases discussed in this chapter again show how negotiations over access to and control over land are shaped by historical evolutions and broader societal events at the local, national and regional levels. This chapter analyses competition over land between different ethnic groups, and examines how these struggles are rooted in a history of violence, cross-border migration, and regional instability. Moreover, contemporary land conflicts can work as a catalyst for the (re)formation of armed groups and for renewed local violence that has the potential to spill over. This chapter further illustrates how successful control over land rights depends upon actors' capacity to mobilize support, requiring an ability to efficiently instrumentalize the legitimacy of a variety of institutions, ranging from the Congolese army to state officials at various administrative levels, as well as to a variety of customary authorities. Although such institutional confusion creates opportunities for the less powerful actors and groups to contest the authorities and the roles of local elites, the latter often find themselves in a 'stronger' position, not only in terms of financial capacity but also, and even more importantly, in terms of formal and informal institutional connectedness. This dimension of political economy needs to be addressed when working towards a more equal playing field.

In Chapter 6, by Mathijs van Leeuwen et al., the focus switches to Uganda ('The Continuities in Contested Land Acquisitions in Uganda'). The authors arrive at similar conclusions as those reached in the chapters on DRC. They stress that current practices of land grabbing in Uganda are not isolated incidents, but are unfolding in a context of internal political and societal developments. In theory, Uganda – alongside Rwanda – has made more progress than the other countries of the Great Lakes Region in providing legal tenure security. In practice, however, civil violence and authoritarian rule have often enabled forms of land grabbing, while the land reforms of the past fifteen years have remained ineffective. Moreover, what appear to be 'new' forms of land grabbing are in fact merely 'the latest episode in a history of contested changes in ownership over the land'. The role of the current government is problematic in two ways. First and foremost, the failure of the Museveni government to effectively deal with injustices from the past has contributed to an overall popular distrust in the ability of formal institutions to deal with land conflicts. Second, the national elites – in addition to elites at the local level – continue to play a major role in common instances of land grabbing through the exploitation of ethnic allegiances and political patronage networks. In addition, the current government's backing for a discourse of development and modernization of the agricultural sector is threatening the tenure security of customary landowners. The new land policy, which was approved in 2013, may create an opportunity to improve this situation, but this will require a degree of 'political will'.

From Uganda, the spotlight turns in Chapter 7 to Burundi, as Aymar Nyenyezi and An Ansoms ('Land Grabbing and Power Relations in Burundi: Practical Norms and Real Governance') consider land conflicts involving political elites and various groups of 'ordinary citizens'. This chapter again shows how history shapes contemporary land conflicts. It highlights how patronage networks, clientelism and nepotism have continued to play a central role in land issues, regardless of which elite group holds power. The actors involved in the land conflicts under scrutiny call upon a broad range of existing normative frameworks: legal provisions, arrangements arising from mediation efforts, provisions from the Arusha Peace Agreement, and customary norms. The chapter also demonstrates that the 'norms' that ultimately prevail in such land conflicts result from the power play amongst the elites. Competing power holders may back up a weaker group in a land conflict to support their own electorate or to undermine political adversaries. When the national-level power constellation changes, the odds in micro-level land conflicts may turn overnight and seemingly settled disputes may be reignited. Competition between different ethnic groups is an important factor, but so too are rivalries between political parties. However, people do tend to act when faced with the risk of losing their land. Power relations may be modified in response to the contestation strategies developed by subordinate actors at the micro level, in their attempts to turn the odds in the land conflict into their favour. Hence the chapter specifically highlights the importance of reinforcing the agency of subordinate groups in the land arena and emphasizes the crucial role of civil society organizations and the media in this respect.

Chapters 8, 9 and 10 deal with Rwanda. First, Chris Huggins ('Land Grabbing and Land Tenure Security in Post-Genocide Rwanda') describes and discusses episodes of contested land transfers and land grabbing in Rwanda since 1994. Huggins analyses a variety of land redistribution processes and places these processes in a broader historical perspective. The land transfers described are often legal and justified by the national authorities on grounds that they serve national economic development, national security, or other national interests. Huggins nonetheless considers such land transfers to be 'problematic' if they lack a regulatory basis, if they are not implemented in accordance with a systematic and transparent process (whereby the same rules apply to all actors involved), or if they are not clearly in the public interest. The author subsequently reflects on the Rwandan government's responses to problematic land transfers. Compared to Burundi and, even more so, the DRC, Rwanda has a strong State, in terms of both its capacity to define a regulatory framework and its power to enforce policy. Moreover, the Rwandan Government has a reputation for 'zero tolerance for corruption'. However, in the land arena, only some of the problematic land transfers have been halted or reversed. Huggins argues that this is due to the underlying belief of Rwandan policymakers that large-scale agriculture (the type of agricultural exploitation pursued by most land grabbers) will eventually replace small-scale subsistence farming. In addition, the author raises the political dimension, drawing attention to the impunity of many high-level government or military officials involved in land grabbing.

Chapter 9, by An Ansoms, Giuseppe Cioffo, Chris Huggins and Jude Murison, ('The Reorganization of Rural Space in Rwanda: Habitat Concentration, Land Consolidation, and Collective Marshland Cultivation'), builds upon the analysis presented in the chapter by Huggins. It further explores the influence of land use regulation policies on land rights and livelihoods of smallholder farmers living in rural settings. It is the Rwandan government's intention to promote a professional, market-driven and efficient agricultural sector, which requires a reorganization of human habitat, land tenure, and cultivation systems. The government is putting in place the legal foundations and is developing its capacity to implement such policies. However, these ambitions contrast with current Rwandan habitat patterns of scattered homesteads across the country's hillside, as well as with most smallholders' risk reduction strategies, such as the cultivation of multiple crops and the exploitation of multiple plots. The government's policy suits a small group of larger, wealthier farmers who often belong to the local elite. However, for most smallholders, opportunities are shrinking as the space of 'modernity' expands. Consequently, the outcome of land use regulation policies is similar to more straightforward cases of involuntary land transfers: smallholders losing access to land and joining a class of unskilled labourers in a context of limited rural and urban employment opportunities.

Chapter 10, by Vincent Manirakiza and An Ansoms ('Modernizing Kigali: The Struggle for Space in the Rwandan Urban Context'), also analyses land use planning in Rwanda, but in the urban context of Kigali. The new Rwandan urban habitat regulations are based on a clear and ambitious conception of what 'modern' urban planning should encompass. Through a reorganization of the urban habitat, the government aims at reconfiguring urban space in line with the needs of a true metropolis. In reality, however, only the better-off actors are able to meet the criteria, thereby enhancing their land rights. Poorer population categories, on the other hand, are unable to abide by the strict planning regulations and consequently are pushed into de facto illegality in terms of urban planning and development, so that they end up living in informal urban areas lacking services or moving to peri-urban areas that, formally, are still rural. Moreover, public-private partnerships allow real estate investors to expropriate and evict more popular, poorer quarters in the 'public interest'. As a result, the poor face land rights insecurity and a short-term risk of (re)displacement.

Several common themes emerge from the chapters as a whole. First, they all indicate that contested land right transfers and outright land grabbing are by no means new phenomena in the Great Lakes Region. In fact, it is essential to a better understanding of contemporary struggles in the land arena that one should adopt a **historical perspective**, stretching back to colonial times, as illustrated in the chapter by Peemans on the DRC. The Ugandan chapter (van Leeuwen et al.) shows how seemingly 'new' forms of land acquisition are merely 'the latest episode in a history of contested changes in ownership over the land'. The chapter on Burundi (Nyenyezi and Ansoms) illustrates how historical evolutions at the political level have shaped the current stakes in the land arena. And the Rwandan chapters, finally, highlight how current policy processes fit within the country's historical heritage.

Awareness of the historical dimension of power struggles, contest and conflict is all the more important because of the **frequent and profound changes in power constellations** in the Great Lakes Region, both during recent episodes of strife and in their aftermaths. All chapters provide vivid examples of how such shifts in power constellations have affected struggles in the land arena, leading to further conflict. Actors who at some point lost land rights often tend not to seek immediate confrontation, but to wait for the 'coins of power to turn'. All chapters show that actors' capacity to gain the upper hand in a conflict over agricultural land or a mining site is influenced by regime change and the actors' ability to connect to the 'power holders of the day'. In line with these past trajectories, people will continue to speculate over future power shifts, and the potential impact of those shifts on their positions in the land arena. Consequently, seemingly definitive resolutions of land contestations are never definitive in the heads of those who feel disadvantaged by the outcome.

By placing land grabbing within a historical framework, the chapters also succeed in demonstrating that land acquisitions are not sterile projects 'imposed' from above or from the outside without facilitation by local actors. Even 'megadeals' seldom take place without involvement of local elites. All chapters pay particular attention to the **roles of local elites** in current land grabs, an element increasingly recognized yet still under-researched in the international literature. Interestingly, local elites' strategies to control land are remarkably similar across the four countries, despite considerable differences between their institutional and normative frameworks. All chapters point at the ability of local elites to instrumentalize the opportunities embedded in the growing commodification of land, in private sector investment, and in the adoption and implementation of new policies and legislation. In addition, local elites gain influence when they manage to position themselves as gatekeepers between local populations on the one hand and the central government, multinational companies, NGOs, etc. on the other. The challenge that presents itself is how to balance or even call into question this gatekeeper role by improving local governance and accountability in the technocratic but also the political sense. Otherwise, all efforts to improve outcomes by promoting local consultation in debates on 'responsible investments' and commitment to global norms and regulations in terms of corporate social responsibility are likely to fail. The chapter on DRC (Geenen and Hönke) shows that companies also have a responsibility in this respect: if there is limited or no scope for action to prevent investors' 'developmental efforts' from being captured by local elites, then such external capital input in the local economy is likely to lead to more poverty rather than less.

Overall, the exclusionary mechanisms embedded in the current land transfers taking place in the Great Lakes Region, have a profound **impact upon local land rights and livelihood strategies** of the populations concerned. The chapters all convincingly argue that access to land is still crucial to a large majority of the local populations in all four countries. Any viable alternatives to agriculture as an income-generating activity are largely absent. It would therefore seem rather illusionary in any of the four countries to aim for economic progress without taking into account the productive capacity of smallholder farmers. On the contrary, such forms of economic progress may be highly exclusive, and would likely feed local-level frustration in an already conflict-prone region.

The complexity and muckiness of many land disputes and land grabs requires careful and in-depth analysis. Such analysis should also contribute to the identification of consistent solutions, not only in the long run, but also within a shorter timeframe. Solution strategies should focus first and foremost on the **crucial position of smallholder farmers** in the social and economic fabric of the Great Lakes Region. There would now appear to be a window of opportunity opening to raise the role of smallholder farming at the international level: not only has 2014 has been designated the UN's International Year of Family Farming, but discussions are ongoing on the elaboration of a Peasants' Charter at the UN level. However, a paradigm shift in relation to the future of agriculture – and the central role of family farming – seems at this point not to be in the offing.

Moreover, the practical reinforcement of smallholder farming is a complex challenge. Solutions could focus on the one hand on ensuring that local authorities are held accountable for upholding local land rights, promoting transparency in land transactions, and curbing illicit actions by elites. Central and local governments also need to work towards securing rights of local people and communities. However, lessons learned from the chapters suggest that modifications within the formal regulatory framework and ensuring the accountability of national policymakers alone will not trigger **sustainable solutions** for improving local livelihood outcomes. In fact, there is a crucial role to be played by local communities themselves. Local people do act, even if not always in immediately visible ways. Subordinate groups have some agency and, by networking with media and civil society organizations, they may succeed in improving their bargaining position (cf. the chapter on Burundi) or in influencing policy (cf. the contribution by Peemans). However, the window of opportunity for those groups remains narrow. At the same time, the rights of the 'strongest' often prevail, as these 'stronger' actors are more resilient in terms of financial capacity and even more importantly, in terms of formal and informal institutional connectedness.

Some of the chapters in the book suggest that alternative pathways should focus on the **empowerment** of all types of local actors' agency, on the enhancement of smallholder farmers' capacity to make their voices heard within the policy arena, and on the reinforcement of their ability to connect to strategic allies within civil society and among the media. Local level resistance to non-transparent land transfers creates an opportunity for acknowledging the legitimacy of smallholders' interests in the land arena and to recognize their capacity to contribute to the development of their country.

2

Land Grabbing & Development History

The Congolese Experience

JEAN-PHILIPPE PEEMANS

Introduction: land grabbing and the place of the agrarian question in development studies

The literature of 'land grabbing' expanded at the end of the last decade. One of the most promising fields in the latest discussions is the renewal of very old research themes, such as agrarian transition and the role of enclosure in primitive accumulation (Hall, Hirsch and Li, 2011), the relationships between land use and property rights (Borras and Franco, 2012), between the role of the State, market and institutions in the access to common goods and their management, between modes of production and social relations (Bernstein 2010), and between dispossession, impoverishment and proletarianisation of small farmers (Li, 2011).

Figures revealing the extent of the threat, have added a dramatic character to these arguments. They indicate that from 2008 to 2011, between 30 and 60 million hectares were given into concession, including 20 million in Africa (Baxter, 2010; Brown, 2011). Between 2000 and 2010, the total allotted, sold or leased land would amount to more than 200 million hectares (Oxfam, 2011).

Discussions around the theme of 'land grabbing' have stimulated a movement of empirical research and theoretical reflection. It gives the 'agrarian question' a central place, while taking into account its multiple economic, social, environmental and cultural dimensions. Various studies have highlighted the multiplicity of stakeholders in North and South, the complexity of the chains of interest connecting them, and also the heterogeneity of local contexts, including the differences in attitude and behaviour between categories of actors involved.

However, despite its stimulating critical perspective, and its empirical and theoretical contributions, much of the recent research remains focused almost exclusively on the recent 'land grabbing' wave, as if it was a sui generis event, whose unexpected magnitude disrupts the conditions for the development of agriculture in the South, and poses a threat of an unprecedented scale for the future of the peasantry. Despite scattered references to the history of enclosure in the formation of agrarian capitalism, the historical perspective in most contemporary literature is very limited. However, when considering that historical perspective, one could state that 'land grabbing' is only one of the components of a very old offensive against the small-scale peasantry.

In the next part, we point to the importance of such historical perspective in the case of the DRC (Democratic Republic of Congo). This allows us to reframe the current waves of land grabbing as an episode within a long history of developmental policies aiming to 'capture' the African peasantry. The third section focuses on the particular forms of land grabbing in the Belgian colonial system in relation to a particularly ambitious attempt to 'capture' the peasantry, and thereafter on the uniqueness of the relationship between the State and the peasantry in Congo-Zaïre after the independence, and its impact on the specific forms of land grabbing in the DRC. The fourth section highlights recent developments in the DRC, and places the question of land grabbing in a historical political economy context of rural development, recognizing the central place of the peasantry in the ongoing evolution. The overall argument of this chapter is that the current challenge for development studies is to develop a political economy of rural development which includes the peasantry as an actor in the history of agrarian change, and not only as the object of a successful or failed agrarian transition, of which the current phase of land grabbing would eventually be the ultimate episode (Sikor and Lund, 2009).

Land grabbing as yet another episode in the long history of efforts to 'capture' the African peasantry

A historical approach is needed to replace the current phase of 'land grabbing' in the long term process through which land resources of peasant communities have been continuously transferred to actors guided by a logic of accumulation (Harvey, 2003). The logic of enclosure was of major importance to the development of capitalism in Europe, after which the process was repeated for centuries in colonial and post-colonial systems (Braudel, 1985). It is obviously a major phenomenon in the history of capitalism in the North and South (White and Dasgupta, 2010). These historical waves of enclosure cannot be isolated from an ideological framework which, for many generations, has presented a negative view of the peasant world. Throughout history, this ideology has legitimized the enclosure movements, and these have strengthened the evolution towards the marginalization of a weakened peasantry.

Modernization theories – at the heart of the formation of development thinking after World War Two – were the most obvious illustration of that thinking (Peemans, 2002). Almost all the national development processes in the North and the South have been based on mobilizing human and material resources of the rural world as instruments for industrialization and growth (De Schutter, 2011). For example, Hyden – a highly influential author in African studies in the 1980s – did not hesitate to attribute the failure of development policies in Africa to the inability of States to capture the African peasantry. He saw a 'free peasantry' as the cause of failure to advance towards capitalism, development and modernity (Hyden, 1983, 1985, 1986). In his view, it was problematic that peasants could ensure their own production and reproduction without the support of other social classes as this allowed them to withdraw into their subsistence economy, while escaping market forces and the pressure of the State (Hyden, 1983).

Indeed, also in Africa, the capture of the peasantry has a long history. It was at the heart of the colonial vision of modernization, relayed by the post-colonial view of it. The first wave of massive dispossession of the peasantry was made by foreign settlers supported by the colonial State machine. After independence, national and local development projects played a central role in the further dispossession of smallholder peasants. They allowed diverse layers of national and local stakeholders to seize control of land resources. This post-colonial move was supported by the fact that since independence, the ideology of modernization was shared by many categories of African elites, and therefore the anti-peasant vision had become widespread. Multiple agricultural initiatives of States and foreign cooperation, in combination with attempts to 'modernize' property rights by imposing new land codes, continued to destabilize the peasant mode of production. Even when major modernization projects failed, land grabbing continued through the alliances formed between foreign, national and local actors to privatize land.

The 2008 World Development Report seemed to present a shift in the discourse on the potential of smallholder farmers, given the World Bank's plea in favour of a green revolution in smallholder agriculture for Sub-Saharan Africa. However, critics have pointed to the way in which the commercially-oriented, entrepreneurial logic of such a green revolution will only apply to a minority of smallholder farmers (see e.g. Akram-Lodhi, 2008). They frame the report as a reformulation of the old modernization policies, 'view[ing] the peasantry by and large as an anachronism' (Veltmeyer, 2009: 395). Another shocking illustration of the fact that modernization theories continue to be core in policy circles, is provided by Collier who does not hesitate to affirm the need for the eradication of resources wasted on small farmers, as he considers that only large-scale farming operations can be beneficial to growth and to the protection of the environment (Collier, 2010). It is a sad irony to see the 'new' environmental argument supporting the old thesis of the 'capture of the peasantry', as it was elaborated by Hyden more than thirty years ago.

The permanence of the anti-peasant bias illustrates that land grabbing cannot be separated from the ideological and political arsenal that continuously reinforced a negative identity of the peasantry. It is important to highlight the cultural dimension of anti-peasant strategies, because, on the opposite side, in the recent manifestations of peasant resilience, land is part of the reconstruction of a positive identity, not only for its material importance, but also because the heritage of collective values embodied in it.

The following sections will present some elements to aid the understanding of the intertwined dimensions of land grabbing in the case of the Democratic Republic of Congo (DRC). The historical dimension is particularly instructive in this case, both because the multifaceted process of 'land grabbing' has a very long history, and because the vitality of the peasantry and their resilience and initiatives are particularly evident.

Land grabbing and attempts to capture the peasantry: the specific case of the Congo (DRC)

Before becoming a theoretical concept after World War Two, modernization already had a long history as an idea and project, exercising a powerful fascination upon the elites of the North and the South. In the case of the Congo, historian I. Ndaywel è Nziem highlights the effects that this fascination with a modern way of life, exerted on the leading groups of many pre-colonial political entities. He attributes the disintegration of the Kingdom of Kongo, in the seventeenth and eighteenth centuries, to the unintended consequences of a too confident opening up to the outside world (Ndaywel, 2010). He emphasizes the destabilizing effect of that modernization desire, even before the imposition of the colonial form of dependence, and many centuries before the influence of the ideology of modernization after independence.

In his book *Histoire du Congo*, Ndaywel paints an impressive fresco of the millennial history of Congo, focusing on the construction of its civilizations, rooted in the mastering of their natural environments. He shows the relationship between the construction of 'territories of life' by local people, agriculturalists and pastoralists, hunters and fishermen, and the construction of complex social and political institutions, which were the roots of identity and culture. It is within such a historical background, that the colonial and post-colonial attempts to 'capture' the peasantry have to be examined. The case of the DRC is particularly interesting, because it identifies no fewer than five waves of land grabbing since the beginning of the colonial period, and preceding the present wave. Interestingly, there is quite a clear relationship between these various waves. They were all based on the ambition to capture the peasantry or marginalize it, leading to a continuous dispossession of the peasant world.

The five waves of land grabbing in question are:

(1)   the decree on vacant lands and the politics of forced labour under the EIC ('État indépendant du Congo') regime 1885-1908;

(2)   the policy of the major agricultural, forestry and mining concessions 1910-1940, including the CNKi ('Comité national du Kivu');

(3)   the policy of the *paysannats indigènes* 1945-1960;

(4)   the Land Acts of the 1970s; and

(5)   attempts to implement a 'farmer model of modernization' after 1980, and the informal and multiform 'land grabbing' of the years 1990 to 2000.

Three waves of land grabbing and attempts to capture the peasantry during the colonial period 1885-1960
From the point of view of the long history of human development in the Congo, the attempt of the colonial State to control the peasantry was the most strategic vector between 1885 and 1960. It introduced a radical break in the secular lifestyle of peasants' worlds in the Congo, not so much in the sense of the theory of modernization (breaking up a 'backward traditional society'), but – as described by Ndaywel (ibid.) – in the construction of the link between 'territories and identities' .

There is obviously no place here for even a summary description of the historical events that have marked the military conquest of the Congo by the troops of the 'État indépendant du Congo' (EIC), first African mercenaries and then local recruits. Once the conquest had succeeded, the apparatus of repression played a decisive role in the mobilization of human resources to undertake natural resource exploitation. The most important elements were the appropriation of the peasant communities by the *State Land Decree* (1885), and the establishment of the State monopoly on the trade of the main export products (1892).

The decree of 1 July 1885 of the General Administration of the EIC on so-called 'vacant land' gave the State the right to dispose of all land that was not occupied by indigenous communities. It gave the State the right to directly exploit or to grant the use of all land, other than what was visibly occupied by villagers and their crops. Through this decree, the State gave colonists the legal means to acquire vast tracts of land, while Congolese peasants were prohibited from any initiative beyond subsistence production. In some cases, they were forced to leave their allotted land (Peemans, 1997: 62-65). In addition, the 1892 decree obliged the indigenous population to harvest, gather and hunt marketable products and deliver them to the agents of the State (Peemans, 1974). This historical approach in fact illustrates that the founding act of the colonial system was first and foremost a huge operation of 'land grabbing', through the institutional coup of decreeing most of the peasant communities' land – considered by themselves as their common heritage – 'vacant'.

The usefulness of this measure was clearly seen by the colonial administration after 1908. The 1918 annual report on the colony claimed that 'in the interest of the indigenous peoples themselves, too large indigenous reserve must not make it impossible or difficult to grant land to Europeans, or distract the natives from industrial sites' (Congo belge, 1918). The human impact of this period of 'founding violence' was very heavy, as assessed by Ndaywel: 'The regression of the population [from 1885] until 1920 [...] has been no less than one-third of the total population, and may even have reached half' (Ndaywel, 2010: 107).

During the 1920s the peasant question was the subject of heated debate between different factions of the colonial policy makers and various groups of opinion and metropolitan lobbies involved in colonial politics (Poncelet, 2008). These debates converged towards the idea that even if one had to recognize that the Congolese people had many features of a civilization prior to colonization, it was in any case needed to advance the requirements of 'progress'. In other words, the idea of modernization in its colonial interpretation played a key role to justify the forced mobilization of the peasant world, according to the objectives of the colonial administration. And these goals could not be separated from the partnership established between the administration and the financial groups controlling the majority of the colonial economy. At the beginning of the years 1930, four Belgian financial groups controlled 75 per cent of the capital invested in the Congo, with the main group ('Société Générale') controlling 60 per cent (Peemans, 1974).

From 1920 onwards, the systematic deconstruction of the peasant economy by the colonial administration continued. Administrative coercion sought to break the centuries-old relationship between village communities and local and regional markets which were embedded in a dense web of social relations and provided ways to diversify livelihood strategies. Moreover, the period was characterized by a second wave of 'land grabbing', contributing to the dispossession of the peasantry – particularly in the Kivu area. Between 1920 and 1945, more than 12 million hectares (almost double the estimated area cultivated by the peasantry in 2010) were granted by the 'Comité national du Kivu' to colonial interests, with a strong predominance of large corporations (Dehoux, 1946). In addition to dispossession, the deconstruction of the peasant world had a very important cultural aspect. This rationale was based on the idea of a necessary authoritarian education for the transition towards progress, an argument with which the colonial power radically denied the identity of the Congolese peasantry (Leplae, 1929, 1933).

After World War Two, a new colonial policy emerged based on the idea that the stabilization of the colonial system required a certain improvement of the living standard of the African proletariat. At that point, colonial authorities became interested in the promotion of a small peasantry through improved production techniques and increased revenues, and the promotion of low ranking employees (the so-called *évolués*) in the public and private sectors. International economic conditions drawn by the strong demand for raw materials in the 1950s, created a favourable climate for economic progress. However the benefits of economic growth – stimulated by external demand – concentrated mainly in urban areas (Peemans, 1980). In rural areas, a new policy of authoritarian agricultural modernization was attempted, with the so-called *paysannats indigènes* (indigenous peasant settlements) model. This model was supposed to bring a minority of peasants to progress under heavy supervision by colonial agronomists (Malengreau, 1949). This new and final variant of the colonial model of modernization led to a third wave of 'land grabbing', since it assumed a form of partial privatization of communal land. But it had very limited results for various reasons (Drachoussoff, 1965). The main feature of the end of the colonial era was therefore the relative stagnation of the rural world, comprising the vast majority of the population. This stagnation maintained the economic base of the colonial system in narrow limits. The countryside remained largely dominated by the legacy of the authoritarian indigenization model implemented during the interwar period.

Overall, it can be said that while the colonial period paralyzed the Congolese peasantry, it failed to break or 'capture' it. In the end, the vast majority of the peasantry kept an informal but real control over their communal land. Much more pervasive, however, were the consequences of the attack carried out against the identity of the peasants' world, through the systematic presentation of a demeaning, even humiliating, degrading image of peasants. Peasant behaviour was locked in authoritarian infantile injunctions, which in some cases resulted in some self-depreciating from the side of the peasants themselves. As Ndaywel writes: 'The Congolese memory kept the bad memory of European, accompanied by agricultural monitors and agronomists, sanctioning the disobedience and the indiscipline of the peasants, a memory that eventually kept them away from agricultural work' (ibid.: 141). However, peasants overall proved to be resilient to such self-deprecation. While they were repressed in the public expression of their identity, colonial repression could certainly not reject or destroy their vitality, often only expressed clandestinely between peasants themselves (cf. the 'hidden transcript' concept of Scott, 1990).

This resilience should not be reduced to forms of resistance expressed in a sporadic manner through more violent revolts during the colonial period. The latter have often been privileged by foreign observers, given their obvious political consequences in the period following independence[1] (Jewsiewicki, 1980, 1987). More recently, Congolese researchers have highlighted less spectacular but more sustainable forms of resilience. They include the various forms of community work, and group savings organizations, inherited from the pre-colonial period but often repressed by the colonial authorities who saw it as an obstacle to

---

[1] Think for example of the rebellions of the Kwango-Kwilu (Mulelist Movement) and the East (Lumumbist Movement).

more individualistic forms of production and savings promoted under the ideology of 'modernization under tutelage'. Indeed, these practices have survived through all vicissitudes. They are expressed through a large vocabulary reflecting the richness and diversity of these peasant practices in the various regions of the Congo. Think for example of *ekirimba* (in *nande* language in the Northeast) or *likelemba* (in *lingala*), referring to various informal associative practices learned through the informal school of customary life: *kyaghanda* (Kakule, 2006: 95-97). These words refer to a strong articulation between ways of life focused on 'living together' and cultural identity, which is at the heart of resilience, and often invisible to the eyes of the foreign actor.

The post-colonial State and two forms of 'land grabbing': 1960-2000
In most African countries, political independence did not deeply change the socio-economic legacy of colonization in terms of agricultural structures. African post-colonial elites who took an active role in the State apparatus after independence were penetrated by the ideology of modernization. The focus on the expansion of agricultural export surplus and on food production thus continued in the 1960s, within a techno-economic context inherited from the end of the colonial period. At the end of the 1960s and the beginning of the 1970s, most African States attempted to speed up the pace of accumulation. They tried to circumvent the peasantry's resistance to the ongoing forms of agricultural surplus extraction through the implementation of large agro-industrial projects. Such projects were often accompanied by another particular type of 'land grabbing', given that fertile land areas were often attributed to such agro-industrial concerns, regardless of their status and their usefulness to local communities.

At the same time, however, the post-colonial dynamics within Congo-lese agriculture were somewhat a-typical in comparison to most other African countries – where the State generally increased its control over the agricultural surplus for exports. One of the reasons for this was that the colonial State collapsed immediately after independence. After 1965 – the takeover of power by General Mobutu – there was an attempt to rebuild the State that was partially successful until the late 1970s. While the ideology of the regime was certainly very imbued by the vision of modernization, it originally focused exclusively on the potential of the mining sector to support industrial projects and infrastructure (Peemans, 1975). Agriculture was not a priority, and therefore, there was no attempt to restore control of the State over the peasantry until the early 1970s.

From 1973 onwards, the State tried to follow the path of other African countries to control the agricultural surplus through the establishment of an extensive array of State offices (the so-called *Zaïreanization*) (Peemans, 1986). A new land law (73-021 of 20 July 1973) was adopted, which strengthened the State's control on the attribution of land rights. It was supposed to be an indirect instrument for the modernization of land institutions, as it allowed the privatization of land that was until then governed by customary arrangements (Kazadi, 1991). The initial idea was that the new land law would stimulate private investment in agriculture. The appropriation of land was thus rationalized and legitimized as a technical instrument to legally secure other actors than the peasantry, because they were supposed to be more efficient. When placed within the historical context, one could consider this modernization rhetoric of the land law as a reactivation of the Decree on 'vacant land' of the EIC in 1885. In any case, it opened up the way for a new phase of 'land grabbing', the fourth since the beginning of the colonial era. Unlike other African countries, where the State apparatus was directly involved as a contractor in large agricultural projects, the State apparatus in Zaïre acted in symbiosis with initiatives of national private entrepreneurs, especially the so-called 'barons' of the regime. That singular stage in the 1970s pioneered multifaceted attempts of land grabbing, and a proliferation of sources of land conflicts between 'grabbers' and peasant communities. In fact from the point of view of the peasants, the new land legislation was essentially a new instrument of 'land grabbing'.

In the 1980s, policies imposed by the IMF's structural adjustment programme (SAP) further reduced the direct intervention of the State in the management of agricultural production and agro-industrial projects. The promotion of a market economy – freed from State interventions – lay at the basis of these policies. The aim was to stimulate agricultural innovation, increase production, and help a minority of dynamic producers to become engines of change and progress. According to the dominant approach of the 1980s, this required both the privatization of commercial channels, the means of production and in particular land (World Bank, 1989). In fact, these SAP liberalization policies sought to create the conditions for the emergence or consolidation of the 'farmer model of modernization' (FMM) in Africa. Attempts at an 'africanization' of the FMM from the 1980s, resulted in the privatization of many formerly public projects, a privileged access to credit and industrial inputs for a few so-called 'more efficient' actors, as well as on the unlimited employment of cheap labour provided by impoverished peasants. This evolution was accompanied with a new fifth wave of 'land grabbing' in Africa. The liberalization policies were used as new devices by new layers of national 'land grabbers', seeking by all means to expand or consolidate their grip on land, including through the concentration of traditional user rights, when full property reclamation proved to be too complex or costly.

The evolution of Zaïre in the 1980s was not completely different to changes seen elsewhere in Africa, although it had very specific aspects derived from the context of the Zaïrean agrarian crisis inherited from the 1970s. A Zaïrean variant of the 'farmer model of modernization' (FMM) was accompanied, as elsewhere in Africa, by a virtual abandonment of reference to the small peasantry as an actor in agricultural and rural development. Often the tendency was concealed behind a screen of unconscious or deliberate confusion, between 'peasants' and 'farmers', the latter being the rural minority that could actually profit from the liberalization policies. From the 1990s, the 'peasantry' as a collective actor had lost all visibility within the public development discourse, being reduced permanently to a mass of poor people waiting for assistance by NGOs (non-governmental organizations) to survive. The peasantry became a sort of passive object or recipient of the competing actions of the myriads of specialized brokers vying for a market share in the field: of local governance promotion, civil society support, programmes of micro-credit, micro-initiatives, micro-enterprise in rural areas, and other variants focusing on the 'local', on 'participation', or on the 'empowerment' of rural poor women etc. Local populations were seen, in the vast majority of cases, as victims or people to-be-assisted. Even when the term 'peasant' appeared, it was to evoke top-down projects firmly framed by the injunctions of external donors. In fact, what occurred could be described as a sort of 'identity grab'; it robbed the peasantry of any quality as autonomous actors in the development process. In the case of the DRC, this reduction of the peasantry to the status of assisted non-actor contributed significantly to the concealment of peasant resistance.

Within this context, 'land grabbers' used diverse strategies to take control of land resources. One of them was, since the 1980s, the de facto privatization of land resources liberated by the dismantling of public agricultural offices and their aborted projects. These were taken over by powerful coalitions of actors (Shikayi, 1994). The private appropriation of land was achieved either through the links that could be established with the traditional chiefs, or through the registration of land rights following the new legislation. In most case, both strategies were combined through the corruption of customary and official authorities. Land grabbing in a very fluid socio-economic context, worked through the re-composition of networks including different actors in political, administrative, judicial and customary circles of power, in order to ensure land security in various overlapping and competing modes of ownership.

On top of this, virtually all rural areas of the DRC were affected by conflict over land during the 1980s and 1990s. The multiplication of conflicts was most often framed as a result of State decline, of ethnic clashes, or the proliferation of armed bands supported by foreign stakeholders. However in reality, land disputes often played a central role in political instability and social violence. Securing access over land became a major objective for actors who wanted to consolidate their economic or political positions (politicians, army officers, civil servants, traders). Taking control over land did not only represent a takeover of property, but also reinforced power, status, prestige and even proof of a local identity (Mafikiri, 1994). In fact, for actors seeking a regional social identity and social prestige to be recognized as 'big men', the accumulation of land reserves was as important – or even more important – than the productive potential of that land. As a result, the majority of land resources in Kivu

– captured by traders, soldiers, politicians in the 1990s – were under-utilized. At the same time, the majority of peasants had an insufficient area to ensure family needs (Mafikiri, 1994: 119-20). These phenomena further fuelled ethnic tensions and led to more violent conflicts.

Behind the apparent institutional chaos in Congo, there was in fact an important structural tendency towards land concentration that accelerated in the 1990s and beyond. As a result of this fifth wave of mainly informal 'land grabbing', many peasant families lost their access to land on the basis of customary principles, while not having the means to secure land rights in line with the new procedures. However, given that access to land remained a vital question for the peasant populations' survival, they tried to defend their rights through passive or active resistance to the purchasers or grabbers. To defend their rights, they often invoked the bond existing between the occupied land and the long tradition of occupation by their ancestors. Indeed, resistance took a new form by insisting on the overt reference to cultural values and practices attached to the land itself. Land grabbing was reframed in terms of 'soul and identity grabbing' of a community.

The importance of the regional dimension in the long historical process of land grabbing: the case of Eastern DRC
The Democratic Republic of Congo represents an area that is larger than the euro zone in the European Union. It is therefore important to take account of the great diversity of situations in the various regions of the DRC. This is particularly the case for the eastern regions, and especially the Kivus. The current situation is difficult and seems locked in a logic of negative factors reinforcing each other in a kind of irreversible entropic evolution: population growth, exacerbation of ethnicity, land disputes, etc. (Vlassenroot and Raeymakers, 2009). However, these factors should be framed within the long term historical evolutions that have had a significant impact on the specific type of agrarian crises endured by this region.

Ndaywel, for example, has shown that in the long term history, there was a rather great fluidity in the human occupation of the region, with a lot of East to West migration (within the Kivu region itself, but also between the Kivus and what would later become Rwanda and Burundi), and multiple political influences. The region was not frozen in rigid ethnic structures, but very open, both to international trade (Swahili networks), and to the emergence of new political institutions that combined centralization with local power (Ndaywel, 2010). The colonial period, however, brought a sharp break in these fluxes by dividing up the region into delineated territories. The legacy of this break up marked the post colonial regimes. The question of landownership, and its corollary land dispossession, played a central role.

For instance, the eastern part of the country has been particularly affected by colonial 'land grabbing'. Kivu peasants' living conditions were severely impacted by the massive dispossession of land, transferred through the 'Comité national du Kivu' to Belgian settlers and large colonial agricultural and mining companies. Another factor, affecting the land arena, was the authoritarian policy of 'Rwandan' populations forced resettlement in the Kivu region in the period 1935-1950, with the establishment of nearly 100,000 immigrants in the Kivu region. A new wave of massive immigration took place after the violent ethnic conflicts that marked the 1960s and 1970s in Rwanda and Burundi. Several hundred thousand additional refugees settled in the Kivu regions. But pressure rose to its maximum at the occasion of the influx of nearly two million refugees from both countries in the 1990s. These massive immigration fluxes have deeply affected the tenure security of local populations, adding a new dimension to the tensions already caused by the land grabbers of national and local origin. As a result, the availability of arable land per capita in the mountainous regions of Kivu decreased by 60 per cent between 1960 and 1990 (Mafikiri, 1994), and the situation further deteriorated in the 1990s. This tenure insecurity has contributed to a pervasive climate of violence, where ethnic tensions and land conflicts are inextricably intertwined. In such a climate, new actors of land grabbing appeared, among which were not only warlords, but also humanitarian agencies claiming land for refugee resettlement.

Overall, it is therefore important to note that in the case of the Kivus, the increasing scarcity of available land cannot be attributed only to endogenous population growth. Various forms of socio-political violence accumulated through ancient and recent history. These historical evolutions played a central role in the dispossession of the peasantry (Mafikiri, 1996; see also Claessens et al.'s chapter in this book).

Also in Ituri, another region in the DRC that has frequently been plagued by conflict and violence, the role of local land grabbers has played a detrimental role in the escalation of ethnic conflicts. Indeed, ethnic tensions were, and still are, often rooted in or linked with land disputes. In a context of pervasive multiplication of armed groups, local elites, charismatic and populist leaders have manipulated and exacerbated ethnic tensions – in the name of securing 'autochthon' access to national or local land – in order to strengthen their positions (RCN, 2009, see also Fahey's chapter in this book).

This historical dimension of 'land grabbing' in the eastern part of the DRC allows us to put the current sixth wave of 'land grabbing' into perspective. The potential impact of this latest wave is certainly not to be underestimated, but a historical perspective underscores that attempts to enclose local communities' lands, and to capture the peasantry, are old realities. As we will show in the next section, peasants in the region have faced these realities for generations. In the face of these threats, they have developed unique, inventive, often hidden forms of resistance, of which the intensity is highly variable depending on the local context. In fact, it is probably because of the particular historical heritage of the eastern parts of Congo (DRC), that this region has the most diverse and most active forms of peasant resistance against 'land grabbing' by the State, national and local elites and foreign invaders.

The political economy of the sixth wave of land grabbing in the DRC

Up to this point, this chapter has alluded to the interest of a historical political economy approach to better understand the current wave of 'land grabbing'. The historical approach obviously should not lead to a denial of the threats brought by this wave. On the contrary, it shows its extreme potential violence in line with the previous waves of land grabbing that took place throughout history.

The scale of the sixth wave of land grabbing
Many features of the sixth wave of land grabbing present similarities with the first and second waves that took place during the colonial period and were characterized by their megalomaniac character (remember the 12 million hectares of concessions granted by the 'Comité national du Kivu') and their non-sustainability. According to a recent evaluation, the six most important Congolese land concessions – granted to foreign investors in recent years – could represent up to 11 million hectares. This would include an 8 million hectares project attributed to associations of white South African farmers fearing the threats of land redistribution in their own country (Global Land Project, 2010), which would give such land acquisition projects a special neo-colonial flavour. These projects, if implemented, would represent almost 50 per cent of the arable land of the DRC (which is equal to 22 million hectares of arable land out of a total of 227 million hectares (FAOstat, 2010). However, many of these so-called projects are never realized; they often remain vague announcements and rumours. Nevertheless, these rumours, true or false, denote a context where the DRC is seen as a potential new Eldorado for large foreign land grabbers.

This new type of agrarian neo-colonialism reuses the old (post-) colonial discourse of massively available 'vacant land'. The deliberately repeated invocation that only 6.7 million hectares (or 3 per cent of the country area) are currently cultivated, falsely gives the impression that the peasantry will not be threatened by these large concessions (New Agriculturist, 2009).[2] The argument of massively available yet under-utilized land seems to justify some tolerance in land concession granting. However, one has to be extremely careful with figures in the debates on

---

[2] One has to note that in other evaluations the total cultivable land is much more important (75 millions hectares), but they agree that the effectively cultivated land is below 10 million hectares (Tecsult and Aecom, 2009).

land grabbing, given the lack of appropriate definition of 'cultivated' and 'utilized' land. In reality, the utilized communal lands of the villages do not only consist of cultivated land, but also of land left fallow (to avoid erosion), and land from which diverse products – required to support a peasant way of living – are extracted (for example non-timber forest products). In addition, communal lands are also part of a sort of 'imagined territory', with all the cultural and identity dimensions attached to this heritage.

At first sight, the role of the State in this sixth wave of land grabbing until 2010 bears great resemblance with the role played by the State during colonial and post-colonial times. Indeed, the State authorities, who have granted these land concessions, consider land and the relations between land and the peasantry in the same way as the colonial authorities and the Mobutu regime. The principles of land management governed by the 20 July 1973 Act – and reinforced by the 18 July 1980 law (law n° 80-008, governing general property, tenure and real estate security) – are still fully relevant: the State is the paramount owner of all land and has the power to decide on its attribution through concessions; the land occupied by local communities, according to customs, is considered as part of the State domain. However, placing this sixth wave into a historical perspective allows us to identify at least one significant difference with the colonial and early post-colonial era. At that time, massive land grabbing could take place because of the overwhelming power of the State. The current post-colonial, post-Mobutu State is far less powerful, despite its recent efforts towards 'reconstruction'. Moreover, the currently weak State faces a new historical situation: the increased local resistance embedded in the historical resilience of the peasantry in many parts of the country.

A specific feature of the DRC: a non-passive peasantry facing the sixth wave of land grabbing

In recent years, the realities of Congo's rural regions have appeared in a new light through a set of studies carried out by Congolese researchers. These studies have highlighted the existence of socioeconomic rural realities far more complex than those put forward by analyses that focused too exclusively on the reduction of poverty (Mirembe, 2006). These studies have revealed that Congolese peasants' resistance is not just passive; it formulates responses and initiatives from the side of the peasant world.

The collapse of the colonial State and the difficulties of the post-colonial State, have gradually opened up space for a certain autonomy of action by peasant populations. The disintegration of the post-colonial State during the 1970s and 1980s, and the profound violent crises of the 1990s, accelerated this trend. A very broad emancipation of the peasantry took place, an autonomy that is primarily manifest in the search for minimal security conditions for families, lineages and communities living in a natural environment that has been theirs for generations. These peasants have very complex strategies to defend and expand their land rights, to preserve a minimal food security, while trying to grow a surplus for marketing whenever circumstances permit. These local-level activities embedded within the informal sector, or better, the people's economy, account for about four-fifths of the actual activity of the Congolese population but weigh little in official statistics (Peemans, 1997). This makes peasant activity rather invisible in the eyes of policy makers and foreign observers. However, their blindness contrasts sharply with the visibility of the weight of the peasant population: the rural population multiplied around five times between 1960 and 2000, from ten to fifty million people (New Agriculturist, 2009). The numerous studies, carried out by Congolese researchers in recent years, incite us to seriously consider the multiple economic, social and cultural aspects of this dynamic popular economy that most of the time is invisible to outsiders.

The resilience of the peasantry has further manifested itself in the proliferation of informal associations. The functions of these associations are multiple: economic, social and political; and they also often promote cooperation and mutual assistance among their members. The interest of the peasantry for these initiatives can be observed through the increasing number of fields in which they are active (informal health care associations, small informal cooperatives, rotating saving clubs, various groups of women and young people, etc.). The growing number of associations reflects a strong desire and capacity to collectively face uncertainties and risks. In fact, one could say that these associations are a sort of reinvention – more than a revival – of former customary institutions geared to ensure group security and solidarity. They are not to be confused with the kind of imported solidarity promoted through externally-driven development initiatives, so richly adorned in some NGO's discourses (Laurent, 1996). In fact, the economic efficiency of these associations is based upon trust between their members. They enable a mobilization of collective work to achieve small-scale infrastructure projects (like water pipes), and the establishment of collective management (e.g. assemblies of water users to fix the royalties and maintenance). Often these associations are rooted in the ancient spirit of the *likelemba*, reflecting the importance of practices of reciprocity in labour organization and resources management (Kakule, 2006). Equally important to their 'security-enhancing' role, is the social role of these groups. They contribute to the collective consciousness of a lineage, a village, a group, and ensure its unity, despite all the pressures. They show continuity between the centuries-old standards of customary governance, and attempts to invent new standards of local governance adapted to contemporary problems. This provides some counterweight to the standards of governance imposed by external stakeholders (Peemans, 1997).

Alongside these associative 'horizontal networks' that defend the 'locale territories' of the peasant economy, there are also important 'vertical networks' of clienteles that play a central role in relationships between old and new players who cooperate or compete in the rural areas. These networks are at the heart of the popular economy in the Congo. The connections between horizontal and vertical networks link both rural areas and urban centres. These networks are at the heart of the popular economy in the Congo, and include the overwhelming majority of economic activities and social relations (de Villers, Jewsiewski and Monnier, 2002).

These complex and dense networks point to the need to recognize peasants as actors, and not to reduce them to passive rural dwellers, entrapped in backwardness and poverty. In fact it is peasants' behaviour – in the Congo as elsewhere – that reinforces this argument. Peasants, especially the young ones, do not hesitate to emigrate to the cities or mining areas. In some mining areas, particularly in Kasai, Kivu and Katanga, the revenue from labour in the mining sector is higher than that provided by agricultural production. This has contributed to a decline in agricultural production in these regions, often interpreted as evidence of a failure of the village economy. But the revenues transferred to the villages mean that families are not confined to self-sufficiency, as they are part of a continuous flow of labour and cash.

According to recent estimates, peasant-miners alone represent two million workers, supporting eight to ten million dependants (Geenen, 2011). Therefore, today's peasantry, in Congo as elsewhere, must not be seen as a 'pure' homogenous peasantry, but as part of a mobile and hybrid peasantry, more or less strongly associated, according to different regions, with networks linking urban, semi-rural and rural economies.

The megalomania of a dummy State facing rising socio-political awareness about the land question

Since the Peace agreements of 2002, attempts to rebuild the central State in DRC have been numerous but with very problematic consequences. At first glance, the years 2002 to 2010 saw an economic recovery with sustained growth and a dramatic reduction of inflation. The investment/GDP ratio rose sharply, mainly because of a massive increase in foreign investments into the mining sector and in some projects related to electricity production. After the end of the war, the country also benefitted from debt reduction in the framework of the Heavily Indebted Poor Countries Programme. But despite this positive evolution, the national level of income and investment per capita remains well below the levels of the early 1980s. In fact, despite some improvements in the health and education sectors, it seems that the increased flow of foreign resources has mainly been invested in the reconstruction of the central administration with very limited results in terms of improved governance efficiency on the ground. The major focus upon rebuilding a strong military and security apparatus has also led to limited results (Marysse and Omasombo, 2012).

The decision-making process remains concentrated within presidential circles. People with key positions at this level are able to strike big deals with foreign investors in the fields of land and mining concessions and large infrastructural projects. But despite massive attention going to a couple of such 'prestige' projects – of which the realization depends entirely on foreign operators – the State apparatus remains largely disorganized and chronically inefficient. As a result, the implementation of central authorities' decisions remains very problematic. This is particularly the case in the field of agriculture and rural development, despite the fact that President Kabila declared these domains to be the new national priority after his re-election at the end of 2011.

Institutional cacophony is an obvious feature in the field of agriculture and rural development. The Ministry of Agriculture (Tecsult and Aecom, 2009) is involved in many conflicts of jurisdiction with the Ministry of Rural Development. The two ministries are plagued by overlapping competences, and are both confronted with a profound lack of financial means – in continuity with the limited means directed to agriculture since independence. Moreover, both ministries have been submitted to the logics of decentralization, as promoted and imposed by the foreign donors' governance model. Provinces have theoretically received large competences in the domain of agricultural policy, but in practice national authorities have been reluctant to transfer competences and funding (ACE, 2011).

Next to these largely powerless official actors, there is also a multitude of initiatives by foreign actors who sponsor a wide range of projects or programmes, each responding to its own logic. These projects and programmes are not only funded by major donor countries, but also by hundreds of NGOs with a great autonomy of action, but very little involved in a dialogue with national and local authorities. In recent years there have been the 'Document de stratégie de croissance et de réduction de la pauvreté' (DSCRP, 2006-2009), where agriculture received little attention, the 'Plan d'actions prioritaires' (PAP) of 2008, the 'Plan national pour la sécurité alimentaire' of 2010 formulated with FAO support, established with ABD support, and the 2011 DRC version of the PDDAA ('Programme détaillé de développement de l'agriculture africaine'*)*, elaborated in the framework of NEPAD (New Partnership for Africa's Development). This institutional cacophony has translated among others into a multiplicity of uncoordinated plans and interventions in the agricultural sector. But despite the exuberant production of projects and programmes, agricultural production itself – with an estimated annual supply of 20 millions tons – only provides 75 per cent of national food needs, while the remaining 25 per cent of needs has to be covered through imports at a cost of almost 1 billion dollars a year.

It is within this very confused institutional context that the granting of large tracts of land takes place. In fact, these concessions are often granted by central authorities through quite opaque negotiations with foreign players without consulting the local population. Moreover, the land transfers are based upon a superficial evaluation of its value, without considering the specificities in terms of local occupation. On top of this, there is no clear institutional mechanism that regulates the way in which these land concessions are implemented on the ground. This implies that investors have to negotiate with actors at the provincial and local level (both official authorities as well as customary chiefs), who are well accustomed to extracting some lucrative benefits from the arbitration between traditional land customs and the rights displayed by the new holders of concessions. The new wave of large-scale concessionaires will probably not be able to derogate from this decade-old tradition.

It is certain, however, that this wave of large concessions reflects a long-lasting preference of the national political elite for agricultural, livestock or forest projects managed by large mechanized farms in line with the FMM (farmer model of modernization). In this way, they share the preferences of a significant part of the donor community, who promote the very same model even when disguised beneath the surface of a 'pro-peasant' rhetoric. These ambitions are also reflected in the recent legislative framework. The first drafts of the agricultural code, developed after 2006 in an attempt to update the 1973 Act and the 1980 law, focused on large-scale exploitation of land, based on private property, mechanization and the use of industrial inputs to increase productivity. The aim was to create a stimulating environment for private operators, national and foreign, capable of developing modern agriculture on so-called 'vacant land'. As a result, the majority of the law articles concentrated on the problems encountered by modern enterprises in terms of the management of land and water resources, of access to infrastructures and energy, and in terms of the dealing with fiscal and accountability problems. References to the preoccupations of small peasants were largely absent.

The first version of this law was voted in in 2010, but it was confronted with fierce protests from a variety of actors. The law was seen as an instrument in favour of speculative foreign investment in land concessions, with negative consequences on the chances of Congolese citizen to secure access to land. These concerns were shared by larger-scale national landowners as well as peasant associations. In fact, resistance to the sixth wave of 'land grabbing' came from an unusual coalition of actors. On the one hand, local elites who had accumulated land during the post-colonial period wanted to avoid the competition for land that would result from the uncontrolled arrival of foreign investors with unlimited financial means. On the other hand, peasant associations shared this aversion for unlimited access to land for foreign investment. But in addition, and with the support of some foreign NGOs, they asked for recognition of communal land entitlements and for special support measures for peasant producers (*La voix du paysan congolais*, 2012).

A new version of the law was voted by the end 2011, and signed by the president immediately after his much debated re-election. An important change with the previous version was the introduction of revised articles 16 and 82. Article 16 stipulates that access to land is reserved for nationals or for enterprises of which 51 per cent of their capital is in the hands of nationals. Article 82 stipulates that the law also applies to those who hold former concessions, but with some time for adaptation (RDC, 2011). These apparently technical changes seem to represent a kind of U-turn in Congo's land concession policy. At least, this can be concluded on the basis of the violent criticisms the FEC (Federation of Congolese Enterprises), formulated against the new law throughout the year 2012. This federation represents, among others, big enterprises – of which many are in the hands of foreigners – in the agricultural, livestock and forestry sectors. Its main argument concentrated on a presentation of the law as a new form of 'Zaïreanization', the failed attempt at nationalization of foreign enterprises in the 1970's. The FEC led a campaign denouncing the new law as discriminatory, contrary to the free circulation of capital, and threatening the future of investment needed for the modernization of agriculture.

On the other hand, diverse groups defending the rights of national producers (like CONAPAC – 'Confédération nationale des producteurs agricoles du Congo') have welcomed and defended the new law. Also many peasant associations have expressed their support of the law's priority in protecting national interests in agriculture. But at the same time, they have sharply criticized the formulation of article 19, which recognizes the existence of communal lands, but refuses to explicitly grant such land a sort of legal status. For peasant associations, this means that peasant communities' land rights are not legally protected in the confrontation with national investors' attempts to privatize this land. In fact, these national investors are now better equipped than before. For local peasants, it makes little difference whether their land rights are eroded or denied by powerful foreign actors, or by more modest national and local actors.

The importance of the discussions goes way beyond the law's contents, given that it is only a state law among so many others, of which a great number have never been really been applied in the DRC. However, the symbolic aspect of the discussion is much more important. It has mobilized different kinds of actors around the land question. It has been a sort of 'hinge moment' that clearly framed the stakes around the land question in a very open debate. These debates around the role of foreign investment, the role of national producers, the type of landownership, private or communal, have brought ideas and demands to the table which have been simmering for a long time. These ideas and demands had, up until now, never been deployed with such force. The future of agriculture and of the peasant world has reappeared as a central theme in national politics. The discussion is taken well beyond the technicalities in which national and foreign experts had encapsulated the agricultural debate for decades.

What is clear is that the debate has not led to a consensus among all groups of concerned actors. Powerful actors, like big (foreign) enterprises in the agricultural sector, will continue to lobby for the dismissal of the articles which limit concessions to large foreign investors. National elites will lobby in favour of the protection of Congolese citizen's land rights, but are not particularly fond of the idea of giving communal land a legal status. Peasant associations, backed by some foreign NGOs, seem dedicated to a continued fight for the recognition of peasant communities' rights. As a result, the land grabbing question is now clearly incorporated in a larger political process. The evolution of this process will depend upon the evolving power relations between these different actors.

Conclusion: the long road ahead for the Congolese peasantry to obtain recognition as a central actor in the search for sustainable agricultural development

The twists and turns that have accompanied the elaboration and proclamation of the 2011 agricultural code, and the subsequent controversies around it, illustrate that an important part of the DRC peasantry is clearly aware of the necessity to mobilize and fight for the recognition of peasant rights. Such mobilization is in line with the Charter of Peasants Rights objectives as proclaimed by the Via Campesina Movement (Declaration of Rights of Peasants), 2009. This charter has contributed to the definition of a coherent alternative to 'land grabbing' at the international level (Holt, Gimenez and Shattuck, 2011). The principles of the charter are fundamental, since they clearly frame family farming within the collective land rights context of peasant communities. In other words, the charter recognizes the peasant actor in both their individual and collective dimension. This allows moving away from the seeming contradiction at the core of all modernization approaches between a 'farmer model of modernization' and a 'peasant development model'.

The Declaration of Rights of Peasants also gave a new dimension to the important topic of legal pluralism. It freed the reference to 'custom' from its archaic connotations that all variants of the modernization discourse attributed to it. Customary law in a broad sense keeps a strong legitimacy in the eyes of village communities. According to the principles of customary law, land is not just a commodity, but a component of a territory of life, a basis for the social and cultural identity of the community. They are the roots of its legitimacy.

But given the many corrupt practices of the present customary power, communal land management will require more and more new forms of complementary or even countervailing powers exerted by peasant associations. It is only in these conditions, that legal pluralism would provide a new empowering space to peasant communities, and that a bridge could be established between the heritage of a historical governance which still provides legitimacy, and the requirement of an invigorated institutional framework providing security to the community.

In such conditions, a framework of legal pluralism could increase the capacity of action (agency) of weaker stakeholders, through a kind of 'institutional bricolage' that opens a space for real negotiation (Cleaver, 2003). It can secure individual land rights within a framework of collective security offered by community rights bequeathed by history. This requires a new legal creativity that is based upon procedures of negotiation between all actors concerned (including peasant communities) on an equal footing (De Schutter, 2011). Indeed, the recognition of customary practices by outside actors – next to the formal regulatory framework – does entail the recognition of the peasant community as an equal player in the land arena (Friedrich-Ebert-Stiftung, 2012).

However, it is clear that empowering forms of 'institutional bricolage' can only occur through continued peasant mobilization at local and national levels. For example, some achievements reached through the mobilization of peasant organizations in 2010 and 2011 – in the context of the elaboration of the DRC agricultural law – will only be secured through continued pressure. Other interesting initiatives have also been taken up by peasant associations. The 'Union paysanne pour le développement intégral' in Kivu – an organization of thirty-three collectives with five hundred and ninety-eight base organizations and seventeen thousand members – has actively involved itself in the question of land disputes. It has put in place a system of courts of arbitration, managed by the peasants themselves, who try to resolve land conflicts before they escalate. By the end of 2010, seven hundred and sixty-eight arbitration efforts had already been validated and received enforcement by the State's judiciary.

Peasants' organizations will have to build and assert themselves continuously as somewhat aggressive collective actors, to be respected and incorporated in an inclusive process of 'substantive democracy' (Gathii, 2000). It will rest on the peasantries' ability to mobilize their own forces, and not be dependent on the urban civil society initiatives embedded in a top-down pro-poor ideology (Ngalamulume, 2011). Indeed, civil society organizations are often unable to recognize the peasantry as players in their own right, with their own vision of rural development. At the same time, most of the external stakeholders and national elites are more than ever fascinated by rural modernizing projects, despite their destructive extravagance (Van Hoof, 2011).

The construction or reconstruction of peasants' 'territories' will in the future depend on the ability of the peasant communities to strengthen their autonomy over local natural resources management, linking this aspect to their cultural identity and to the legacy of 'historical governance' of those resources by the very same peasant communities. A local governance model[3] based on associative networks and local communities can provide an alternative to the mishaps and pitfalls of imported governance (Peemans, 2008), and could play an important role in supporting 'a peasant way of sustainable development'. Local governance may be registered in the establishment of 'charters of local development', recognizing the rights and obligations of the State and local communities. While recognition of the peasantry as actors in their own right is not likely top of the agenda of the ruling elites, it will certainly be at the heart of many conflicts and struggles to come. The outcome of those struggles will frame the future balance between the continuation of land grabbing processes and the construction of a 'sustainable way of peasant development'.

[3] In the DRC, recent local governance institutions like the CARG ('Conseils agricoles et ruraux de gestion'), created in the wake of the awkward decentralization process, could be a first step in that direction, if duly recognized and adequately funded (ACE,2011). In some cases, those *conseils* have indeed functioned as a tool for empowerment by autonomous local peasant associations. They could be used as a forum to oppose attempts at land grabbing. But strangely (or understandably) enough the CARG have received no place in the institutional settings of the 2011 law on agriculture.

Bibliography

ACE Europe, 2011. *De la gouvernance du secteur agriculture en RD Congo, Rapport final*. Mechelen (Belgique).

Akram-Lodhi, A., 2008. '(Re)imagining Agrarian Relations? The World Development Report 2008: Agriculture for Development'. *Development and Change*, vol. 39, no. 6, pp. 1145-161.

Baxter, J., 2010. 'Ruée sur les terres africaines'. *Le Monde diplomatique*, no. 670, p. 18.

Bernstein, H., 2010. *Class Dynamics of Agrarian Change*. Kumarian Press, Halifax.

Borras, S. M. Jr and Franco, J. C., 2012. 'Global Land Grabbing and Trajectories of Agrarian Change: A Preliminary Analysis'. *Journal of Agrarian Change*, vol. 12, no. 1, pp. 34-59.

Braudel, F., 1985. *La dynamique du capitalisme*. Arthaud, Paris.

Brown, L., 2011. 'The New Geopolitics of Food.' *Foreign Policy* (May/June 2011).

Cleaver, F., 2003. 'Reinventing Institutions: Bricolage and the Social Embeddedness of Natural Resource Management'. *Securing Land Rights in Africa*, eds, Benjaminzen, T. A. and Lund, C. Cass, London.

Collier, P., 2010. *The Plundered Planet: How to Reconcile Prosperity with Nature*. Allen Lane, London.

Congo belge, 1918. *Rapport annuel sur la Colonie présenté aux Chambres législatives*. Documents parlementaires [s.d.], Bruxelles.

Declaration of Rights of Peasants, 2009. 'Women and Men' (proclaimed at the *La Via Campesina Jakarta Conference*, June 2008). Document adopted by the Via Campesina International Coordinating Committee in Seoul, March 2009.

Dehoux, E., 1946. *L'effort de paix au Congo belge*. Robert Stoops, Bruxelles.

De Schutter, O., 2011. 'How not to Think of Land Grabbing: Three Critiques of Large-scale Investments in Farmland'. *The Journal of Peasant Studies*, vol. 38, no. 2, pp. 249-279.

de Villers, G., Jewsiewski, B. and Monnier, L. (eds), 2002. 'Manières de vivre. L'économie de la débrouille au Congo-Kinshasa'. *Cahiers africains*, no. 49-50.

Drachoussoff, V., 1965. *Agricultural Change in the Belgian Congo, 1945-1960*. Food Research Institute, Stanford.

FAOstat, 2010. *Land Resource Database*.

Friedrich-Ebert-Stiftung, 2012. *Plaidoyer pour une réforme du régime juridique des cessions de terre à grand échelle en Afrique centrale*. Document cadre, Yaoundé.

Gathii, J. T., 2000. 'Representations of Africa in Good Governance Discourse: Policing and Containing Dissidence to Neo-liberalism'. *Third World Legal Studies*, vol. 1998-99, Post colonialism, Globalization and Law, Intworlsa, pp. 65-108.

Geenen, S., 2011. 'Local Livelihoods, Global Interests and the State in the Congolese Mining Sector'. *Natural Resources and Local Livelihoods in the Great Lakes Region of Africa, A Political Economy Perspective*, eds, Ansoms, A. and Marysse, S., Palgrave Macmillan, Basingstoke (UK), pp. 149-169.

Global Land Project, 2010. 'Land Grab in Africa'. *GLP Report*, no. 1. GLP International Project Office, University of Copenhagen, Department of Geography and Geology.

Hall, D., Hirsch, P. and Li, T., 2011. *The Powers of Exclusion*. National University of Singapore Press, Singapore.

Harvey, D., 2003. *The New Imperialism*. Oxford University Press, Oxford.

Holt Gimenez, E. and Shattuck, A., 2011. 'Food Crises, Food Regimes and Food Movements: Rumblings of Reform or Tides of Transformation?' *Journal of Peasant Studies*, vol. 38, no. 1, pp. 109-144.

Hyden, G, 1983. *No Shortcuts to Progress. African Development Management in Perspective*. Heinemann, London.

Hyden, G., 1985. 'La crise africaine et la paysannerie non capturée'. *Politique africaine*, no. 18, p. 95.

——, 1986. 'The Anomaly of the African Peasantry'. *Development and Change*, vol. 17, no. 4, pp. 677-705.

Jewsiewicki, B., 1980. 'Political Consciousness among African Peasants in the Belgian Congo'. *Review of African Political Economy*, no. 19, pp. 23-32.

——, 1987. 'Pour une histoire comparée des révoltes populaires au Congo'. *Rébellions-Révolutions au Zaïre, 1963-1965*, tome 2, eds, Coquery-Vidrovitch, C., Forest, A. and Weiss, H., L'Harmattan, Paris, pp. 130-156.

Kakule Kaparay, C., 2006. *Finance populaire et développement durable en Afrique au Sud du Sahara, Application à la région Nord-Est de la RDC*. Presses universitaires de Louvain, Louvain-la-Neuve (Belgique).

Kazadi, T., 1991. *Les déterminants de la crise agraire en Afrique sub-*

saharienne et la spécificité zaïroise. CIACO, Louvain-la-Neuve (Belgique).

Laurent, P.-J., 1996. 'Institutions locales, processus identitaires et quelques aspects théoriques à partir de l'exemple du Burkina Faso'. *Démocratie, enjeux fonciers et pratiques locales en Afrique, Cahiers Africains,* no. 23-24, eds, Mathieu, P. et al., CEDAF, Bruxelles, pp. 45-62

La Voix du Paysan Congolais, 2012-2013, n° 17-21, Kinshasa.

Leplae, E., 1929. 'Les cultures obligatoires dans les pays d'agriculture arriérée'. *Bulletin agricole du Congo belge,* vol. XX, no. 4, pp. 449-478.

——, 1933. 'Histoire et développement des cultures obligatoires du coton du riz au Congo belge de 1917 à 1933'. *Congo,* vol. XXIII, tome I, no. 5, pp. 645-753.

Li, T. M., 2011. "Forum on Global Land Grabbing: Centering Labor in the Land Grab Debate". *Journal of Peasant Studies,* vol. 38, no. 2, pp. 281-298.

Mafikiri Tongo, A., 1994. 'La problématique foncière au Kivu montagneux (Zaïre)'. *Cahiers du CIDEP,* n° 21, L'Harmattan, Paris.

Mafikiri Tongo, A., 1996. 'Mouvements de population, accès à la terre et question de la nationalité au Kivu'. *Démocratie, enjeux fonciers et pratiques locales en Afrique, Cahiers Africains,* no. 23-24, eds, Mathieu P. et al., CEDAF, Bruxelles, pp. 180-201.

Malengreau, G., 1949. *Vers un paysannat indigène : les lotissements agricoles au Congo belge.* Éditions Van Campenhout, Bruxelles.

Marysse, S. and Omasombo, J., 2012. *Conjonctures congolaises. Chroniques et analyses de la RDCongo en 2011.* Musée royal de l'Afrique centrale/L'Harmattan, Tervuren (Belgique)/Paris.

Mirembe, O. K., 2006. *Échanges transnationaux, réseaux informels et développement local. Une étude au Nord-Est de la RDC.* Presses universitaires de Louvain, Louvain-la-Neuve (Belgique).

Ndaywel è Nziem, I., 2010. *Histoire du Cong. Des origines à nos jours.* Afrique Éditions, Kinshasa.

New Agriculturist, January 2009. 'Democratic Republic of Congo'.

Ngalamulume, G., 2011. *Projets de développement agricole, dynamiques paysannes et sécurité alimentaire. Actions globales et initiatives locales au Kasaï occidental, RDC.* Presses universitaires de Louvain, Louvain-la-Neuve (Belgique).

Oxfam, 2011. 'Land and Power. The Growing Scandal Surrounding the New Wave of Investments in Land'. *Briefing Paper,* 22/09/2011.

Patel, R., 2006. 'International Agrarian Restructuring and the Practical Ethics of Peasant Movement Solidarity'. *Journal of Asian and African Studies,* vol. 41, no. 1-2, pp. 71-93.

Peemans, J.-Ph., 1974. 'Capital Accumulation in the Congo under Colonialism: The Role of the State'. *Colonialism in Africa,* vol. IV, eds, Duignan, P and Gann, L. H., Cambridge University Press, Cambridge.

——, 1975. 'The Social and Economic Development of Zaïre since Independance: An Historical Outline'. *African Affairs,* no. 295, pp. 148-179.

——, 1980. 'Imperial Hangovers: Belgium. The Economics of Decolonization'. *Journal of Contemporary History*, vol. 15, no. 2, pp. 257-286.

——, 1986. 'Accumulation and Underdevelopment in Zaïre: General Aspects in Relation to the Evolution of the Agrarian Crisis'. *The Crisis in Zaïre: Myths and Realities*, ed. Nzongola-Ntalaja, Africa World Press, Trenton (NJ), pp. 67-84.

——, 1997. *Le Congo-Zaïre au gré du XXᵉ siècle. État, économie et société, 1880-1990*. L'Harmattan, Paris.

——, 2002. *Le développement des peuples face à la modernisation du monde*. Louvain-la-Neuve (Belgique)/Paris, Academia-Bruylant/L'Harmattan.

——, (2008). 'Territoires et mondialisation: les enjeux en termes de développement'. *Alternatives Sud*, vol. 15, no. 1. Éditions Syllepse/Centre Tricontinental, Paris/Louvain-la-Neuve (Belgique), pp. 7-38.

Poncelet, M., 2008. *L'invention des sciences coloniales belges*. Karthala, Paris.

Réseau citoyens-Citizens Network (RCN) Justice & Démocratie, 2009. *Les conflits fonciers en Ituri : de l'imposition à la consolidation de la paix*. Cellule d'appui à l'Ordonnateur national du Fonds européen de Développement. COFED, Kinshasa.

République démocratique du Congo (RDC), déc. 2011. *Loi portant sur les principes fondamentaux relatifs à l'agriculture*. Kinshasa.

Scott, J., 1990. *Domination and the Arts of Resistance: Hidden Transcripts*. Yale University Press, New Haven.

Shikayi, L., 1994. *Initiatives de développement local et pouvoir paysan. Étude d'une dynamique locale de développement: le rôle des associations villageoises, des organisations non-gouvernementales et des micro-projets dans la vallée de la Ruzizi (1978-1989), Sud-Kivu/Zaïre*. CIACO, Louvain-la-Neuve (Belgique).

Sikor, T. and Lund,C. (eds), 2009.'The Politics of Possession: Property, Authority and Access to Natural Resources'. *Development and Change*, Special Issue, vol. 40, no. 1, pp. 1-217.

Tecsult and Aecom, 2009. *Étude du secteur agricole. Rapport préliminaire – Bilan-diagnostic et note d'orientation*. Ministère de l'agriculture, pêche et élevage (MAPE), Kinshasa.

Van Hoof, F., (2011). *Changer l'agriculture congolaise en faveur des familles paysannes, Des dynamiques paysannes dans les différentes provinces de la RDC*. Alliance Agricongo.

Veltmeyer, H., 2009. 'The World Bank on "Agriculture for Development": A Failure of Imagination or the Power of Ideology?' *Journal of Peasant Studies*, vol. 36, no. 2, pp. 393-410.

Vlassenroot, K. and Raeymaekers, T., 2009. 'Kivu's intractable security conundrum'. African Affairs, no. 432, pp. 475-484.

White, B. and Dasgupta, A., 2010. 'Agrofuels Capitalism: A View from Political Economy'. *Journal of Peasant Studies*, vol. 37, no. 4, pp. 593-607.

World Bank, 1989. *Sub-Saharan Africa: From Crisis to Sustainable Growth*. World Bank, Washington DC.

3

This Land is My Land Land Grabbing in Ituri (DRC)

DAN FAHEY

Introduction

The most famous song by the celebrated American folk singer Woody Guthrie – *This Land is Your Land* (1940) – was a response to dispossession and alienation during the Great Depression in the United States, but its message transcends space and time. Guthrie sought to remind Americans of massive land grabs by government agencies and private interests (Terrell, 1972; Reisner, 1993; Brown, 2001), which deprived millions of people – including indigenous populations – of land and livelihood. Guthrie's song provides a useful starting point for understanding land grabbing in the Ituri District of Northeastern Democratic Republic of the Congo. The people of Ituri experienced three distinct phases of land grabbing, starting with Belgian colonizers, continuing under the post-independence rule of Mobutu Sese Seko, and expanding during the war (1996-2007) and post-war (2007-present) periods. Over time the perpetrators have shifted from international to national to local actors, creating multiple layers of land conflict that limit post-conflict reconciliation and development, and threaten to reignite violent conflict.

The story of land grabbing in Ituri highlights several themes about how and why people take land from each other, and thus has relevance for similar situations in other places. These themes include (1) the importance of historical context in understanding current issues, (2) the incorporation of land into broader power struggles in ways that produce violence, and (3) the challenges faced by post-conflict efforts to resolve land conflicts. In addition, (4) perception is a key element in understanding claims about which land is 'your land', which land is 'my land,' and whether the land was created 'for you and me,' or just for 'me.'

Many contemporary episodes of land grabbing have ties to historical events and processes. For example, in highly publicised cases in Zimbabwe (Moyo, 2005) and the West Bank (Blanche, 2008), current land grabs are intimately tied to and should be understood in relation to their historical contexts. In Eastern Sudan, the post-independence state continued colonial land use policies that exacerbated local conflicts, thus linking recent land grabs to perceptions of historical injustice and increasing the likelihood of violent conflict (Fahey, 2007; El Hadary and Samat, 2011). Also in Ituri, many recent land grabs have ties to historical policies that favoured certain groups over others. This chapter will illustrate how disputes over boundaries, ownership, or access are often interpreted through perceptions of past greed and grievance.

The case of land grabbing in Ituri also highlights how local struggles for political and economic power may incorporate land disputes in ways that produce violence. That is, seemingly 'ordinary' land disputes may become enmeshed in broader conflicts and processes, providing a motivation for people to initiate violence. This phenomenon has been seen in many places, such as Chiapas, Mexico, where 'land occupations and often violent responses to them are not just struggles over scarce land for production', but also struggles for power and over the relationship between land and identity in rural areas (Bobrow-Strain, 2001: 184-185). In post-independence Kenya, the government used land as a 'patronage asset', contributing to a 'land grabbing mania' that underscored deepening corruption and produced escalating violence (Klopp, 2000). Another example concerns the potential for interstate war over the Spratly Islands in the South China Sea, which are claimed by six countries including China and Vietnam. Several countries have occupied barren rocks to establish their claims, which are based on perceptions of historic ownership and economic interests in the area's fishing grounds and oil and gas reserves (Garver, 1992; Storey, 1999).

Additionally, the story of Ituri's land conflicts illustrates some of the challenges of addressing disputes in a 'post-conflict' situation. The dysfunction and neglect of the Congolese State, as well as the lack of a comprehensive process of local reconciliation, have produced a situation in which most of the land conflicts that pre-date the war or were caused by the war are unresolved, containing the seeds of future violence. This is similar to the situation in post-war Mozambique, in which 'the end of the war [...] ha[d] neither resolved struggles over resources nor, more importantly, been accompanied by a process in which land laws are clarified, made transparent, and effectively administered by a capable state apparatus' (Myers, 1994: 631). In Mozambique, as in DRC, persistent land disputes limited post-conflict reconciliation and peace building, and sustained disagreements that had the potential to reignite armed conflict.

The final theme of this chapter is that community perceptions shape land conflicts and influence how they may trigger violence; and it is foundational for understanding land grabbing and its effects. In the context of land disputes, perception may refer to 'the process by which we form impressions whether positive or negative of other people's traits and personalities' (Azuimah, 2011: 261). Perception and misperception can contribute to the onset of violence and armed conflict through 'inaccurate inferences, miscalculations of consequences, and misjudgements about how others will react to one's [actions]' (Jervis, 1988: 675). For example, in northern Ghana, where ethnic conflicts included many disputes over landownership, there was 'deep resentment [among local communities] based on perceptions of economic and political inequalities, social and cultural prejudices, and competition for limited resources' (Azuimah, 2011: 265). Although the relationship between perception and armed conflict is based on controversial assumptions about what constitutes 'rational' behaviour and decision-making (Levy and Thompson, 2010: 134-138; Levy, 1983), the story of land grabbing in Ituri suggests that community perceptions – and manipulation of those perceptions – can play an important role in escalating land conflicts and determining the onset of violence.

In this chapter, I analyse historical and contemporary land grabbing in the Ituri District of Eastern DRC. In the first part, I provide an overview of Ituri and its history of land conflicts. In the second part, I examine contemporary land disputes, and provide detailed assessments of three conflicts. In the final part of the chapter, I review the themes that emerge from my analysis of land grabbing in Ituri.

Historical context

The Ituri District takes its name from the Ituri River, which runs south and then west through the heart of the district and empties into the Congo River. Ituri is well endowed with natural resources, including fertile land, forests, gold and fish (in Lake Albert). Administratively, Ituri is within Oriental Province; the capital of Ituri is Bunia. Ituri contains five territories,[1] each of which has several collectivities.

The Ituri District encompasses an area that includes people from numerous ethnic groups. The original inhabitants of Ituri are the Mbuti (pygmies), but starting in the sixteenth century, other groups arrived from the East (present-day Uganda) and North (present-day Sudan) (Meesen, 1951: 174-181). The two populations of greatest relevance for this chapter are the Lendu and the Hema. The Lendu arrived in Ituri during the sixteenth century from Sudan (Southall, 1953: 152). Some Lendu settled in an area that later became Northern Ituri (in present-day Mahagi and Djugu territories), while others travelled farther south and settled in present-day Irumu territory near Gety; the former are called Lendu or Bbale, while the latter are known as Ngiti. The Hema arrived during the eighteenth century from Uganda (Meesen, 1951: 179).[2] Like the Lendu, some Hema settled in Northern Ituri (present-day Djugu territory), while others settled in Southern Ituri (present day Irumu territory); the former are referred to as Gegere, while the latter are simply called Hema.

In the late nineteenth century, the Iturian social landscape changed profoundly because of the arrival of one of the greatest land grabbers in

---

[1]   These are Aru, Djugu, Irumu, Mahagi, and Mambasa.

[2]   Pottier (2009: 33) states the migration took place starting in the late 17th century.

history: Belgium's King Leopold II. King Leopold nominally acquired the territory of Congo as a result of the 1885 Berlin conference (Martelli, 1962: 87-127), and called his new possession the Congo Free State.[3] On 29 May 1885, King Leopold issued a decree from Brussels that declared all 'vacant' land to be property of the State, but without defining what constituted vacant land (Hochschild, 1998: 117).[4] Starting in 1891, Leopold issued a series of decrees that established his hegemony over vast territories and the human, plant, animal, and mineral resources contained therein. In response to international concerns about the free trade status of Congolese territory (Pakenham, 1991: 393-412), in 1892 Leopold created a new land policy that reserved some 'vacant' lands for the exclusive use of the State while allowing commercial companies to operate in other areas (Martelli, 1962: 139-141). Leopold also 'claimed as state property all wild plants and animals on these lands – notably elephants and wild rubber plants – and imposed a labour tax on the Congolese people to be paid in ivory and latex or in other labour services' (Northrup, 1988: 40-41).

Around 1894, the Congo Free State first established a presence in Ituri.[5] Leopold's initial interests in Ituri were to procure ivory, of which there was still plenty in Ituri at that time, and to extend his authority through Northeastern Congo to the Nile River (Martelli, 1962: 144-145). During the next decade, colonial authorities increased their presence in Ituri and carved the region into administrative zones (Thiry, 2004: 30), claiming on maps an authority it did not yet fully possess on the ground.

The 1903 discovery of gold by colonial agents marked the beginning of a new era in Ituri. In July 1905, foreign engineers employed by King Leopold started mining gold in Ituri, in an area of present-day western Djugu territory known as the Kilo belt. The State had previously designated this area as part of the 'domaine privé', which made commercial activity the exclusive right of the Congo Free State, but in 1906 the designation was changed to 'Fondation de la Couronne', which made it the personal property of King Leopold (Meesen, 1951: 60). In 1908, after an international movement exposed the brutal policies used to extract Congo's rubber and ivory, King Leopold transferred the Congo Free State to the Belgian government, thus creating the Belgian Congo (Pakenham, 1991: 656-668).

Colonial land policy continued to evolve, but followed the same general pattern of facilitating maximum benefits for the colonizers and marginalizing local populations. A 3 June 1906 decree formally recognized

---

[3] The Congo Free State was the name of the organization controlling the territory of the Congo, and was under the direct control of King Leopold. The Congo Free State ran Congo from 1885 to 1908, when control of Congo was transferred to the Belgian government (Hochschild, 1998: 258-259).

[4] The ambiguity in definitions of what constitutes 'vacant land' is still extremely relevant in contemporary debates on land grabbing. See e.g. De Schutter, 2011.

[5] Meesen (1951: 55) puts the date of first colonial occupation as 1894, but Southall (1953: 281) states the State established a presence in 1893 at Mahagi; Thiry (2002: 88) puts the first occupation in 1895.

'native lands' as those that were inhabited, cultivated or exploited in any manner by native Congolese people.[6] All land that was not 'native land' or otherwise registered was considered vacant and therefore 'public land'.[7] The Belgian Congo promulgated regulations in 1910 and 1911 that enabled the colonial government to lease vacant (public) lands to private individuals or corporations; these lands were known as 'concessions' (Geographical Section, 1920: 287).

In order to better control the local populations and protect the growing extraction of gold in the Kilo belt, Belgian colonial authorities created new tribal and administrative units in Ituri.[8] During 1917-1918, colonial authorities in Ituri organised the Lendu populations into several autonomous groups, thereby separating them from the Hema chiefs who previously ruled over them (Southall, 1953: 152-153; Bakonzi, 1982: 762-763; Thiry, 2004: 30-31). As a consequence of this colonial intervention in local politics, there were power struggles among Lendu clans, which the colonial authorities suppressed using the 'Force publique', as well as increased tension between the Hema and Lendu (Bakonzi, 1982: 175-176; Thiry, 2004: 31-32). The State tried to physically separate Hema and Lendu populations, believing this would quell latent conflict between the communities; this process continued into the 1930s (Thiry 2004: 32; Pottier, 2009: 38-39;). Despite this effort, many Hema and Lendu continued to live together in the same territories and villages, and intermarriage was common (UNSC – United Nations Security Council, 2004: 7-8).

As the State established its authority over the territory and population of Ituri, it granted concessions for gold mining, plantations, forestry, and fishing. The first white settlers in Ituri, who arrived between 1910 and 1920, were Belgians, British, Greeks and Afrikaners who variously raised cattle, grew food crops (for other white settlers and for gold miners), and planted coffee (Bakonzi, 1982: 113, 138, 178). During the 1910s, there were severe food shortages in the Kilo mining area, as well as in the Moto gold mines in neighbouring Haut-Uélé district (the entire gold mining area in Northeast Congo and the company exploiting gold became known as Kilo-Moto). As a result, in 1922 the State decided to encourage more white settlement in Ituri to grow foodstuffs for the Kilo-Moto operations (ibid.: 213).

To more easily orient the region's overall production to support gold mining, in 1928 the colonial government altered district boundaries to place the Kilo and Moto goldmines in one district, called Kibali-Ituri (Northrup, 1988: 123). The colonial government also created new

---

[6]   In 1934 and 1935, colonial decrees prohibited Congolese from selling their land rights to private parties (cf. Office d'information, 1959: 206).

[7]   Lands could only be considered vacant after an official inquiry, which by decree of 31 May 1934 included a two-year waiting period for public comment on the disposition of the land.

[8]   On 1 January 1920, the colonial government created a new administrative Territory called Nizi that was later renamed Djugu (Thiry, 2004: 32).

economic zones throughout Congo, which restricted African labour in Ituri for work in the mines (Bakonzi, 1982: 267-269). Starting in the late 1920s, colonial authorities granted many new concessions in Ituri to white settlers (ibid.: 411-412), including concessions for coffee. By 1933, the State had allocated more than 15,000 hectares in Ituri for fifty-nine coffee plantations (Leplae, 1936: 207).

The colonial State exercised its control over Ituri using a form of indirect rule that organized administrative districts under the control of ethnic chiefs. Racial stereotyping heavily influenced the function of colonial rule in Ituri, for example by favouring the Hema over the Lendu, but it also forced many groups to physically separate, creating the notion that they could not live together. Although the separation was incomplete, particularly in rural areas (UNSC, 2004: 7-8), it nonetheless exacerbated historical inequalities, such as between Hema and Lendu in Ituri (Thiry, 1996: 116-118, 245-247, 279-284). Pottier (2009: 49) has noted:

> If negative stereotyping about Lendu continued throughout the colonial era, this had to do with the fact that Lendu, Lendu-Bindi [Southern Ituri] especially, showed indifference, resistance and hostility toward the European occupier [...] Facing ardent hostility, the convenient option for the coloniser was to create and perpetuate the myth of physical-cum-intellectual superiority that would put Hema in the ascendancy in matters of education, administration, and commerce. And on that myth the dominant discourse may have grafted another, that of Lendu subjugation since time immemorial.

The effectiveness of Belgian mythmaking is evident today. Some leaders of the Hema community articulate Hema superiority over the belligerent and lazy Lendu,[9] while some Lendu leaders speak of victimhood and exclusion at the hands of greedy Hema.[10]

The November 1965 ascendancy of Mobutu Sese Seko to power in Congo/Zaïre marked the beginning of significant changes for the entire country, including Ituri. Shortly after Mobutu took power, the Zaïrean government began a process of redistributing agricultural concessions in Ituri (and elsewhere) to those with strong ties to the regime, which in Irumu and Djugu territories were Hema businessmen. On 7 June 1966, President Mobutu approved the so-called Bakajika Law, which annulled all land titles granted before independence and required prior titleholders to reapply to the Zaïrean government. While this law was part of the State's effort to extend its political sovereignty into the economic realm, it also served to create an inventory of lands and their current uses (Young and Turner, 1985: 281). Then, on 30 November 1973, President Mobutu

---

[9] Interviews with Hema community leaders and academics, July 2009, Bunia.
[10] Interviews with Lendu elders, politicians, administrators and teachers, June and July 2009, Kpandroma.

unveiled his 'Zaïreanization' plan, which nationalized 'farms, ranches, plantations, concessions, commerce, and real estate agencies' (Young and Turner, 1985: 326).

Starting in the mid-1960s, some Ituri businessmen acquired concessions from the State and from expatriate concession owners, but Mobutu's Zaïreanization plan resulted in a large-scale reallocation of concessions and industries into the hands of those with political connections. Hema businessmen benefitted most from this process due to their political ties to the Mobutu regime.[11] In Djugu territory, where the Ituri war started in 1999, the State gave contracts for many concessions to Hema businessmen, while other concessions became government property or were retained by churches.[12]

The problems created by the history of land grabbing in Ituri were multiplied by the polywar of international and internal conflicts that began in 1996. The first Congo war (1996-97) left the Ituri District relatively unscathed, and resulted in the Rwandan-led 'Alliance des forces démocratiques pour la libération' (AFDL) taking power in Ituri (and the entire Congo). The AFDL exercised authority over Ituri until August 1998, when the invading Ugandan army (Ugandan People's Defence Force, or UPDF) took de facto power at the start of the second war (1998-2003). The UPDF initially ran Ituri with the assistance of the Congolese rebel group 'Rassemblement congolais pour la démocratie' (RCD), but after RCD split in 1999, the UPDF used the splinter group RCD - Mouvement de Libération (RCD-ML) to manage Ituri until UPDF's withdrawal from Ituri in May 2003 (ICJ 2005: 60).

The war in Ituri continued after the UPDF's withdrawal. In 1999, a 'war within the war' had started in Ituri, involving a localized conflict that spread due to the actions of UPDF, RCD-ML, and Hema and Lendu elites. This conflict spawned new armed groups, most of which had an ethnic agenda, but all of which pursued political and/or economic agendas. The UN Organization Mission in the Congo (MONUC) deployed in earnest in 2003 to Ituri, but had little impact until 2005, when MONUC pursued a 'robust approach' that combined vigorous military attacks against armed groups with political negotiations and a disarmament process (Fahey, 2011: 166-204). The war largely ended in November 2007, after more than 20,000 rebels were disarmed and Ituri's rebel group leaders were variously incorporated into the Congolese army (FARDC – 'Forces armées de la République démocratique du Congo') or arrested. As of late 2012, armed groups continued to cause instability, death and displacement in Ituri; some groups reportedly receive support from the Rwandan government (Tamm, 2012; UNSC, 2012). In addition, FARDC is also exploiting

---

[11] One prominent Hema politician, D'zbo Kalogi, served as national vice-minister of agriculture from 1970-1974, minister of mines from 1974-1977, and minister of agriculture and rural development from 1986-1987.

[12] It remains unclear how many concessions Hema businessmen obtained, but various sources suggest they acquired a majority of the concessions in Ituri's Irumu and Djugu territories.

local populations and demonstrating its inability (or unwillingness) to fully establish security in Ituri.

The legacies of colonialism, post-independence rule, and war have profoundly influenced contemporary land grabbing in Ituri. As a result of these processes, land conflicts in Ituri are often incorporated into local power struggles, tied to ethnic identity, and linked to perceptions of injustice. In addition, the corruption of governance in Ituri during the last several decades has sustained land disputes and facilitated new land grabs, as shown in the cases discussed in the next section.

Contemporary land grabbing in Ituri

The concept of land in Ituri is complex and multidimensional. As in Eastern DRC more generally, land in Ituri 'is significant as a means of production for subsistence or commercial sale; an area where political authority is expressed and taxes may be raised (the concept of "territory"); a means by which families and individuals maintain social influence and status; and also as a source of feelings of ancestral "belonging"' (Huggins, 2010: 10). These various aspects of land – the economic, the political, the social, and the spiritual – continuously interact, informing narratives that justify and contest land grabs. In addition, perception over land rights can be as important – or more important – than rights 'legally' conferred by a government authority.

Van Puijenbroek and Ansoms (2011: 62) highlight the great variety of contemporary land conflicts in Ituri. These arise from 'a unique and locally specific combination of governance aspects, demographic aspects, cultural aspects, historical aspects and local socio-economic interdependencies'. The persistence and widespread nature of land conflict is tied to competition for power at various levels, ranging from the household, to the community, to the ethnic group, to hierarchies of political and economic structures (Camm, 2011; RCN – 'Réseau citoyens' - Citizens Network, 2009).

The multifaceted nature of land conflicts in Ituri makes them difficult to resolve. Huggins (2010: 5) notes: '[l]and is essential to most rural livelihoods, but it is also bound up very strongly with issues of "identity and power".' Individuals and groups that acquired or grabbed land as a result of war, seek 'to avoid having wartime transactions and population movements scrutinised and potentially undone, for example through the establishment of land commissions, mediation processes, the return of IDPs and refugees, or other state or non-state interventions.' Indeed, 'such actors will likely attempt to gain influence with politicians or maintain a certain level of "instability" in order to prevent international and local NGOs and state services from gaining a foothold in areas under their control, to prevent the return of those claiming landownership.' As a result of the displacements and land grabbing that took place during the polywar in Ituri, as well as the land grabbing during the colonial and Mobutu eras, there are well in excess of one thousand active land disputes in this region.[13]

Contemporary land conflicts generally fall under one of three categories. One category involves problems between communities, which evolved before, during and after the wars in Ituri. This may include disputes between villages or larger administrative units, involve political elites, and have an ethnic dimension (Van Puijenbroek and Ansoms, 2011). These problems generally concern a disputed boundary, rights of access or use, or the inability of a displaced community to return to its place of origin due to resistance from the current residents (Camm, 2011). A second category involves disputes between individuals. These include conflicts over access, use, property boundaries, succession disputes, and illegal selling of property. The third type of land dispute involves problems at concessions between concession owners and local communities; many of these problems began in the 1970s following Zaïreanization. Land conflicts involving concessions have received the most attention from scholars (e.g. Pottier, 2008: 435; Veit, 2010: 123), although they represent only a small fraction of the overall land conflicts in Ituri (Van Puijenbroek and Ansoms, 2011). Nonetheless, problems at concessions contributed to the outbreak of war in 1999 in Ituri (Fahey, 2011), and according to practitioners in the field,[14] are among the most difficult conflicts to resolve; therefore they deserve special attention.

There are four dimensions to problems at concessions in Ituri. The first involves concessionaires who illegally (and/or unethically) expanded their concessions into neighbouring lands. This reportedly happened most commonly at concessions that were cattle ranches, where increasing numbers of cows required more land. Local populations often did not consent or have knowledge of these land grabs, which were obtained through political connections and/or corruption. As a result, local populations resisted the expansions through various violent and non-violent means. The second dimension pertains to land access and use. In some locations, concessionaires sought to end local use of concession lands for farming or animal husbandry. Such use had been customary since the colonial era at many concessions, but when possession changed hands after independence, the new concessionaires at some sites ended the practice, provoking resentment. The third dimension of disputes at

---

[13] A 2009 study by the Congolese group Haki na Amani and IKV Pax Christi identified 1,318 active land conflicts throughout the Ituri district (Van Puijenbroek and Ansoms, 2011: 50; IKV Pax Christi and Haki na Amani, 2009). As of February 2012, the Land Commissions established and supported by UN Habitat had identified approximately 1,000 land conflicts in Djugu and Mahagi territories alone. Interviews with staff from UN Habitat and Land Commissions, Ituri, January and February 2012.

[14] Interviews with staff from UN Habitat and Land Commissions, Ituri, January and February 2012.

concessions is tied to social relations. Colonial era concessionaires often had good relations with local communities, but the businessmen who grabbed the concessions during the Mobutu era sometimes disrupted those traditional relations and treated local chiefs and populations disrespectfully. In addition, local political and customary leaders incorporated land issues into their struggles for political and economic power, which contributed to problems between concessionaires and local populations. The final dimension concerns animal trespassing. There are numerous stories in Ituri of cattle wandering off concession lands into neighbouring lands, where they consumed and trampled villagers' crops, and provoked ire from local communities.

In what follows, I concentrate on three disputes that illustrate broader themes about land conflicts. The first example involved mutual accusations of land grabbing between a concessionaire and a local community, where the former is Hema and the latter Lendu. The second example is a boundary dispute between two administrative units – one Hema and one Lendu – with ties to larger political and economic power struggles. The third example highlights a case of a Hema concessionaire trying to grab land from a Hema village. These examples illustrate why and how land grabs take place, how they can produce violence, and why disputes persist.

Land and violence
In 1999, a land conflict at a concession called Leyna resulted in violence and contributed to the start of the Ituri war. Leyna is also known as Aboro, after the large nearby mountain, southeast of the town of Kpandroma in the Walendu Pitsi collectivity of Djugu territory. In 1948, the Belgian government gave permission to a man named Frans Nicolai to establish the 480-hectare concession at Leyna. At some point after independence (but no later than 1985), a Hema businessman acquired the rights to Leyna. During the 1990s, it was used primarily as a coffee plantation, and secondarily for timber harvesting, agriculture, and cattle.

There are divergent accounts of the causes of the events at Leyna,[15] but general agreement on the central facts. For several years in the late 1990s, some Lendu villagers from Gosenge, a village abutting the northwest corner of Leyna, accused the concession owner of trying to illegally expand his concession into Lendu lands and Gosenge village (the concessionaire denies these charges). Interestingly, most of the concessionaire's employees were Lendu, and many lived in Gosenge village. In April 1999, the concession owner convened a meeting with local communities to try to resolve the matter, but the two sides failed to come to agreement. In early May, some Lendu attacked crops and cattle on the Leyna concession. On 14 May 1999 (UNSC, 2004: 9), the

---

[15] Unless otherwise specified, this discussion is based on interviews conducted with local officials and villagers during May and June 1999 in the Ituri District; cf. Fahey, 2011.

concession owner asked police and the Ugandan army to push some Lendu farmers off of disputed land, near the hill known as Dju. After this action, some Lendu attacked the Leyna concession a second time, destroying buildings and some crops; the owner abandoned the concession at that time.

There are two narratives about the causes of the problems at Leyna, and much remains unknown. From the Lendu perspective, the concessionaire was trying to illegally grab land that belonged to neighbouring Lendu communities, including land between the hill known as Dju and the central part of the concession used by villagers from Gosenge for farming. When the Lendu resisted eviction from land they claimed belonged to them, the concessionaire used the police and soldiers to attack them, resulting in one person being wounded. The Hema account (related by the concessionaire and other Hema leaders) asserts that the concession owner sought to use land that was within the concession boundaries, but that had been farmed by local Lendu villagers under an informal arrangement. According to this account, the villagers were misinformed about the concession's boundaries and were manipulated by local Lendu politicians who wanted to seize the concession. When the Lendu refused to cease farming the land within the concession, and then committed vandalism, the concession owner summoned security forces to protect his property.

Official maps of Leyna appear to support the Hema version of events, although they may not tell the entire story. The original map of the concession from 1948 and a map updating the concessionaire's contract in 1992 show identical borders, and I have not seen any evidence suggesting that the concession owner was trying to expand the boundaries of his concession and grab local lands. Moreover, both the 1948 and 1992 maps clearly show that the hill called Dju is within the boundaries of the concession, and that the disputed gardens used by the Gosenge villagers were also within the concession. During a June 2009 visit to Leyna and Gosenge, local Lendu leaders and villagers told me that Dju and the disputed gardens were Lendu lands belonging to Gosenge village, and were situated outside the concession boundaries; however, the maps contradict this claim.

Based on reviews of available documentation, a visit to the site, and interviews with approximately two-dozen people, I hypothesize that two separate factors led to the conflict at Leyna. First, the local population believed that after years of farming within the boundaries of the concession (perhaps since colonial times), the land became theirs by right of use. This is an example of legal pluralism, in which 'various institutional frameworks (both formal and informal) interact, reinforce, and compete with each other' (Ansoms and Claessens, 2011: 17). The map represents an official tool of control and rights, but customary use created perceptions of rights that are as real as the map. This factor interacted with a second, which is the probability that local Lendu elites incited the local population against the concession owner.[16] This hypothesis is supported by interviews, including statements made by Lendu elites in Walendu Pitsi collectivity about their desire to reclaim 'Lendu lands' from Hema concessionaires. Indeed, a 1995 report from the Zaïrean intelligence service[17] about the Walendu Pitsi branch of the Lendu group LORI[18] noted: 'The tribal character of the Association is at the foundation of its members' projects to expropriate the concessions and fields of non-Lendu, particularly of the Hema' (SNIP – 'Service national d'Intelligence et de Protection', 1995).

In this context, in which the concessionaire and local communities were accusing each other of land grabbing, and in which there was a dispute about access and use of concession lands, violence erupted that increased tensions locally. The conflict at Leyna caused fear among Hema concession owners in the area, leading them to employ UPDF (Ugandan People's Defence Force) soldiers to protect their concessions. This in turn led to resentment and fear among Lendu populations, who perceived the occupying Ugandan army as backing land grabbing Hema elites (Fahey, 2011). A month after the violence at Leyna, the mounting tensions led to attacks on two nearby villages, which marked the start of the Ituri war.

Disputing (ethnic) boundary lines
The border dispute between Walendu Bindi and Bahema Sud collectivities in Irumu territory demonstrates the links between historical claims and contemporary political and economic agendas. At issue are claims by Walendu Bindi officials that several villages with Lendu populations (Nombe, Lakpa, and Lagabo – roughly half-way between Bunia and Lake Albert) are wrongly considered part of Bahema Sud collectivity, and that Walendu Bindi has historical claims to land along the shore of Lake Albert. Bahema Sud officials assert these claims lacks merit and are simply an attempt by the Walendu Bindi authorities to grab land and gain access to the lake. The claims are tied to long-standing ethnic tensions, the legacy of war in this corner of Ituri, and the start of oil exploration near Lake Albert.

The origins of this dispute can be traced back to 1911 or earlier, when the colonial district commissioner (called 'Chef de Zone') appointed a Hema chief named Bomera to be 'Grand Chef' for the populations in present day Irumu territory south of Bunia. Pottier (2009: 43) states that the 'Chef de Zone' established the new chiefdom because he disliked the political fragmentation in the area, while Bakonzi (1982: 762-763) asserts that the colonial government ordered its administrators to establish chiefdoms as a form of indirect rule. The action by the 'Chef de Zone' followed

---

[16] Geenen and Hönke (see chapter in this volume) observed a similar dynamic of elites playing a very active role in land disputes. They point to the way in which the commercialization of land interacts with a reconfiguration of local politics.

[17] Service national d'Intelligence et de Protection (SNIP).

[18] Libération des opprimés et rejetés de l'Ituri (LORI).

a directive from his superiors to more firmly establish control over local populations via a local chief, who would be paid a salary by the State, and effectively act as a state agent. In addition, the appointment of Bomera in Southern Ituri coincided with Belgian efforts to clearly establish Congo's boundaries with Uganda and Sudan (ibid.: 763).

The Chef de Zone's selection of Bomera was immediately controversial. After his arrival around 1900 from Western Uganda, Bomera had stolen cattle, stolen land, and killed people – particularly Lendu – thereby creating enemies and increasing tensions in the area (Thiry, 1996: 223-228). Belgian authorities arrested Bomera in 1910 because of his actions; however, in a strange reversal of fortune, the 'Chef de Zone' appointed Bomera to be a state agent and local leader, based in part on the recommendation of a Canadian missionary (ibid.: 229).

Bomera did not have much popular support among Hema clans in Southern Ituri, which supported other Hema chiefs (Pottier, 2009: 43), but Bomera's actions were even more problematic for Lendu populations. After his appointment, Bomera exacted revenge upon Lendu villages with whom he had prior disputes, stealing cattle, burning at least one village, and killing people (Thiry, ibid.: 230-231). Lendu clans revolted and, on 4 December 1911, killed Bomera and two hundred Hema villagers in a decisive battle. The colonial authorities reacted swiftly and brutally, and with the help of a chief from the Bira ethnic group, stole cattle from Lendu populations that were then given to Hema people (ibid.: 234-235). In 1914, the Belgian authorities abandoned the idea of establishing one chief, creating instead nine chieftaincies: six under Lendu chiefs and three under Hema chiefs (ibid.: 237). Two of the chieftaincies the Belgians created were Tsiritsi (with a Lendu chief) and Bandihango (with a Hema chief).

During the 1920s and 1930s, the Belgian colonial government repeatedly shifted authority over a small enclave of land between Tsiritsi and Bandihango. This enclave included the villages of Nombe and Lakpa, as well as the place where the village of Lagabo now stands, along the road from Bogoro to Gety. During the 1920s, Nombe and Lakpa villages were allegedly part of Tsiritsi *chefferie*, which had a Lendu chief (Van Puijenbroek and Ansoms, 2011: 57). Nonetheless, a December 1931 colonial government document identifies Nombe and Lakpa as being part of the Bandihango chieftaincy, which had a Hema chief.[19] In 1933, another administrative change moved Nombe and Lakpa back into the chieftaincy of Tsiritsi. But in 1940, the colonial government again moved Nombe and Lakpa into the chieftaincy of Bandihango, which became part of Bahema Sud collectivity, run by a Hema chief. Two colonial maps from

---

[19] The remainder of this discussion is based upon nearly two-dozen interviews with villagers in Nombe and Lagabo, and interviews with local officials in Geti and Kasenyi, during January and February 2012. It also draws upon many documents and maps obtained in Ituri (Jan-Feb. 2012) and at the Belgian Royal Museum of Central Africa in Tervuren, Belgium (Feb. 2012).

1959 (8 May and 31 December) show the Nombe-Lakpa-Lagabo enclave as part of Bandihango collectivity, and Bahema Sud collectivity.

In 1966, violence erupted over rightful administration of the three disputed villages. Walendu Bindi authorities initiated protests based on the claim that the provincial governor had wrongfully allowed Bahema Sud to 'annex' Nombe, Lakpa, and Lagabo. In addition, they claimed that in 1960, a colonial administrator had reassigned the three villages to Tsiritsi chieftaincy, under the administration of Walendu Bindi (Kabaga, 2000: 4). The Bahema Sud authorities insisted that the villages had been part of their collectivity since 1940 at the latest. Mobutu's soldiers violently suppressed the Lendu protestors, but there continued to be conflicts over the enclave during the 1970s and 1980s; Mobutu's security and political apparatus also contained these protests.

In 1993, rising tensions over the boundary issue led the then-Governor of Haut-Zaïre (Oriental Province) to come to Bunia to meet with representatives of Bahema Sud and Walendu Bindi. Both sides signed a peace agreement on 18 July that included allowing the people of Nombe, Lakpa, and Lagabo to vote in a non-binding referendum about their administration; Walendu Bindi was also required to relinquish all claims to the shore of Lake Albert in Bahema Sud collectivity. On 19 September, the people of the enclave reportedly voted overwhelmingly to be administered by Walendu Bindi. In 1994, territorial administrators forwarded the results of the referendum to the Ministry of Interior in Kinshasa, but the Ministry never took action on the issue before the AFDL took control of Ituri in December 1996 (see above), or before Mobutu's government fell in May 1997.

The war that started in June 1999 in Walendu Pitsi soon spread one hundred kilometres southwest to Walendu Bindi and Bahema Sud. The conflict's ethnic dimension was particularly intense in Irumu, with its long history of ethnic tension. The worst attack in the area of the enclave took place on 24 February 2003, when Lendu militia killed more than two hundred Hema villagers in the town of Bogoro (ICC – International Criminal Court, 2012), 4 kilometres north of Lagabo village. Lendu militias also attacked and destroyed several concessions south of Bogoro, after which Lendu villagers from Lagabo harvested timber from the concession grounds.

Supporting the Walendu Bindi claims about the Nombe-Lakpa-Lagabao enclave are two facts: the enclave was at one time under the rule of a Lendu chief, and the population of the villages voted to be administered by Walendu Bindi in a 1993 referendum. Supporting the Bahema Sud argument are numerous documents and maps showing the enclave as being within the Hema-run areas of Bandihango and Bahema Sud for more than seventy years. Both sides in this debate fervently believe the other side is guilty of land grabbing, and in these perceptions lays the potential for conflict between Lendu and Hema to reignite in this area.

In March 2002, Lendu authorities created their own map to assert control over a swathe of Bahema Sud from the disputed enclave to Lake Albert. There appear to be two motivations for this action. First, there were longstanding grievances in Walendu Bindi about the lack of access to Lake Albert, which limited Lendu populations' ability to acquire fish from the lake, and prevented Lendu authorities from collecting taxes from fishing. This claim is tied to Ngiti (Southern Lendu) historical claims of having arrived in the region prior to Hema populations, as well as perceptions of lost territory and rights. Second, the timing of this map coincided with the signing of a contract for oil exploration along the shores of Lake Albert. On 10 June 2002, Congo's president Joseph Kabila signed a contract with Heritage Oil to explore for oil along the Congo side of Lake Albert and the shore of the lake in Ituri (Johnson, 2003: 19). In this context, it appears Walendu Bindi's claim that its territory extended to the shores of Lake Albert was an attempt to position itself to obtain rents from oil exploration and production.

In 2012, a militia closely affiliated with the Lendu community occupied nearly the entire area on the 2002 map that Lendu leaders had claimed as part of Walendu Bindi. Since 2007, a splinter group of the FRPI ('Forces de résistance patriotique d'Ituri') militia that refused to disarm had operated in Walendu Bindi. This group, which numbered fewer than one hundred combatants, gained strength after the 2010 return of its leader, Cobra Matata, who had deserted the Congolese army. Following a February 2012 mutiny of FARDC soldiers in Southern Irumu, the army chief of staff withdrew nearly all soldiers in Ituri to four sites to prevent a spread of the mutiny (Fahey, 2012; Tamm, 2012). Cobra's men filled this power vacuum, occupying all the territory between Gety and Nombe (government troops retained control of Lakpa and Lagabo), and extending roughly due east to the lakeshore at Nyamavi.[20] In September 2012, Cobra received a jeep and other inducements to join a disarmament programme (UNDSS – United Nations Department of Safety and Security, 2012), but he failed to integrate. While his land grab enabled Ngiti access to Lake Albert and its fishing grounds, it also prevented further oil exploration by the French firm Total. In August 2013, FARDC launched a major offensive against FRPI that succeeded, by October 2013, in recapturing most of the towns previously occupied by FRPI. As this book goes to press, the conflict continues, but even if it is resolved, the boundary dispute will persist.

Love thy neighbour?
The land grab at the village of Nyali demonstrates the challenges of resolving land grabs in a post-conflict environment. It also highlights a situation in which a Hema concessionaire sought to take land from Hema villagers, which runs counter to the oft-repeated notion that Hema concessionaires exclusively sought to grab land from Lendu villages

---

[20] Interview with MONUSCO official, Bunia, August 2012.

(Pottier, 2008: 435; UNSC, 2004: 8). By failing to mention that anyone other than Lendu villagers may have been affected by Hema concessionaire land grabs, many authors have imputed an ethnic motivation to the concessionaires' actions in addition to their economic agendas. While there is copious evidence that some Hema concessionaires sought to grab land from Lendu communities, the case of Nyali suggests that land grabbing in Ituri can be blind to the ethnicity of targetted villagers.

Nyali is a village in south-central Walendu Pitsi collectivity, in Djugu territory, adjacent to a concession called Tsa.[21] Nyali became a village in 1955, after a man by that name led a group of people to that site from neighbouring Bahema Nord collectivity.[22] The village numbered several hundred people, who were predominantly Hema. It occupies a space on the western side of the Tsa concession, which was started in 1937 by an American named Charles Trout. Trout used the concession to raise cattle.

In 1971, after the Bakajika Law annulled all land titles granted before independence, a Hema businessman obtained the rights to Tsa concession from the Zaïrean government and used it for cattle ranching. He immediately sought to expand Tsa's boundary westward to include several hills near Nyali, and obtained local permission to use (but not own) one of the hills. In 1972, the businessman also established his residence at the Tsa concession. For the next twenty-five years, the concessionaire raised cattle at Tsa and used some of the hills belonging to Nyali village through an informal agreement with the village chief.

In May 1997, just as Mobutu fell and the AFDL assumed political control of Ituri, the concessionaire invited some of the new AFDL officials from Bunia to Tsa, with the purpose to formally take land from Nyali village. The concessionaire sought to annex approximately 100 hectares around three hills, which would normally have required him to apply to the provincial government. However, the concessionaire divided the area he sought into eight smaller plots (one for himself, and one each for seven of his sons), thereby enabling him to seek only district level approval for his land grab.

The AFDL officials determined that the lands in question were 'vacant' or not in use, and awarded property rights to the concessionaire. The villagers from Nyali immediately disputed this finding, stating that they in fact used the fields and hills, and that the village elders were not properly consulted about the status of the land. In late 1997, the population sought relief from the provincial governor in Kisangani, and from the court in Bunia, for what they considered to be an illegal land grab. On 25 February 1998, the court ('Tribunal de grande instance') in Bunia denied the claim made by the Nyali villagers, thus validating the

---

[21] This section is based on interviews conducted during January and February 2012 in Ituri, with residents of Nyali, local politicians, and others. It is also based on numerous primary source documents in my possession, which I obtained in Ituri.

[22] A settlement known as Yiko (or Jiko) existed in the general area prior to the arrival of Nyali, but the population significantly grew in 1955 with the arrival of Nyali and his followers.

concessionaire's annexation. Village officials appealed this decision, and continued to live in Nyali and farm the fields that had officially become part of the concessionaire's property.

In August 1998, the Ugandan army invaded Congo and took over Ituri, thus preventing any AFDL action to evict the Nyali villagers. The villagers' appeal wound its way through the courts until 2001, when, in December, the appeals court ('Cour d'appel') in Kisangani deemed the villagers' claims inadmissible, and awarded the concessionaire and his sons $2,603 (current $US) in court costs. The villagers claim they were unable to take part in the court proceedings in Kisangani because of the war; the concessionaire, on the other hand, had a lawyer present during the court proceedings.

During 2001, the intensification of the war in Ituri finally forced the Nyali villagers to flee. At some point that year, Lendu militias attacked Nyali and burned down the village; Lendu militias also stole or killed most of the cows in the Tsa concession. The residents of Nyali scattered to various parts of Ituri, including Bunia, leaving the village uninhabited until late 2003. In February 2004, a survey by the territorial agricultural service noted that eighty people had returned to Nyali; the survey also recorded quantities of trees and plants cultivated by village residents in fields in the disputed area around three hills. The Nyali villagers assert that the concessionaire used violence and intimidation against the returnees, who by early 2006 numbered approximately three hundred people, in order to keep them off the land.

The dispute took an interesting turn one night in May 2007, when FARDC soldiers entered Nyali looking for local residents who were reportedly part of Joseph Kony's Lord's Resistance Army (LRA). The soldiers pillaged several homes in Nyali and arrested five men, who were held in detention for one week and released following payment of an undisclosed sum. The Nyali villagers point to this event as an example of the strategy of intimidation and violence inflicted upon them by the concessionaire, who they claim started the rumour about LRA operatives in Nyali. In January 2011, a group of men attacked and injured several villagers in Nyali; the villagers claim the concessionaire ordered this attack. Another incident took place in June 2011, when the concessionaire brought a group of young men to the contested lands in order to enclose the fields; in the process some villagers' crops were destroyed.

In November 2010, the case had gone back to court when the concessionaire sought action against the 'illegal and anarchic' occupation of the disputed land. On 29 August 2011, the court handed down its judgement, finding the concessionaire's claim to be valid based on the authorization he received in 1997 from the AFDL. The court also found the villagers' claims invalid, and ordered them to compensate the concessionaire for his court costs. The court held that the concessionaire possessed the proper documentation to support his claim to the land; however, the villagers contend this documentation was obtained through illicit means.

A 2011 investigation conducted by an official from the district government lends credence to the villagers' claims. In a September 2011 report, Ituri's economic and finance commissioner, Avo Eka, corroborated numerous irregularities in the process whereby the concessionaire obtained the rights to the land in 1997. Moreover, he stated that the annexation would deprive the people of Nyali of their 'means of subsistence', and recommended that the provincial government annul the annexation. The significance of this report remains unclear, and as of January 2013, had not produced any governmental effort to solve the problem.

Like the case of Leyna, described above, the whole story about the alleged land grab at Nyali will probably never be known. This case highlights the way in which a concessionaire was able to take advantage of a change in government to obtain authorization for a land grab, which has since been upheld by courts but disputed by the villagers and a senior district official. As of late 2012, the concessionaire has still not been able to fully assert his claim to the disputed lands because of the potential for violent resistance of the Nyali villagers.

Conclusion

Land grabbing in Ituri blends historical patterns of land administration with contemporary struggles for political and economic power among local elites. In a pattern similar to that in Ghana, '[t]he important currencies in debates [about land] are history and tradition, while the negotiation and argument follow paths laid out by contemporary concerns, institutions and opportunities' (Lund, 2008: 177). Both land grabbers and those who resist land grabs often invoke pre-colonial or colonial history to justify their actions and claims, but debates over land rights are frequently a means through which current power struggles play out in Ituri. The case of Ituri shows how these power struggles may incorporate land issues in ways that produce widespread violence and inhibit 'post-conflict' peace.

In places with extensive land conflicts, like Ituri, the challenge faced by governments and local communities in post-conflict situations is how to sort out complex property claims in a context of contemporary power struggles and perceptions of historical rights and injustices. Indeed, the State may not exist 'as a set of congruent and hegemonic institutions capable of enforcing one particular interpretation of property' (ibid.: 178), but rather as a pluralistic configuration of interests, each struggling for its own legitimacy and power (Ansoms and Claessens, 2011: 17-18), thus limiting its ability to address land disputes. Similarly, local communities may be unable to resolve land grabs and boundary disputes, particularly in a place that lacks a broad reconciliation process and experiences widespread insecurity, poverty, and corruption.

War may graft new land conflicts onto old disputes over boundaries, ownership and access, creating multiple claimants and complicating resolution efforts (Myers 1994: 603). In such situations, the tough decisions about boundary lines and ownership that are required to resolve land grabs are difficult to achieve. This has certainly been the case in Ituri, where the State lacks the legitimacy and will to resolve land disputes, and where local resolution efforts have proved inadequate due to internal power struggles, lack of means, perceptions about land rights and ownership, and opposition from elites who benefitted from the grabbing (Huggins, 2010: 31).

Customary authorities, local organizations, international agencies and even government initiatives have successfully addressed some land disputes in Ituri. However, the more difficult and explosive cases – such as those at Leyna, the Walendu Bindi-Bahema Sud border, and Nyali – are unresolved. The debates over which land is 'your land' and which is 'my land' in Ituri are unfortunately likely to go on for the foreseeable future, continually causing instability and threatening to reignite war.

Bibliography

Ansoms, A. and Claessens, K., 2011. 'Land Relations and Local Livelihoods in the Great Lakes Region'. In: *Natural Resources and Local Livelihoods in the Great Lakes Region of Africa: A Political Economy Perspective*, eds, Ansoms, A. and Marysse, S., Palgrave Macmillan, Basingstoke (UK), pp. 3-25.

Azuimah, F., 2011. 'Perception as a Social Infrastructure for Sustaining the Escalation of Ethnic Conflicts in Divided Societies in Ghana.' *Journal of Alternative Perspectives in the Social Sciences*, vol. 3, no. 1, pp. 260-278.

Bakonzi, A., 1982. *The Gold Mines of Kilo-Moto in Northeastern Zaïre: 1905-1960*. PhD Dissertation. University of Wisconsin-Madison, Madison.

Blanche, E., 2008. 'West Bank Land Grab'. *The Middle East* (June), pp. 26-28.

Bobrow-Strain, A., 2001. 'Between a Ranch and a Hard Place: Violence, Scarcity, and Meaning in Chiapas, Mexico'. *Violent Environments*, eds, Peluso, No. L. and Watts, M., Cornell University Press, Ithaca (NY), pp. 155-185.

Brown, D., 2001. *Bury My Heart at Wounded Knee: An Indian History of the American West*. Henry Holt and Company, New York.

Camm, M., 2011. 'Conflict in Congo'. *World Policy Journal* (Winter 2011-2012).

De Schutter, O., 2011. 'How Not to Think of Land Grabbing: Three Critiques of Large-scale Investments in Farmland'. *The Journal of Peasant Studies*, vol. 38, no. 2, pp. 249-279.

El Hadary, Y. A. E. and Samat, N., 2011. 'Pastoral Land Rights and Protracted Conflict in Eastern Sudan'. *The Journal of Pan African Studies*, vol. 4, no. 8, pp. 74-90.

Fahey, D., 2007. 'The Political Economy of Livestock and Pastoralism in Sudan'. *IGAD LPI Working Paper*, no.6-8.

——, 2011. *Rethinking the Resource Curse: Natural Resources and Polywar in the Ituri District, Democratic Republic of the Congo.* PhD Dissertation. University of California, Berkeley.

——, 2012. 'The Mai-Mai Lumumba: Okapi killers or self-defense forces?' *Congo Siasa blog* (6 September). Online at: http://congosiasa.blogspot. be/2012/09/guest-blog-mai-mai-lumumba.html [date of last access: 14 October 2012].

Garver, J. W., 1992. 'China's Push through the South China Sea: The Interaction of Bureaucratic and National Interests'. *The China Quarterly*, no. 132, pp. 999-1028.

Geographical Section of the Naval Intelligence Division, Naval Staff, Admiralty, 1920. *A Manual of Belgian Congo.* His Majesty's Stationery Office, London.

Hochschild, A., 1998. *King Leopold's Ghost.* Houghton Mifflin Company, Boston and New York.

Huggins, C., 2010. *Land, Power and Identity: Roots of Violent Conflict in Eastern DRC.* International Alert, London.

IKV Pax Christi and Reseau Haki na Amani, 2009. *Conflits fonciers en Ituri : Poids du passé et défis pour l'avenir de la paix.* IKV Pax Christi, Utrecht.

International Criminal Court (ICC), 2012. *Case Information Sheet: Situation in the Democratic Republic of the Congo. The Prosecutor v. Germain Katanga and Mathieu Ngudjolo Chui.* Case n° ICC-01/04-01/07. Updated 25 June. ICC, Den Haag.

Jervis, R., 1988. 'War and Misperception'. *Journal of Interdisciplinary History*, vol. 18, no. 4, pp. 675-700.

Johnson, D., 2003. *Shifting Sands: Oil Exploration in the Rift Valley and the Congo Conflict.* The Pole Institute (March), Goma.

Kagaba, B., 2000. *Proposition de solution pour une paix durable aux conflits inter-ethniques entre les Hema et Lendu dans le territoire d'Irumu, District de Ituri, Province Orientale.* Unpublished manuscript.

Klopp, J. M., 2000. 'The Problem of Land Grabbing in Contemporary Kenya'. *Africa Today*, vol. 47, no. 1, pp. 7-26.

Leplae, E., 1936. *Les plantations de café au Congo belge.* Institut royal colonial belge, Bruxelles.

Levy, J. S., 1983. 'Misperception and the Causes of War: Theoretical Linkages and Analytical Problems'. *World Politics*, vol. 36, no. 1, pp. 76-99.

Levy, J. S. and Thompson, W. R., 2010. *Causes of War.* Wiley-Blackwell, West Sussex.

Lund, C., 2008. *Local Politics and the Dynamics of Property in Africa.* Cambridge University Press, Cambridge.

Martelli, G., 1962. *Leopold to Lumumba: A History of the Belgian Congo, 1877-1960.* Chapman & Hall Ltd, London.

Meesen, J. M. Th., 1951. *Monographie de l'Ituri: histoire, géographie, économie.* Publication de la Direction de l'agriculture, des forêts, de l'élevage et de la colonisation, Bruxelles.

Moyo, Sam. 2005. 'Land and Natural Resource Distribution in Zimbabwe: Access, Equity and Conflict'. *African and Asian Studies,* vol. 4, no. 1-2: 187-223.

Myers, G. W., 1994. 'Competitive Rights, Competitive Claims: Land Access in Post-war Mozambique.' *Journal of Southern African Affairs,* vol. 20, no. 4, pp. 603-632.

Northrup, D., 1988. *Beyond the Bend in the River: African Labor in Eastern Zaïre, 1865-1940.* Ohio University, Athens (Oh).

Office d'information et des relations publiques pour le Congo belge et Ruanda-Urundi, 1959. *Belgian Congo,* vol. 1. [Translated from the French by F.H. and C. Heldt]. Office d'information et des relations publiques pour le Congo belge et Ruanda-Urundi, Brussels.

Pakenham, T., 1991. *The Scramble for Africa.* Avon Books, New York.

Pottier, J., 2008. 'Displacement and ethnic reintegration in Ituri, DR Congo: Challenges ahead'. *Journal of Modern African Studies,* vol. 46, no. 3, pp. 427-450.

——, 2009. 'Representations of Ethnicity in the Search for Peace: Ituri, Democratic Republic of Congo'. *African Affairs,* vol. 109, no. 434, pp. 23-50.

RCN Justice et Démocratie (RCN). 2009. *Les conflits fonciers en Ituri: de l'imposition à la consolidation de la paix.* RCN, Bruxelles.

Reisner, M., 1993. *Cadillac Desert: The American West and its Disappearing Water.* Penguin, New York.

Service national d'Intelligence et de Protection (SNIP), République du Zaïre, Département Intérieur, Poste Principale de Bunia. 1995. *Note d'information au Commissaire S/Régional de L'Ituri à Bunia – Concerne: cas de l'association culturelle 'LORI' dans la collectivité des Walendu/Pitsi.'* No. 05/00/451/SNIP/DI/462/95 (30 November).

Southall, A. W. 1953. *Alur Society: A Study in Processes and Types of Domination.* W. Heffer & Sons Limited, Cambridge.

Storey, I. J., 1999. 'Creeping Assertiveness: China, the Philippines and the South China Sea Dispute'. *Contemporary Southeast Asia,* vol. 21, no. 1, pp. 95-118.

Tamm, H., 2012. 'Coalitions and Defections in a Context of Uncertainty. A Report from Ituri (Part II)'. *Congo Siasa* blog (27 August). Online at: http://congosiasa.blogspot.com/2012/08/coalitions-and-defections-in-context-of_27.html [date of last access: 10 October 2012].

Terrell, J. U., 1972. *Land Grab: The Truth about 'The Winning of the West'.* The Dial Press, New York.

Thiry, E., 1996. *Une introduction à l'ethnohistoire des Hema du Sud (Haut-Zaïre).* Musée royal de l'Afrique centrale, Tervuren (Belgique).

——, 2002. *Éléments de l'ethnohistoire des Nyali.* Musée royal de l'Afrique centrale, Tervuren (Belgique).

——, 2004. *Une introduction à l'ethnohistoire des Hema du Nord.* Musée royal de l'Afrique centrale, Tervuren (Belgique).

United Nations Department of Safety and Security (UNDSS), 2012. *UNDSS Briefing. Coordination humanitaire.* UNDSS (14 September), Bunia.

United Nations Security Council (UNSC), 2004. *Special Report on the Events in Ituri, January 2002-December 2003.* S/2004/573. UNSC (16 July), New York.

Van Puijenbroek, J. and Ansoms, A., 2011. 'A Legacy from the Past Hindering the Future: Land Conflicts in Ituri (DRC)'. In: *Natural Resources and Local Livelihoods in the Great Lakes Region of Africa: A Political Economy Perspective,* eds, Ansoms, A. and Marysse, S., Palgrave Macmillan, Basingstoke (UK), pp. 49-67.

Veit, A., 2010. *Intervention as Indirect Rule.* Campus Verlag, Frankfurt and New York.

Young, C. and Turner, T., 1985. *The Rise and Decline of the Zaïrean State.* The University of Wisconsin Press, Madison.

4

Land Grabbing
by Mining Companies

Local Contentions &
State Reconfiguration
in South Kivu (DRC)

SARA GEENEN & JANA HÖNKE

Introduction: mining, land grabbing and politics in the DRC

Large-scale foreign direct investments in land are not new, as Peemans demonstrates in this volume. Foreign investors and concessions granted to multinational companies were crucial in the *mise en valeur* of 'vacant lands' in the nineteenth and early twentieth centuries (Vellut, 1983). More recently, a 'new [resource] scramble for Africa' has been observed (Southall and Melber, 2009), targeting primarily oil and mineral-rich regions. As such resources are in high demand and becoming scarcer, multinationals continue to prospect for reserves and are seeking to gain and secure access to strategic mineral and energetic resources in more risk-prone environments.

Risk is a reality and, according to Price Waterhouse Coopers (PWC, 2011: 1), 'projects become more complex and are typically in more remote, unfamiliar territory'. These 'unfamiliar territories', in which mining companies find it difficult to operate, are often inhabited by local communities who make their own claims to the land. They frequently clash with multinational mining companies over issues such as land use, dispossession, relocation, environmental pollution, degradation of communities' resources, human rights abuse and the loss of livelihoods (Hilson, 2002: 68; Ballard and Banks, 2003: 289). Such contestations are now occurring all over the world, as demonstrated in case-studies from Australia (O'Faircheallaigh, 1995), Papua New Guinea (Banks and Ballard, 1997; Hilson, 2002), Peru (Bury, 2004), Ghana (Hilson and Yakovleva, 2007; Aubynn, 2009; Bush, 2009), Tanzania (Carstens and Hilson, 2009) and the DRC (Geenen and Claessens, 2013; Hönke, 2013).

The DRC is known for its large reserves of mineral resources, including over 10 per cent of the world's copper and 49 of the world's cobalt reserves, situated mostly in the underground of the province of Katanga (USGS – United States Geological Survey, 2009). Moreover, the province of Kasai holds a considerable share of the world's diamond reserves and the eastern provinces host substantial reserves of coltan (tantalum ore), cassiterite (tin ore) and gold, although these are hard to estimate because few geological surveys have been conducted (World Bank, 2008).

Since colonization, the Congolese economy has relied extensively on the industrial exploitation and export of raw materials (Bezy, Peemans and Wautelet, 1981; Geenen, 2011a). Mining companies such as 'Union Minière' in Katanga governed their vast concessions as private domains. But from the 1920s onwards, they turned from an outright coercive mode of governance to a more paternalist model, providing electricity and water, schooling, healthcare and recreational facilities to workers and their families (Hönke, 2010, 2013). After independence in 1960, Mobutu sought to centralize political and economic power in the hands of the State and hence he nationalized some important companies. But in the mid-1970s industrial production dwindled as a result of a combination of factors, both internal (perverse effects of nationalization measures, neopatrimonial practices, lack of productive investment and deteriorating infrastructure) and external (commodity price fluctuations, such as the fall of copper prices in 1975) (Geenen, 2011a). At the same time, individual Congolese started to extract minerals in an artisanal way, as a way of coping with the ever intensifying economic crisis. Their artisanal production was smuggled out of the country through parallel and 'informal' trade networks and consequently generated no revenue for the State. By the mid-1990s, many industrial companies were facing bankruptcy and the State was forced to sell off a number of concessions to private investors (Kennes, 2002; Nest, Grignon and Kisangani, 2006). The 1996-97 and 1998-2003 wars eventually brought industrial production to a standstill, especially in the eastern provinces. At the same time, existing 'informal' trade networks linked up with armed groups and external war financiers, such as neighbouring Uganda and Rwanda (see various United Nations [UN] reports and Marysse, 2005). At the local level, the war created 'new local complexes of power, profit and protection', disrupting traditional social and economic structures (Vlassenroot, 2004: 40).

In 2002, the Kabila government introduced a revised Mining Code[1] and attendant Mining Regulations.[2] These laws were in line with the liberalization, privatization and industrialization policies that the World Bank had been promoting since the 1980s. The primary aim, to attract foreign direct investments, was to be achieved by a very liberal tax and customs regime, transparency and efficiency in granting licences, and the provision of investment security (Mazalto, 2009). The Code recognizes artisanal mining as a production mode, and provides for the designation of special 'artisanal mining zones' where miners'

---

[1] Loi n° 007/2002 du 11 juillet 2002 portant sur le Code Minier ('Mining Code').

[2] Décret n° 038/2003 du 26 mars 2003 portant sur le Règlement minier (Mining Regulations). For a detailed analysis of the laws and policies, see Mazalto (2009).

cooperatives may apply for research permits. However, it also stipulates that such zones may be converted into an industrial concession if 'a new deposit necessitating large-scale exploitation has been discovered'.[3] This implies that industrial companies ultimately have the right to take over artisanal mining zones, which is obviously a source of insecurity for the artisanal miners involved.

Since the end of the war, a number of companies have taken a renewed interest in Congo's minerals. In Katanga, many foreign private investors have engaged in copper and cobalt production since 2004-2005, and industrial output is now at unprecedented levels (Hönke, 2009; Marysse and Tshimanga, 2013). In the more conflict-ridden eastern parts of the country, foreign companies have hesitated longer. But thanks to the booming gold price in recent years – the average price increased by almost four times between 2003 and 2010 (PWC, 2011: 22) – Congo's gold deposits have become potentially profitable and thus increasingly attractive to foreign investors. A few companies have engaged in gold exploration activities, including Anglogold Ashanti in Ituri and Kilo Goldmines in Haute Uele (Van Puijenbroek, Mongo and Bakker, 2012), Loncor Resources in North Kivu and Casa Mining in South Kivu (Misisi). However, the first company to start effective gold production was the Canada-based multinational Banro Corporation. In South Kivu, Banro holds exploitation permits for more than 2,790 km² in total,[4] and further research permits for an even larger area.[5] In 2005, Banro started intensive exploration in Twangiza, a mine situated about 40 kilometres southwest of Bukavu, the provincial capital. The exploration phase, which focused primarily on the chiefdom of Luhwindja but extended into the neighbouring chiefdoms Burhinyi and Ngweshe, took six years. In November 2011, the first gold ingot was produced.

This makes Banro an important case study that can shed light on some of the dynamics induced by large-scale land use by multinational companies. These dynamics include tensions between transnational, national and local politics, as well as impacts on local livelihoods and cohabitation challenges with local communities. Such effects may also be expected to manifest themselves at many other mining sites in Eastern DRC as more companies move towards production. Section two of this chapter presents two arguments concerning the reconfiguration of politics. First, we argue that selling mining rights to multinational companies and promoting industrial mineral extraction by a limited

---

[3]   Mining Code, T. 4, Ch. 1, Art. 110.

[4]   Divided as follows: 1,216 km² for Twangiza Mining, 653 km² for Lugushwa Mining, 766 for Kamituga Mining and 172 for Namoya Mining. Another small part of their concession lies in Maniema province.

[5]   By comparison, there are seven artisanal mining zones in South Kivu, with a total surface area of 219km². Hence most artisanal miners – they are estimated to be one hundred thousand to two hundred thousand in South Kivu – do not work in these zones, but outside or inside industrial concessions (World Bank, 2008: 56).

number of large companies is commonly associated with a reconfiguration of national politics. For the Congolese State, it constitutes a strategy for extending its governance into areas previously out of state control. Second, we propose that this strategy involves negotiations with local elites, including customary chiefs. Hence such land acquisitions also imply a reconfiguration of local politics. As argued in section three, these reconfigurations are shaped by transnational norms and regulations. However, reference to corporate social responsibility (CSR) by Banro to some extent remains superficial and produces ambiguous results in practice. We demonstrate how the presence of a company such as Banro affects local communities and how CSR is used and contested at the local level.

The empirical parts of this chapter are based on fieldwork in South Kivu, more precisely in the chiefdom of Luhwindja, where Banro has concentrated its activities so far, and in Bukavu. The fieldwork included in-depth interviews, focus groups, collection of documents and primary observations during four periods in January to February and October to November 2011, and May to July and September to October 2012.[6]

Mining companies, land and the reconfiguration of politics

This section revolves around two arguments. First, it is asserted that selling mining rights to international investors is conducive to a reconfiguration of national politics. Giving mining areas into concession to industrial companies enables the Congolese government to (re) centralize control over revenues from mineral extraction. In so doing, it also facilitates the extension of state control into areas previously out of state reach. In Eastern DRC, the Central State has been a distant absentee for a long time. Yet, despite its dysfunctions, the state administration remains home to many powerful political players (Trefon, 2007). These take part in broader political, military and economic struggles, including struggles for control of the mining areas. The alliances between politicians at the national level and these local elites reflect the negotiated nature of the Congolese State (Hagmann and Péclard, 2010). Thus far the literature has focused mainly on the various strategies deployed by the State to establish control over distant territories (Boone, 2003). In this regard, research on the DRC has highlighted the role of state ideology, repression, and military and clientelist networks – including customary chiefs – as mechanisms for keeping control over

[6]   The authors wish to thank the researchers at CEGEMI (Centre d'expertise en gestion minière), a project at the Catholic University of Bukavu sponsored by VLIR (Flemish Interuniversity Council [Vlaamse Interuniversitaire Raad]) for their help with the fieldwork.

the country's vast territory (Young and Turner, 1985; Schatzberg, 2001; Englebert, 2003). However, multinational companies can also play a role in the expansion of government control (Hönke, 2010), in particular in areas Catherine Boone has described as *l'Afrique utile* (Boone, 1998). This stands in contrast to the limited control of government over artisanal mining. The majority of artisanal production and trade currently occurs outside the official economy, especially in the case of high-value low-volume minerals such as gold.[7] Hence giving mining areas in concession to multinational mining companies can yield central government privileged access to mineral rents (Hönke, 2010; Reno 2001).[8] The gold concessions in South Kivu are part of this 'useful Africa' and the case study, described below, illustrates the relationship between local conflict over land and state reconfiguration.

The second argument contends that the land grabs by mining companies are also related to a reconfiguration of local politics. In order to establish control over the concession and to build a stable working environment, companies are inclined to negotiate with local elites. These elites will in turn seek to consolidate their power, reinforce their authority and maintain their access to economic gains through such negotiations. Overall, the wars of the 1990s increased the autonomy of local actors in Eastern DRC. At the same time, traditional patron-client relationships were undermined and superseded by new relationships based on economic gain and wealth accumulation (Vlassenroot, 2004). Certain customary chiefs, for example, succeeded in repositioning themselves and were able to acquire additional power due to the breakdown of institutional capacities, public infrastructure, and the distance to the capital city (Tull, 2005). They used their political and economic power to grab opportunities and to turn negotiation processes over access to land and resources to their own advantage.[9] In the case of land given in concession to mining companies, local elites use their power and authority to benefit from the large-scale investments involved. This implies 'legitimizing practices' (Sikor and Lund, 2009: 8) through which they seek recognition and a 'minimum of voluntary compliance' with the new 'extractive order' (Hönke, 2009: 274) that they have helped negotiate and maintain. In the area under study, customary chiefs traditionally governed and distributed the land, thereby creating patron-client relationships and inducing dependency among their 'subjects' (Geenen and Claessens, 2013). These traditional patterns were put under serious pressure by the war and by the introduction of a legal system in which the State de jure owns all land. In practice, though, customary chiefs retained some control over land allocation because the law was never fully implemented (Utshudi and Ansoms, 2011). As the

---

[7] It is estimated that 98 per cent of the gold from the eastern provinces is smuggled out to neighbouring countries (UN, 2014).
[8] On how governments have used the privatization of the economy in the context of neoliberal political reforms to (re)gain privileged access to rents, see Hibou (1999); Tangri (1999).
[9] On elite capture in other contexts, see Peters (2004); Wong (2010).

economic value of this land tends to increase with mining opportunities, the local chiefs will generally try to cash in (see also Borras and Franco, 2011: 49). As we will show, the case of Luhwindja is paradigmatic for these mechanisms.

Reconfiguration of national politics: Sominki, Sakima and Banro
This section describes the troublesome process through which Banro acquired its mining titles and demonstrates how the sale of concessions is related to a reconfiguration of national politics.[10] In the early 1990s, Sominki ('Société industrielle et minière du Kivu'),[11] which operated gold and cassiterite concessions in North and South Kivu, was looking for a buyer. The Canadian junior company Banro Corporation, specializing in exploration and in speculation on promising deposits, was interested but only in the gold concessions.[12] In the first instance, Banro concluded a partnership with the British firm Cluff Mining, which provided most of the financial capital. Subsequently Banro negotiated with both the moribund Mobutu regime and rebel leader Laurent Kabila. The latter had launched the AFDL ('Alliance des forces démocratiques pour la libération du Congo') offensive in the East and he promised Banro that, if he were to seize power, he would respect the titles to the gold concessions. After months of negotiations and pressure, Banro managed to remove Cluff from the contract so that in February 1997, all of Sominki's concessions were eventually transferred to Banro.[13] Sominki was liquidated on 29 March 1997. On 6 May 1997, just a few days before Kabila took Kinshasa, a new company was created under the name of Sakima ('Société aurifère du Kivu-Maniema'), with 93 per cent of the shares belonging to Banro and 7 per cent to the Zaïrean State.

After the accession to power of Laurent Kabila, Sakima effectively started large-scale exploration works in Twangiza, the major mining site studied in this chapter. But the company failed to honour any of its obligations towards former Sominki personnel and supply companies, resulting in a wave of protest. This prompted Laurent Kabila on 31 July 1998 to strip Banro of its mining titles and to establish a new state-owned company called Somico ('Société minière du Congo').[14] This could be interpreted as a strategy on the part of the new regime to gain control of and centralize mining revenues. However, there was also a more fundamental, 'nationalist-inspired' rationale behind the move, as the Kabila regime

---

[10] This section is based on a number of documents, letters and notes from the personal archives of Serge Lammens, former Administrator-General Director of Sominki. See de Failly (2001).

[11] The company was 28 per cent state-owned, 72 per cent privately owned.

[12] Sominki (1996). 'Procès-verbal de la quarante-huitième réunion du Conseil d'Administration tenue à Kinshasa le samedi 10 août 1996'. Unpublished.

[13] 'Convention minière entre la République du Zaïre et la Société Minière et Industrielle du Kivu (SOMINKI) et Banro Resource Corporation' (13 February 1997).

[14] The president issued four decrees: Decree n. 101 annulling the Decree that created Sakima, Decree n. 102 annulling the Agreement of 13 February, Decree n. 103 creating Somico and Decree n. 104 nominating Somico's president.

aimed to reform the mining sector and make it more independent from Anglo-American companies (Kennes, 2002). It was also symptomatic that Kabila appointed the mwami (customary chief) of Luhwindja, Philemon Naluhwindja, as director of Somico. Naluhwindja had always contested the concession rights of Sominki on land that he governed under customary law, and thus represented the 'traditional' rights holder, as opposed to the external investor. Two days after the creation of Somico, the RCD ('Rassemblement congolais pour la démocratie') uprising broke out, and it was not long before large parts of South Kivu fell to the rebels. Banro sided with the RCD rebels, while Somico allegedly supported local defence groups, Mayi-Mayi, and FDLR ('Forces Démocratiques pour la Libération du Rwanda'),[15] and received backing from the Kabila government. In other words, access to the gold mines had become the stake in a highly politicized and militarized conflict. Banro failed to fully control the concession and the gold mines were then alternately occupied by the abovementioned armed groups.

Banro's position only improved after 16 January 2001, when President Laurent Kabila was assassinated and succeeded by his son Joseph, who sought to collaborate with the company. Amidst the war, this could be seen as an attempt by the regime to re-establish control over the region. However, the new president also wanted to avoid having to pay USD one billion in damages to Banro as a result of a lawsuit that the company had successfully filed with the United States Federal Court.[16] The rapprochement between both parties resulted in the signing on 18 April 2002 of a 'gentlemen's agreement' whereby all titles and rights were given to Sakima (of which Banro owned 93 per cent). Sakima Sarl now became a fully state-owned enterprise, retaining the rights to thirty-five tin concessions. Banro, for its part, as a private company, retained the titles to twelve gold concessions in Twangiza, Kamituga, Lugushwa and Namoya. The gentlemen's agreement also extended the duration of the contract from twenty-five to thirty years and preserved the extensive tax holidays.[17]

---

[15] Kabila's former allies Uganda and Rwanda turned against him in 1998 and supported the RCD rebellion in the East, which eventually led to RCD occupying a large part of the Congolese territory. The Mayi-Mayi were local defence groups that fought against foreign occupation. However, there was also FDLR activity in the East. FDLR is made up of Hutu rebels who fled Rwanda after the genocide and whose presence in Congo was used by the new Rwandan regime as a justification for invasion. Alliances between the different military groups were unstable and violent confrontations and atrocities against the population were frequent.

[16] The case was first presented to the ICSID, a member of the World Bank Group that is an international institution for arbitration of legal disputes between international investors: https://icsid.worldbank.org/ICSID/Index.jsp [date of last access: 20 January 2015]. It proclaimed itself incompetent in this case in 2000 and Banro subsequently turned to the US Federal Court in 2001, invoking the 'Foreign Sovereign Immunities Act'.

[17] 'Avenant n. 1 à la convention minière du 13 février 1997'. Unpublished document, 18 April 2002.

The deal should be seen in the context of Kabila's overall approach to the mining sector at the time. He embraced a policy of promoting privatization and liberalization with the aim of attracting investment by multinational companies, as was also reflected in the aforementioned Mining Code. This was part of an attempt to regain control over mining areas and to recentralize mining rents in the hands of the government. Giving mining areas into concession to industrial companies also opened up the prospect of extending government control into areas previously out of reach, either because they had been occupied by rebel movements or because they were so distant from the capital. In the next section, we consider how the process at hand induced a reconfiguration of local politics.

Reconfiguration of national and local politics: Banro's Twangiza concession

The struggle over the mining concessions in Twangiza involved actors at the national, regional and local levels and had profound repercussions on political configurations, especially locally. As previously stated, mwami Philemon Naluhwindja, who was appointed by Laurent Kabila as director of Somico, had always contested the fact that the mining titles were in 'foreign' hands. The death of the mwami triggered a succession struggle, as the eldest son had not yet attained the age of majority and was residing in Europe.[18] The 'bagingi'or elders appointed the mwami's younger brother Justin as regent and his widow Espérance Barahanyi as 'mwamikazi' or guarantor of the customs. The two would become embroiled in a fierce struggle for authority and control over the mining site. Justin continued to support Somico, and nourished the popular narrative that Somico had been created to mine gold on the 'people's land' for the good of Luhwindja's inhabitants. This was his 'legitimizing discourse' (see Sikor and Lund, 2009). However, Somico would never become operational, due to lack of investors. In practice, Justin effectively controlled and derived rents from artisanal exploitation (interview with community leaders, November 2011). Many former artisanal miners, who subsequently lost their jobs with the arrival of Banro, are still grateful to him for opposing the installation of 'foreigners'. According to their narrative, Justin's main concern was to 'make sure that any newly arriving company would be accountable to the community', meaning that it would create jobs and foster community development (interview with community leader, October 2011).

However, the war also drove local actors to enter into strategic military alliances. Justin contracted FDLR to provide personal security guards. He is also believed to have incited civilians to arm themselves and to set up a self-defence movement. At the time, the RCD, backed by the Rwandan regime, controlled many of the urban centres in the area and

---

[18] Naluhwindja was murdered in December 2000 in France, in mysterious circumstances. Some speculate that Banro was involved. It has also been suggested that he was smuggling minerals or that it was a personal reckoning.

it also tried to obtain tight control over the mines. Yet it would never succeed in gaining full control of the gold sites, let alone in monopolizing the gold and coltan trade (Vlassenroot and Raeymaekers, 2004), since well-established networks of artisanal miners and traders continued to channel most of the minerals to the international markets via 'informal' trade routes that had been in place since the 1970s, bypassing the RCD administration. Many rural areas, on the other hand, were controlled by Mayi-Mayi and FDLR, who apart from pillaging miners and traders, sometimes also cooperated with local traders in order to channel the precious metals out of the region without paying taxes to the RCD. The case of Luhwindja and Justin seems to fit into these patterns.

As previously mentioned, Joseph Kabila had, in the meantime, come to a new agreement with Banro and now intended to facilitate the company's effective control over the concessions. There were however a number of obstacles to clear. While the war had officially ended in 2003, large parts of South Kivu remained under the control of rebel groups. Hence, in July 2005, the Congolese army carried out a military operation whereby the FDLR was driven from Luhwindja. At the same time, Banro was effectively installed and subsequently protected by special military forces, who also took violent action against community members suspected of sympathizing with FDLR. Justin fled to Kinshasa. Banro was faced with a rather hostile environment when it started to build its first exploration camp in Luhwindja in October 2005. However, the company had just announced a massive exploration programme and had listed its shares with the New York and Toronto stock exchanges, so investors needed to be reassured that the region was safe and ready for investment. It would therefore be in the interest of the company if the local situation could be appeased, and it was felt that an alliance with loyal members of the local elite would further that cause.

Before the military campaign, Joseph Kabila had already contacted the *mwamikazi*, widow of Philemon Naluhwindja, who was residing in Belgium at the time. If the population were to recognize her as the legitimate customary chief, she could act as an intermediary and facilitate Banro's work in Luhwindja. From Kinshasa, however, Justin tried to maintain some political power and control. He emerged from the 2006 elections as a member of the country's national parliament, but it was not long before the Supreme Court cancelled his mandate because of electoral irregularities. His supporters claim that the ruling was part of an obvious ploy to sideline him (interview, 06 June 2012), and Justin retained his popularity among a section of the population.

The mwamikazi also took up a political position and returned to Bukavu. She was co-opted in the provincial assembly after the 2006 elections. The electoral system provides for thirty-two directly elected deputies and four co-opted representatives of the customary chiefs, to be nominated by the president. As the mwamikazi maintained excellent relations with the president himself, as well as with his political counsellor and current governor of South Kivu Marcellin Cishambo, she was appointed to the provincial parliament (personal communication, 15 January 2013). Apart from fulfilling her political functions, the mwamikazi was also active in business and in development projects.[19] She set up a subcontracting company that provided day labourers to Banro, Cinamula, with the specific aim of creating employment for the population in Luhwindja. She was also a majority shareholder in 'Chez Bibbas', a subcontractor that built houses for the resettled population. She was involved in the construction of the Nabuntalaga market through a company called Arcadis, as well as the market of Cinjira (the resettlement village) and a primary school at Luchiga, the hill where the Banro plant was located. Her involvement in development projects went through APEF ('Action pour la promotion des enfants et de la femme'), an NGO that she had created and a privileged partner of Banro's, and through her membership of the local committee of the Banro Foundation and the Community Forum that negotiated resettlement and compensation schemes. Apart from her (probably genuine) concern for community development, it is clear that, through a combination of strategies, she sought power, authority and access to economic gains. However, whereas she was able to gain legitimacy in the eyes of some, part of the population felt abandoned and accused the mwamikazi of merely looking after her own interests.

This also held for the head of local state administration, who likewise acted as an intermediary between Banro and the community and represented the mwamikazi in local politics. Several informants agreed that he was 'a marionette of the mwamikazi who is pulling the strings' (interview with community leaders, October 2011). Others described him as a powerful man who was 'like a king' (interview local NGO, October 2011). He was able to stamp his mark on some of the company's investments in community development, and was allegedly also a key gatekeeper of employment at Banro. In 2010, he appeared before court and was ordered to pay a fine to a man whose house had been demolished without the latter's consent. The sentence was however never implemented and the victim's compensation money had not been paid yet a year after (interview victim, 02 November 2011). These feelings of marginalization and frustration among the population were reinforced and further politicized in conflicts between members of the local elite.

Indeed, the mwamikazi's controversial position gave rise to local opposition. In addition to the succession dispute with Justin, a decade-old dispute with another family in Luhwindja over who was the legitimate mwami resurfaced (interview throne pretender, 10 October 2012). Moreover, in late 2011, a petition calling for the mwamikazi's abdication was launched by a local 'human rights organization' called UJCC

---

[19] 'Pétition de la population de Luhwindja contre Madame Espérance M'Baharanyi La Namunene' (2012).

('Union des jeunes Congolais pour le changement').[20] They accused her of violating customary law, disrespecting the population, serving personal business interests and embezzling money. The petition, bearing 4,044 signatures, was submitted on 24 January 2012. On 17 March 2012, two leaders of UJCC were arrested in Bukavu. The organization was now openly supported by CODELU ('Comité de développement de Luhwindja'), a solidarity association of Luhwindja's elite (businessmen, church and NGO leaders) in Bukavu (interview Codelu, 20 May 2012). They claimed that 'the population had lost confidence in the mwami-kazi'[21] and represented themselves as spokespersons for 'the community', particularly those without a voice. However, the group was obviously also pursuing certain private interests. Some Codelu members had, for example, previously won contracts for construction work for Banro, and now felt they were losing access to these opportunities because of the growing power of the mwamikazi. Others were prominent leaders of NGOs, and possibly had set their sights on the development funds flowing through the Banro Foundation. The opposition forces also gained support from Kantintima, the governor of South Kivu under RCD rule, a former minister of agriculture and member of the national parliament (interview with local elite, 06 June 2012). He probably allied himself with the opposition in order to win political support.

On 19 March 2012, people in Luhwindja protested against the arrests of the initiators of the petition. According to the latter, the manifestation was violently suppressed by the head of the local state administration, assisted by the national police, and nine more people were arrested[22]. In the meantime, forty-two individuals had submitted a complaint with the tribunal, on grounds that their names were on the petition while they had never signed. It was also alleged that the petition contained ficti-tious names and names of underage persons. More protests followed in Luhwindja, and on 28 April eight prisoners were released. Both Codelu and the mwami claimed credit for these releases.[23] The three remaining prisoners were accused of forgery and the unlawful use of signatures. Their case was introduced on 15 May 2012. After hearings in August and September 2012, the defendants were found guilty of forgery and sentenced to a year in prison and five years on probation (interview with lawyer, 2 October 2012), although in practice they were released shortly after.

---

[20] Letter to the President on 'Pétition de la population de Luhwindja contre Madame Espérance M'Baharanyi La Namunene' (2012).

[21] Letter from Codelu to Banro, 'Retrait de la confiance de la population de Luhwindja à Madame Espérance M'Baharanyi' (28 March 2012).

[22] 'Note de plaidoirie pour Mukenge Barhegine Totoro, Bachoke Ganywamulume Gustave et Beka Ngekema. RP 13 802.' Mail by UJCC 'Dossier arrestation' (21 August 2012). Mail by UJCC 'Retroacte de l'arrestation des défenseurs des intérêts et des droits des Bahwindja par la Namunene' (21 August 2012).

[23] 'Rapport de la réunion présidée par sa majesté mwami Naluhwindja Chibwire V Tony en sa résidence à Bukavu avec une délégation de la Codelu en date du vendredi 10 août 2012'.

We may conclude from the foregoing that, upon its installation, Banro unwittingly stirred up the hornets' nest of local politics in Luhwindja. In order to create a stable working environment, it aligned itself with selected members of the local and national elites. But in so doing, it at once contributed to the marginalization of competing voices at the local level, nourishing grievances and frustrations.[24] While the company had initially used the mwamikazi to secure its position and win the population for its cause through a supposedly legitimate intermediary (the customary chief), some company agents now feared that they had become 'far too entangled in local politics' (pers. comm., Banro, June 2012).

This section has shown that, in an attempt to gain control over their concession, and in order to reduce tensions within local communities, companies may choose to align themselves with local elites. Local elites may in turn use their power and authority to gain access to resources. In this instance, the mwamikazi experienced difficulty in gaining acceptance as the legitimate customary chief because of local history and politics. In our understanding, associating herself with Banro, presenting herself as an intermediary and attracting funding and development money for the community were also strategies to augment and legitimize her power, and to gain access to resources. However, her legitimization strategies were only successful in the eyes of some. She received the support of part of the community, and many people were appreciative of her efforts to secure investment in schools, hospitals and roads. Another part of the community, however, openly challenged her position and accused her of embezzlement and abuse of power. The actors opposing the incumbent local authorities, such as Codelu and UJCC, sought access to the financial and development opportunities created by Banro's presence as well. In addition, they sought to renegotiate the legitimate order around industrial mining.

Impact on local livelihoods, transnational norms and local contestations

In comparison to the issues outlined in the other chapters of this book, land use management by mining companies is shaped more by transnational norms and regulations, particularly the notion of corporate social responsibility. However, corporate social responsibility is not clearly defined and may therefore include all sorts of local social investment initiatives by the company concerned. In fact, the notion has given rise to a veritable 'industry' (Welker, 2009), with its own consultancies, dedicated journals and websites, purposely designed initiatives, and fee-based certification and study programmes. Moreover, it can be argued that reference to

---

[24] See Hönke and Thomas (2012) for a broader discussion of potential unintended consequences and externalities of companies' activities.

corporate social responsibility and voluntary standards often remains superficial, and that, in the local arena, ambiguous practices prevail. These result from the prevalence of multiple 'transnational meaning systems' that provide company practitioners, security officers and local political actors with certain 'practical norms', to use Olivier de Sardan's (2008) concept, that engender different sets of 'normal' behaviour (Hönke, 2013). In the local arena, CSR guidelines and voluntary standards have not guided all or even most of company agents' practices. Nor did they necessarily guide the practices of actors closely associated with Banro and entrusted with implementing its security and development policies. Consequently, the case shows that negative effects of the mining project prevailed and remained uncompensated for, and that CSR and voluntary standards could have been better implemented and monitored.[25] In fact, significant parts of Banro's CSR activities failed to live up to the transnational standards for companies, as some increased the power of a small group of elites and mostly benefited these people and their clients with whose support the new extractive order in Luhwindja was constructed. In what follows, we illustrate the impact of Banro's 'land grabbing' on local livelihoods. We examine in particular how the company used transnational norms to manage the negative effects of its large-scale use of land, and the problems and contestations associated with these attempts.

In the context of this chapter, the term 'land grab' refers to Banro's taking control of the Twangiza concession from 2005 onwards, as a result of which the local population effectively lost access to the land. However, the notion of a single land grab does not accurately capture reality in this instance. When Banro acquired the research permits on the gold concessions, the company was granted the right to prospect for gold within this perimeter, within a defined period of time. As the exploration programme proceeded, Banro targeted specific sites for drilling, for setting up the workers' camp and for tracing roads. This way, it initiated a whole series of smaller 'land grabs', each of which drove away farmers or artisanal miners whose livelihoods depended on that land. In this early period (2005-2009), there were no general agreements on resettlement and compensation, so people affected by these small land grabs were not systematically indemnified. This of course led to protest and open resistance from local communities, inspired in part by a more general resentment of the company for the political and historical reasons outlined above. A teacher and fierce opponent of Banro explained why they frequently took the streets during this period:

> Because our rights were being violated, we pulled out all the stops: we opposed Banro, we blockaded the roads, we passed on information to the radio [...], we told them we were ready to die. Because my land is my life! (Interview with a community leader, January 2011)

---

[25]   We do not deal with this matter further in the present chapter, but for a discussion on the shortcomings of transnational standards, see for instance Hönke and Thomas (2012).

Members of the local community thus base their land use claims, or at least their entitlement to compensation for its loss, on 'traditional' rights and reference to their livelihoods (Geenen and Claessens, 2013). From 2009 onwards, Banro intensified its activities, constructing an industrial plan and generally moving towards the production phase. This engendered impacts on a much larger scale. People lost agricultural land and were relocated, houses and shops were destroyed, fields were damaged by drilling, and the environment was affected through erosion, landslides, and the construction of water dams. In the core area, Banro identified four hundred and sixty-three households – some two thousand to two thousand and five hundred individuals out of a total population of fifty-two thousand in Luhwindja – who needed to be moved to a 'resettlement site' (interview with the Banro community relations manager, January 2011). In addition, artisanal mining sites – both underground and alluvial – were closed down. Civil society organizations estimate that the number of artisanal miners working in this core area amounted to six thousand individuals (OGP – 'Observatoire gouvernance et paix', 2008).[26] Overall, Banro's activities directly and indirectly affected the livelihoods of thousands of people: miners and their families, but also traders and shopkeepers, cooks and prostitutes.

In order to mitigate the negative effects, Banro reinforced its community policies, for which it referred to a number of transnational standards. In 2008, for example, the company contracted a renowned consultancy firm (SRK) to conduct an initial social and environmental impact study based on the IFC's (International Financial Corporations) Environmental and Social Performance Standards. Banro also committed to respecting the IFC Guidelines for Resettlement and Compensation (see Szablowski, 2007a, 2007b) and the Equator Principles, a voluntary standard for banks to manage risks in project financing (interview with Banro's community relations manager, January 2011).[27] These guidelines require involving representatives of the local population in negotiations over the modalities of resettlement and compensation. Hence Banro initiated a 'community forum' in 2009, consisting of teachers, religious leaders, customary chiefs, health workers and women (interview with community leader, 8 January 2011). Later this community forum was split up into four committees, devoted to resettlement and compensation, infrastructure building, planning, and artisanal mining respectively.

---

[26] A survey that was carried out jointly by Banro and the Congolese government for the purpose of listing the artisanal miners in the targeted area identified only one thousand two hundred and sixty-seven individuals. However, many miners told us they did not register as a resistance strategy.

[27] The IFC Handbook for preparing a Resettlement Action Plan can be found at: http://www.ifc.org/ifcext/enviro.nsf/AttachmentsByTitle/p_resettle/$FILE/ResettlementHandbook.PDF [date of last access: 20 January 2014]. Information on the 'Equator Principles' is online at: http://www.equatorprinciples.com/index.php/about-ep/about [date of last access: 20 January 2014].

As a result of these negotiations, a Protocol of Agreement on resettlement and compensation was eventually signed in January 2010.[28] The agreement stipulated that the houses (main structures) would not be compensated for in cash, but would be replaced with new constructions in another location, and built *at least* to the same standards as the destroyed homes. They also agreed on the company's contributions to social services in the communities directly affected by the mine. Banro set up local development projects, such as the building of new schools and the initiation of sports projects with marginalized youth. They did this through the Banro Foundation, which was financed by the company and active both within and outside Banro's concessions.[29] On the issue of artisanal mining, Banro agreed to integrate a number of artisanal miners in its workforce, and to assist others in finding alternative livelihoods. The 2010 agreement provided for eight hundred and seventy-five former miners to be employed by Banro in various jobs associated with the construction of the mine. An additional four hundred artisanal miners, who had been identified in a survey carried out in the artisanal sites, would participate in different professional training programmes carried out by local NGOs under the supervision of Banro and the Banro Foundation, with financial support from the company.[30]

With respect to local development, the Congolese Mining Code and the 2010 annex to the agreement between Banro and the government stipulated that Banro should pay to the Congolese State an annual contribution of 4 per cent on its net revenues and 1 per cent royalties, starting from the production phase. The contract specified that the 4 per cent should go to 'infrastructural and development projects in the communities where Banro operates'.[31] The fact that it was not specified through which mechanisms this payment would take place and precisely which communities should benefit gave rise to serious disputes, particularly between local elites. In a letter addressed to Banro, Codelu for example asked to be involved in the set-up of a special fund that would supervise how the money should be managed and spent.[32] This was fiercely contested by the mwami and his allies, who insisted that Codelu had no right whatsoever to represent 'the community'.[33] It thus remained a controversial issue who could 'legitimately' represent the community.

[28] 'Protocole d'Accord passé entre la chefferie de Luhwindja et Twangiza Mining Sarl'. Unpublished document, 28 January 2010.

[29] See http://www.banro.com/s/CorporateResponsibility.asp#foundation [date of last access: 23 September 2012]; interview with Banro Foundation, Bukavu, 10 February 2011.

[30] 'Protocole d'Accord passé entre les comités des creuseurs artisanaux des chefferies de Luhwindja et de Burhinyi et la société Twangiza Mining sarl relativement à l'évacuation de la mine de Twangiza'. Unpublished document, 05 June 2010.

[31] 'Avenant n. 2 à la convention minière du 17 février 1997'. Unpublished document, 13 July 2010.

[32] Codelu 'Mot de circonstance à l'occasion de la remise du premier chèque entre Banro et la communauté de Luhwindja' (10 August 2012).

[33] Letter from Mwami to the Governor of South Kivu on 'Message de la Codelu au Président

Nonetheless, on the basis of these examples, we may conclude that Banro made quite some effort to abide by transnational standards. The company is a medium-sized multinational that is probably less well-known than the leading corporations in the mining sector, such as BHP Billiton or Anglo-American. Yet in the international specialized press, Banro is portrayed by some as a model company, with 'a community development programme that would put many majors to shame, let alone other juniors' (Mineweb, 2007). The Banro case thus confirms an argument in the business and governance literature according to which multinational companies that build on reputation in order to finance their operations at international stock exchanges, and who are likely to be targeted by shaming campaigns, will make an effort to comply with transnational voluntary standards.[34] Banro has also attracted a lot of attention in South Kivu and Eastern DRC more generally. International organizations, bilateral donor agencies and international NGOs have a strong presence in this post-conflict area and are closely watching the company's actions. Therefore, Banro also publicly commits to due diligence and efforts aimed at combatting so-called 'conflict minerals'.[35]

However, despite the efforts described above, Banro was faced with fierce resistance from the local population. The latter heavily contested the 2010 Protocol of Agreement and the way it had been negotiated and implemented on two levels (interviews with community leaders, 10/2011; see Geenen and Claessens, 2013). First, there were deficits proper to the transnational standards and procedures. These were not always adapted to local conditions. In the context of its resettlement and compensation policy, for instance, Banro imposed a moratorium on the building of new constructions or the cultivation of new crops in selected parts of its concession, which made it difficult for people to continue their regular agricultural activities. Furthermore, extended families – with married children and daughters-in-law – often lived together in separate accommodation on a single plot of land. However, these secondary structures were not compensated for by Banro. Even more problematic was the fact that Banro based its compensation scheme on the Congolese land code, according to which only an official land title – not a mere 'occupation' as recognized under customary land rights – entitled people to compensation for the loss of land (interview with lawyer, October 2011[36]). As a consequence, families with a customary title, the majority of the peasant population, were not compensated for their loss of land,

(contd) Directeur Général de la société Banro' (August 2012). Letter by *intellectuels et amis du mwami* on 'Notre réaction aux impertinences continues dans la lettre vous adressée par la Codelu en date du 11 septembre 2012' (21 September 2012).

[34] See for instance Börzel and Thauer (2013).

[35] In its CSR reports (Banro, 2012, 2013), Banro explicitly refers to the Voluntary Principles on Security and Human Rights, the Conflict Free Gold Standard of the World Gold Council and the OECD Due Diligence Guidelines for Multinational Companies.

[36] *Barème des taux d'indemnisation et modalités de remplacement des biens immobiliers.* Unpublished document, 2010.

but only for the loss of crop types having been cultivated on the plot for more than six months and for the loss of primary buildings (interviews in Luciga, October 2011). By late 2011, at least twenty-eight compensation-related cases had been brought before the court in Bukavu, and many more problematic situations are likely to exist, considering that few people have access to litigation (interview with local NGO, October 2011). These findings confirm what Szablowski has argued with respect to the World Bank resettlement guidelines: transnational law is limited in its reach and applicability when it comes to local communities in contexts where customary institutions and land rights are widely used but may be in conflict with state law (Szablowski, 2007).

Second, Banro's community policies provoked resistance because local elites served as gatekeepers between the company and the population at large. These partnerships led to exclusive deals that bypassed large parts of that population. In principle, the community was to be consulted on the implementation of local development projects. However, the community forum that had been set up in 2009 was disbanded after the conclusion of the protocols in 2010. Instead, the mwamikazi installed a local development committee, which has been severely criticized for being made up exclusively of partisans of the mwamikazi (interview with civil society organization, September 2012). Obviously the selection of representatives for such committees is in itself a political process (Ballard and Banks, 2003: 302). It is difficult to ascertain to what extent Banro's management was aware of the clientelist practices employed by the mwamikazi, the head of the local administration and local Banro personnel. We have argued above that one may assume Banro did not actively seek to influence local politics in this way. At least, the headquarters may not have been directly involved and, initially, may not have been aware. However, some local staff members were entrusted with closely monitoring local events, and it is not inconceivable that these individuals were involved in establishing the clientelist arrangements, or may at least have tacitly accepted them. Overall, the company seems not to have monitored or questioned the implementation of community policies as long as they ensured more or less stable working conditions. It was not until the exclusionary arrangements proved unsustainable and protests by parts of the local population grew stronger that the company became more concerned.

The local political power play also weighed heavily on Banro's projects for job creation and the professional reintegration of artisanal miners. About four hundred artisanal miners, who had been identified in a survey carried out in the artisanal sites, would participate in different professional training programmes. These programmes were to be executed by four local NGOs under the supervision of the Banro Foundation, with financial support from Banro. The selection of these NGOs, however, was also co-opted by local elites. At least two organizations were controlled by members of Codelu (LAV, 'Laissez l'Afrique Vivre' and ADMR, 'Action pour le développement des milieux ruraux'). Another was managed by the local catholic priest (ADEPED, 'Action pour le développement des peuples en détresse') and the fourth by the mwamikazi herself (APEF). In addition to problems with the embezzlement of funds in one case (ADEPED), the overall number of people that ultimately received training was also quite small relative to the total number of people involved in artisanal mining, namely six thousand in the core area and up to twelve thousand in the entire chiefdom (Geenen and Claessens, 2013). Thus the perception arose that participation in this reintegration programme was only for well-connected people, which again prompted popular protest.

Apart from these training programmes, the 2010 agreement for the compensation of artisanal miners also stipulated that eight hundred and fifty former artisanal miners would be employed by Banro. These would be 'relatively stable jobs', as the agreement specified, for a period of twelve to fifteen months, corresponding to the period of construction of the industrial plan. By mid-2011, however, almost all these unskilled workers had been laid off, as the exploration phase gradually came to an end. In response, hundreds of miners reoccupied the artisanal sites of Kaduma and Lukunguri, which had been closed down by the company, in April 2011. In order to maintain the social peace, the company tolerated them for a while, but the presence of private security guards served as a reminder to the miners that they were working in Banro's concession. The trespassing of artisanal miners into these sites may be interpreted as another form of protest against the company's policies, in a context where the majority of the population was directly or indirectly dependent upon artisanal mining activities (see Geenen, 2011b).

We have shown in previous sections that the arrival of Banro in the Twangiza concession resulted in a reconfiguration of national and local politics and gave rise to a powerful alliance between local elites, the company and the national government. The protests against the way Banro handled the issues of compensation and resettlement demon-strate that this alliance compromised the company's compliance with CSR guidelines. Its commitment to transnational guidelines with respect to community policies has benefitted the population, as the building of schools and hospitals and some of the compensation and resettlement efforts illustrate. However, it has so far also (re)produced an elite alliance for stability that is fairly exclusive and not percei-ved as legitimate by an important part of the local population. Despite the company's development efforts, many local people who are nega-tively affected by the mining project continue to feel frustrated and disadvantaged.

Conclusion

The concept of the 'global land grab' is often used in the context of large-scale land acquisitions for the mass production and exportation of food and biofuels (Borras and Franco, 2011: 34). However, similar phenomena are observed in the mining sector. In this chapter, we have examined the case of an industrial mining concession in South Kivu, focusing in particular on the political dynamics and contestations that the large-scale land acquisition engendered. The 'land grab' in question implied reallocations of access to land, to resources, and to the revenues that flow from mineral extraction. As Banro, the company involved, was the first to commence gold extraction in Eastern DRC, the dynamics outlined in this chapter are highly relevant for the future of mining and land use in the region more generally. More large-scale land use by mining companies in the near future is likely to give rise to similar problems and conflicts.

We have argued that the Luhwindja case first of all serves as an illustration of the reconfiguration of the Congolese State with the help of foreign direct investment. The return of industrial companies to South Kivu was part of a process of extending control by the incumbent government into areas previously out of its reach, partly because of geographical distance, but mostly through conflict. We propose that, in this case, the granting of vast concessions to multinational companies was part and parcel of a strategy adopted by the Congolese State and designed to (re)centralize control over mining rents. This extension took place through negotiations with local elites, such as the customary chiefs in Luhwindja. This brings us to our second main conclusion, namely that these 'land grabs' also led to a reconfiguration of local politics. In collaboration with Banro, local elites used the opportunities opened up by the arrival of the transnational company for establishing and consolidating their political power, and for gaining access to economic resources. At the same time, they sought to legitimize their position and constitute their authority. In these attempts, they were endorsed by the company, which tried to establish effective control over its concession and to guarantee stable working conditions. The case study illustrates how company practitioners together with local elites sought to fabricate social peace and stability through clientele practices. Two mechanisms were identified in this respect: controlling the distribution of economic opportunities in order to co-opt parts of the local population, and manipulating representation in institutions on which participatory community engagement is built. Such clientele practices remain an integral part of the 'hybrid regime of security practices' (Hönke, 2013) that multinational companies and other local and transnational actors enact in order to protect industrial mining sites.

This does not mean that external investors are all-powerful and co-opt local elites as if the latter had no agency in these matters. The case of Luhwindja illustrates that local elites play an active part in negotiating and appropriating external opportunities. But 'the local elite' is not a homogeneous group, as we have seen, and the selective alliances between company and elite members may give rise to fierce power struggles at the local level. Elite members who are not included in the strategic alliance with the company may protest and contest the ruling authorities. Also 'local communities' – a typically heterogeneous group of farmers, miners, traders and others – exercise some agency. This is exemplified by the violent protests, barring of the streets, participation in the petition, and reoccupation of artisanal mining sites described in the course of this chapter.

Unlike in other land conflicts discussed in this volume, the manner in which multinational companies such as Banro use large chunks of land is mediated by transnational standards. We have shown that transnational voluntary guidelines and the discourse of corporate social responsibility shaped the way in which the impact of 'land grabs' on local livelihoods was managed, guaranteeing compensation and resettlement standards, and assuring a number of development interventions. However, the impact of Banro's land use on local livelihoods has been ambivalent, and the effectiveness of transnational guidelines has been compromised by a number of factors. The chapter has pointed to two problems in particular: the inadequacy of transnational standards to local needs and practices and their coexistence with other 'normal' ways of fabricating local order that allow for the appropriation of corporate compensation and community engagement by local elites and company managers.

Bibliography

Aubynn, A., 2009. 'Sustainable Solution or a Marriage of Inconvenience? The Coexistence of Large-scale Mining and Artisanal and Small-scale Mining on the Abosso Goldfields Concession in Western Ghana'. *Resources Policy*, no. 34, pp. 64-70.

Ballard, C. and Banks, G., 2003. 'Resource Wars: The Anthropology of Mining'. *Annual Review of Anthropology*, no. 32, pp. 287-313.

Banks, G. and Ballard, C., 1997. *The Ok Tedi Settlement: Issues, Outcomes and Implications.* Australian National University, Canberra.

Banro Corporation, 2012. 'A new Direction for the Eastern Democratic Republic of the Congo'. *2012 Corporate Social Responsibility Report.* Banro Corporation, Toronto.

——, 2013. 'Investing in Capacity Building, Jobs and Community Development'. *2013 Sustainability Report.* Banro Corporation, Toronto.

Bezy, F., Peemans, J.-P. and Wautelet, J.-M., 1981. *Accumulation et sous-développement au Zaïre 1960-1980.* Presses universitaires de Louvain, Louvain-la-Neuve (Belgique).

Boone, C., 1998. '"Empirical Statehood" and Reconfiguration of Political Order'. *The African State at a Critical Juncture*, eds, Villalón, L. A. and Huxtable, P. A., Lynne Rienner, Boulder (CO), pp. 129-141.

———, 2003. *Political Topographies of the African State. Territorial Authority and Institutional Choice*. Cambridge University Press, Cambridge.

Borras, S. M. and Franco, J. C., 2011. 'Global Land Grabbing and Trajectories of Agrarian Change: A Preliminary Analysis'. *Journal of Agrarian Change*, vol. 12, no. 1, pp. 34-59.

Börzel, T. and Thauer, C., 2013. *Racing to the Top? Business and Governance in South Africa*. Palgrave MacMillan, New York.

Bury, J., 2004. 'Livelihoods in Transition: Transnational Gold Mining Operations and Local Change in Cajamarca, Peru'. *The Geographical Journal*, vol. 170, no. 1, pp. 78-91.

Bush, R., 2009. 'Soon there will be no-one left to take the Corpses to the Morgue. Accumulation and Abjection in Ghana's Mining Communities'. *Resources Policy*, no. 34, pp. 57-63.

Carstens, J. and Hilson, G., 2009. Mining, Grievance and Conflict in Rural Tanzania. *IDPR*, vol. 31, no. 3, pp. 301-326.

de Failly, D., 2001. 'Coltan: pour comprendre...': *L'Afrique des Grands Lacs. Annuaire 2000-2001*, eds, Marysse, S. and Reyntjens, F., L'Harmattan, Paris. pp. 279-306.

Englebert, P., 2003. 'Why Congo Persists: Sovereignty, Globalization and the Violent Reproduction of a Weak State'. *QEH Working Paper Series*, no. 95.

Garrett, N. and Mitchell, H., 2009. *Trading Conflict for Development. Utilising the Trade in Minerals from Eastern DRCongo for Development*. DFID, London.

Geenen, S., 2011a.' Local Livelihoods, Global Interests and the State in the Congolese Mining Sector'. *Natural Resources and Local Livelihoods in the Great Lakes Region of Africa*, eds, Ansoms, A. and Marysse, S., Palgrave MacMillan, Basingstoke (UK).

———, 2011b. 'Constraints, Opportunities and Hope. Artisanal Gold Mining and Trade in South Kivu, DRCongo'. *Natural Resources and Local Livelihoods in the Great Lakes Region of Africa*, eds, Ansoms, A. and Marysse, S., Palgrave MacMillan, Basingstoke (UK).

Geenen, S. and Claessens K., 2013. 'Disputed Access to the Gold Mines in Luhwindja, Eastern DRCongo'. *Journal of Modern African Studies*, vol. 51, no. 1, pp. 1-24.

Hagmann, T. and Péclard, D., 2010. 'Negotiating Statehood: Dynamics of Power and Domination in Africa'. *Development and Change*, vol. 41, no. 4, pp. 539-562.

Hibou, B., 1999. *La Privatisation des États*. Karthala, Paris.

Hilson, G., 2002. 'An Overview of Land Use Conflicts in Mining Communities'. *Land Use Policy*, no. 19, pp. 65-73.

Hilson, G. and Yakovleva, N., 2007. 'Strained Relations: a Critical Analysis of the Mining Conflict in Prestea, Ghana'. *Political Geography,* no. 26, pp. 98-119.

Hönke, J. 2009. 'Extractive Orders: Transnational Mining Companies in the Nineteenth and Twenty-First Centuries in the Central African Copperbelt'. *A new scramble for Africa?* eds, Southall, R. and Melber, H., KwaZulu Natal Press, Durban. pp. 274-298.

———, 2010. 'New Political Topographies. Mining Companies and Indirect Discharge in Southern Katanga (DRC)'. *Politique africaine,* no. 120, pp. 105-127.

———, 2013. *Transnational Companies and Security Governance.* Routledge, London.

Hönke, J. and Thomas, E., 2012. 'Governance for Whom? Inclusiveness, Indirect Effects and Externalities'. *Working Paper Series,* no. 31. Research Centre SFB 700 'Governance in Areas of Limited Statehood', Berlin.

Kennes, E., 2002. 'Footnotes to the Mining Story'. *Review of African Political Economy,* vol. 29, no. 93, pp. 601-606.

Marysse, S., 2005. 'Regress, War and Fragile Recovery: the Case of the DRCongo'. *The Political Economy of the Great Lakes Region in Africa. The Pitfalls of Enforced Democracy and Globalization,* eds, Marysse, S. and Reyntjens, F., Palgrave Macmillan, New York. pp. 125-51.

Marysse, S. and Tshimanga, C., 2013. 'La renaissance spectaculaire du secteur minier en RDC: où va la rente minière?' *Cahiers africains 'Conjonctures Congolaises 2012. Politique, secteur minier et gestion des ressources naturelles en RDCongo',* eds, Marysse, S. and Omasombo, J., Musée royal de l'Afrique centrale, Tervuren (Belgique).

Mazalto, M., 2009. 'Governance, Human Rights and Mining in the Democratic Republic of Congo'. *Mining in Africa. Regulation and Development,* ed. Campbell, B., Pluto Press, London and New York, pp. 187-242.

Mineweb, 2007. 'Banro – Punching well above its Weight for a Gold Explorer'. Online at: http://www.mineweb.com/mineweb/view/mineweb/en/page34?oid=39910&sn=Detail [date of last access: 16 January 2014].

Nest, M., Grignon, F. and Kisangani, E. F., 2006. *The Democratic Republic of Congo: Economic Dimensions of War and Peace.* Lynne Rienner, Boulder (CO).

Observatoire gouvernance et paix (OGP), 2008. *Potentialités des entités administratives décentralisées: collectivité chefferie de Luhwinja (Sud-Kivu/DRCongo).* OGP, Bukavu.

O'Faircheallaigh, C., 1995. 'Negotiations between Mining Companies and Aboriginal Communities: Process and Structure'. *CAEPR Discussion Paper,* no. 86. Centre for Aboriginal Economic Policy Research, Australian National University, Canberra.

Olivier de Sardan, J.-P., 2008. 'À la recherche des normes pratiques de la gouvernance réelle en Afrique'. *Afrique: pouvoir et politique, APPP*

Discussion Paper, no. 5. Overseas Development Institute, London.

Peters, P. E., 2004. 'Inequality and Social Conflict over Land in Africa'. *Journal of Agrarian Change*, vol. 4, no. 3, pp. 269-314.

Price Waterhouse Coopers (PWC), 2011. *Mine 2011. The Game has Changed. Review of Global Trends in the Mining Industry*. Price Waterhouse Coopers.

Reno, W., 2001. 'How Sovereignty Matters: International Markets and the Political Economy of Local Politics in Weak States'. *Intervention & Transnationalism in Africa: Global-Local Networks of Power*, eds, Callaghy, T. M., Kassimir, R. and Latham, R., Cambridge University Press, Cambridge, pp. 197-215.

Schatzberg, M. G., 2001. *Political Legitimacy in Middle Africa. Father, Family, Food*. Indiana University Press, Bloomington (IN).

Sikor, T. and Lund, C., 2009. 'Access and Property: A Question of Power and Authority'. *Development and Change*, vol. 40, no. 1, pp. 1-22.

Southall, R. and Melber, H., 2009. *A New Scramble for Africa?* KwaZulu Natal Press, Durban.

Szablowski, D., 2007a. *Transnational Law and Local Struggles: Mining Communities and the World Bank*, Hart Publishing, Oxford.

Szablowski, D. 2007b. 'Who Defines Displacement? The Operation of the World Bank Involuntary Resettlement Policy in a Large Mining Project'. *Development's Displacements. Ecologies, Economies and Cultures at Risk*, eds, Vandergeest, P., Idahosa, P. and Bose, P. S., UBC Press, Vancouver and Toronto.

Tangri, R., 1999. *The Politics of Patronage in Africa: Parastatals, Privatization, and Private Enterprise*. Africa World Press, Trenton.

Trefon, T., 2007. 'Parcours administratifs dans un État en faillite: récits populaires de Lubumbashi (RDC)'. *Cahiers Africains*, no. 74. L'Harmattan/ Musée royal d'Afrique centrale, Paris et Tervuren (Belgique).

Tull, D., 2005. 'The Reconfiguration of Political Order in Africa. A Case Study of North Kivu (RDCongo)'. *Hamburg African Studies*, no. 13. Institut für Afrikakunde, Hamburg.

United Nations (UN), 2014. Letter dated 22 January 2014 from the Chair of the Security Council Committee established pursuant to resolution 1533 (2004) concerning Democratic Republic of the Congo addressed to the President of the Security Council: S/2014/12, UN Security Council, New York.

United States Geological Survey (USGS), 2009. *Minerals yearbook. Congo (Kinshasa)*. US Department of the Interior, Washington.

Utshudi Ona, I. and Ansoms, A., 2011. 'Reconciling Custom, State and Local Livelihoods: Decentralized Land Management in South Kivu (DRC)'. *Natural Resources and Local Livelihoods in the Great Lakes Region of Africa*, eds, Marysse, S. and Ansoms, A., Palgrave Macmillan, Basingstoke (UK), pp. 26-48.

Van Puijenbroek, J., Mongo Malolo, E. and Bakker, J., 2012. *Un avenir en or en Ituri? Quel futur pour l'exploitation aurifère en Ituri, RD Congo?*

IKV Pax Christi et Réseau Haki na Amani (RHA), Utrecht.

Vellut, J.-L., 1983. 'Mining in the Belgian Congo'. *History of Central Africa*, eds, Birmingham, D. and Martin, P. M., Longman, London, pp. 126-162.

Vlassenroot, K., 2004. 'Reading the Congolese crisis'. *Conflict and Social Transformation in Eastern DR Congo,* Vlassenroot, K. and Raeymaekers, T., Academia Press, Ghent (Belgium), pp. 39-60.

Vlassenroot, K. and Raeymaekers, T., (2004). *Conflict and Social Transformation in Eastern DR Congo.* Academia Press, Ghent (Belgium).

Welker, M. A., 2009. 'Corporate Security Begins in the Community: Mining, the Corporate Social Responsibility Industry, and Environmental Advocacy in Indonesia'. *Cultural Anthropology,* vol. 24, no. 1, pp. 142-179.

Wong, S., 2010. 'Elite Capture or Capture Elites? Lessons from the "Counter-elite" and "Co-opt-elite" Approaches in Bangladesh and Ghana'. *UNU-WIDER working paper,* no. 82, pp. 1-18.

World Bank, 2008. *Democratic Republic of Congo. Growth with Governance in the Mining Sector.* World Bank, Oil, Gas, Mining and Chemicals Department, Washington.

Young, C. and Turner, T., 1985. *The Rise and Decline of the Zaïrean State.* University of Wisconsin Press, Madison.

5

**Competition
over Soil
& Subsoil**

Land Grabbing
by Local Elites
in South Kivu
(DRC)

KLARA CLAESSENS,
EMERY MUDINGA & AN ANSOMS

Introduction

Population growth, environmental degradation, slow rates of economic development and land grabbing have all contributed to the transformation of Africa from a continent of land abundance into a continent characterized by increasing land scarcity and competition over land (Berry, 2002). However, the contemporary struggles over land vary in nature depending on the specific political, social and economic context in which they occur. Shifts in land access, changing property relations and land distribution patterns can lead to different outcomes in different contexts. For some actors involved in struggles over land, it may open a window of opportunity; for others, it may result in dispossession and displacement (Borras and Franco, 2010).

In this chapter, we focus on the involvement of local elites in cases of land grabbing, a less highlighted topic in the contemporary literature on the global land rush and one that takes full account of the role of external actors who seek to invest in land as a more general response to the ongoing food, financial and energy crises (Hall, 2011; De Schutter, 2011).[1] National elites are also key players in land acquisition processes, either as direct actors or as brokers between the local community and (foreign) investors. However, these elites 'often fall below the radar of global-level studies because they are seldom regulated or facilitated by public agencies, and because individual transactions tend to be smaller' (Anseeuw et al., 2011: 21; Hilhorst, et al., 2011). We explore the role of local elites and their access to and control strategies over land in the absence of foreign investors on the basis of evidence from two case studies in the territory of Kalehe, South Kivu, in the Democratic Republic of the Congo. These cases demonstrate how local groups are strategically framed around issues of land use, land distribution and land control and how their actions unfold within a broader national and regional dynamics.

---

[1] For an analysis of less discussed processes driving the current global land grab, see also Zoomers, A., (2012), Globalisation and the foreignisation of space: seven processes driving the current global land grab. *Journal of Peasant Studies*, vol. 37, no. 2, pp. 429-447.

Local elite members of these strategic groups operate in different political arenas that are vertically and horizontally interconnected. They are thus able to enforce their claims on land at the local level.

We argue that contemporary studies on land grabbing should consider recent evolutions in land relations in their specific historical contexts. Land grabbing is neither a new nor a recent phenomenon. Past cycles of land grabbing in Africa include the colonial conquests and local elites' interest in land as an investment opportunity in response to the structural adjustment programmes (SAPs) of the 1980s (see Peemans in this volume). Local elites invested in land for direct revenue and for future financial security following the devastating effects of privatization measures taken under the SAPs. At various phases in history, local African elites have used their status and power as well as their familiarity with the institutional and legal contexts to acquire large land concessions (Berry, 2002). They are more likely to be able to navigate the complex institutional landscape and thus to gain comparative advantages at the expense of poorer and less well-connected actors.

Furthermore, land transactions do not take place in a political vacuum, as demonstrated by the roles that domestic factors and local elites play in such processes. In its report on the opportunities and challenges of large-scale land acquisitions, the World Bank recognizes that land governance in most developing countries is problematic. However, the report's recommendations are rather technocratic and do not go beyond suggestions for the reinforcement of the legal and institutional framework (World Bank, 2010). Land tenure and land arrangements are nonetheless embedded in an intricate network of local power relations, and are part of a complex institutional landscape. Therefore 'land conflicts reflect more than economic and demographic pressures; [...] land is also seen as a form of political space-territory to be controlled both for its economic value and as a *source of leverage over other people*' (Berry, 2009: 24; our emphasis). The situation is even more complicated in violent contexts, as in our case study setting, where, over several decades or even centuries, deep ethnic, economic and political cleavages have appeared in the social tissue.

In the next section of this chapter, we outline the evolution of tenure arrangements in Eastern DRC through history. Paying particular attention to the land-conflict nexus in the specific context of Eastern DRC, we introduce theoretical concepts that yield insight into the land dynamics unfolding in the case-study settings. In part three, we demonstrate on the basis of our case studies how land relations are negotiated in a context of extreme uncertainty and state failure. We focus in particular on the diverse strategies deployed by the local elites. In conclusion we reflect on the importance of the specific political, historical and institutional context, on the conflict-land nexus, and on the 'victim's' perspective in instances of local land grabbing.

Land tenure in Eastern DRC

In South Kivu, the prevailing land tenure arrangements, based on collective ownership, kinship loyalty and mutual interdependence, have come under serious stress as a result of population growth, opportunistic behaviour by local elites and a growing number of land claims for other than agricultural purposes, such as the exploitation of forestry and mining resources (Utshudi Ona and Ansoms, 2011).

These customary arrangements are generally embedded in a *kalinzi* system, which may be described as 'an institution that legitimizes the whole social organization by absorbing all persons within a given area into a network of dependent relations' (Van Acker 2005: 81). *Kalinzi* is a customary contract, based on a strict hierarchy dominated by the king or *mwami*, who acts as the allocator of land. In order to become integrated into the network of interdependent relationships and obtain inheritable land use rights, one has to address the customary chief to pay a tribute or kalinzi, most often in the form of cattle. By paying the kalinzi, one becomes the 'subject' of the chief. However, although such customary arrangements and the power of customary chiefs to allocate land use rights persist to this day, the system has been severely challenged and has undergone profound change.

The first challenge to customary land arrangements came from the colonial powers and their introduction of a dual system that distinguished between *terres domaniales* or state-owned land governed by state law and *terres indigènes* or indigenous land governed by customary law. This duality was maintained until the introduction in 1973 of the General Property Law, whereby all land, including customary land, was nationalized. While Article 389 of the law provided that land occupied by local communities could remain under customary arrangements by force of a presidential decree, to date no such decree has been proclaimed. Consequently, since 1973, there has been much uncertainty regarding communally held land, specifically in respect of its legal status, its governance and the rights of land users (Mugangu Matabaro, 2005, Uthsudi and Ansoms 2011). Furthermore, due to the weak implementation capacity of the Congolese State, the de facto duality between state-owned land and customary land has persisted. Vlassenroot and Huggins (2005) describe how these historical evolutions have resulted in a profound reshaping of access rights to land and the reorganization of rural society. Traditional patron-client relationships such as the kalinzi contract have gradually become eroded, replaced in part with new forms of patrimonial ties based on economic gain and wealth accumulation. Local customary chiefs have tried to maintain their positions by acting as gatekeepers during the transition from customary control to a modern legal system. The traditional order is thus slowly making way for an order of social stratification. Proximity to the political centre has become key to wealth accumulation. At the individual level, this radical reconfiguration has led to unequal access patterns, growing tenure insecurity, land alienation and ultimately impoverishment. At the institutional level, growing competition over land has created opportunities for customary leaders to instrumentalize customary land tenure by reinterpreting local norms. In the immediate aftermath of the democratization process initiated by Mobutu in the 1990s, land disputes among other issues gave rise to violence between ethnic groups.

The dynamics of land-related issues were further complicated by the Congolese wars, as access and occupation patterns were altered through displacements and growing social and ethnic tensions (ibid. , 2005). Land actually became a structural cause of conflict, as unequal access led to the impoverishment of some population groups and a growing group of landless peasants. In some instances, land continues to be a local cause or source of conflict. As will become apparent later in this chapter, contested land transaction and disputes over resource-rich land have, for example, given rise to strife and violence in the territory of Kalehe. Eastern DRC has witnessed different types of land-related conflicts, mostly of an interpersonal nature and usually involving little physical aggression. However, when such conflicts contain an element of ethnicity and identity they can easily give rise to violence (CRG – Conflict Research Group, 2012).

Today, land tenure in the DRC is governed by a variety of authorities and institutions, all of which issue norms and rules that are intended to shape the behaviour of individual and collective actors. This apparent complexity in the production of rules and norms, and any ensuing contradictions, may be termed 'legal pluralism'. Legal pluralism is a typically empirical concept that we define as 'the normative heterogeneity attendant upon the fact that social action always takes place in a context of multiple, overlapping "semi-autonomous social fields" which [...] is in practice a dynamic condition' (Griffiths, 1986:38). A society is made up of different social fields, including villages, ethnic communities, associations or the State. Each field has different loci of authority that overlap and interact with other social fields. Because of this interaction and overlap, each field is only semi-autonomous, implying that while they each generate internal rules and symbols they also remain sensitive to decisions and rules generated by surrounding social fields (Moore, 1978).

Hence the institutional landscape is by definition heterogeneous, in flux, unstable and dynamic (Bastiaensen et al., 2005). At the same time, powerful actors may use economic, political or social means to instrumentalize the co-existence of different institutions, norms and rules, including in relation to land governance. Customary authorities, for example, occupy a unique position on the crossroads of local and regional governance: not only do they oversee the (transformation of) customary arrangements, but they also have knowledge of, and indeed are integrated into, the decentralized state administration. This may lead to abusive practices, as in instances where land occupied by local communities is declared 'unoccupied' by a customary chief in order that elites could register it in the national land registry (Utshudi and Ansoms, 2011). Clearly, then, access to land and control over resources from that land are negotiated amidst unequal power relations.

To help us understand how access to land is negotiated in a context of increasing competition over natural resources, we rely on the explanatory concept of 'political arena', introduced by Olivier de Sardan. A 'political arena' is a 'space in which real conflicts between interacting social actors occur around common stakes. It occurs within a "local space"' (Olivier de Sardan, 2005: 190). The notion of conflict is key, as Olivier de Sardan considers it to be an intrinsic part of social relations: 'conflicts figure among the best ways of penetrating the intricacies of society, of revealing its structures, norms and codes, or of highlighting the strategies and logics of actors or of groups' (ibid.: 189). Within a particular political arena, individual social actors may gather around a common strategic goal. They may then form 'strategic groups' or the 'social aggregates of a more empirical and variable nature, which defend common interest, especially by means of social and political action' (ibid.: 191). Strategic groups, then, are temporary alliances of individuals who, for a period of time, share certain objectives. They are dynamic: their composition may change and hence so too may their cause. The struggle over access to land may be seen to unfold in such a political arena, a setting where individual actors and strategic groups interact in order to retain, gain and regain access to and control over a natural resource.

In the next section, we analyse local land dynamics and the role of the local elites and their strategic groups in order to gain an understanding of how access to and control over land are negotiated in a context of uncertainty and state failure. We illustrate through case studies the way in which strategic groups are formed and how they operate around the issue of access to land.

Land conflicts in Kalehe

Situated between Bukavu and Goma, the two major regional capitals, Kalehe is one of eight territories constituting the Province of South Kivu in Eastern DRC. It has a surface area of 4082 square kilometres and an estimated population of 524,000 (APC – 'Action pour la paix et la concorde', 2009). The main economic activities in Kalehe are agriculture, cattle breeding and the extraction of mineral resources. The presence of different mining sites and vast concessions of fertile land in the Hauts Plateaux has exacerbated already growing competition between different ethnic groups over both occupied and non-occupied land. The territory is characterized by a strong cultural diversity and the presence of different ethnic groups, including Bahavu, Batembo, Barongeronge, Bahutu, Batutsi and Bahunde. These ethnic groups may be divided into an indigenous and an immigrant population group. The former have frequently vented their frustration at the presence of a substantial Kinyarwanda-speaking population (Hutu and Tutsi) that has entered the DRC in various migratory waves. The first wave of Banyarwanda immigrants arrived in the 1950s, brought in as labourers by the Belgian colonial administration, to work the Kivu region's vast coffee, tea and cinchona plantations. These early immigrants came to Kalehe from Rwanda and from Masisi in the neighbouring province of North Kivu (APC, 2009). Later, various other groups of Banyarwanda arrived as refugees during different episodes of ethnically motivated violence in Rwanda and Burundi.

Since the 1990s, different armed groups have operated within the territory of Kalehe (APC, 2009). At the time of our research (September 2011), there were six such armed groups. Their activities contributed to an atmosphere of continuing insecurity, frequently resulting in displacements of local residents and aggravating their social and economic vulnerability. One recent example is the armed movement *Nyatura*, which was founded in June 2011. In addition to other military and political agendas (competition for grades and high-ranking positions within the national army, refusal to be deployed outside the Kivus), one of the underlying reasons for establishing Nyatura was to serve the land rights of Hutu inhabitants. Nyatura was the successor to PARECO ('Patriotes résistants congolais'), a movement founded in 2008 and originating in the Hutu militia known as *Bakobwa*. Already in the 1990s, the 'combattants' clashed with the Mai-Mai militias of Batembo over issues of identity and land. At the time of our research, however, actors close to Nyatura expressed concern over the return of Congolese Tutsi refugees from Rwanda. These Tutsi had fled to Rwanda in 1994, after the influx in DRC of Hutu refugees from Rwanda, a country then embroiled in interethnic violence between Tutsi and Hutu. Now, almost two decades on, the Congolese Tutsi were returning home and reclaiming the land they had left behind (APC, 2011).

Tutsi-dominated armed groups such as the CNDP ('Congrès national pour la défense du peuple') and the March 23 Movement (M23) have always listed the return of these Tutsi refugees among their political objectives. They argue that the conflicts that have ravaged Eastern DRC can only be resolved if the return of refugees, land issues and nationality are placed on the Congolese political agenda.[2] In the territory of Kalehe, many land conflicts pit Hutu and Tutsi against each other, sometimes resulting in armed clashes. Our empirical evidence indicates that the presence of former CNDP fighters in the Congolese army has facilitated the return of some Tutsi. The CNDP's policy of protecting the Tutsi ethnic group holds the danger of a radicalization of the position of Nyatura and Hutu in general, as in the recent rivalry between Hutu and Tutsi over the civil and military leadership of the village of Numbi.[3]

---

[2] See for details Stearns, J. (2012).
[3] See for details on the struggle for land and village leadership between Tutsi and Hutu: APC, (2012) and Stearns, J. (2013).

Access to land: contestation in the Hauts Plateaux
Many of the land conflicts identified during our research (September 2011) were framed around the return of Kinyarwanda-speaking Tutsi, an evolution that was generally perceived as problematic by the indigenous population of Kalehe. Originally, these Tutsi had settled in Kalehe during successive migratory waves since the 1950s. Over years or even decades of presence in the DRC, many obtained Congolese nationality, and the majority acquired access to plots of land in the Hauts Plateaux through negotiations with local customary chiefs. However, following the Rwandan genocide of 1994, large groups of Hutu refugees arrived in South Kivu as they fled the RPF[4]'s violent retaliations. Their arrival in turn prompted a reverse migratory wave of Congolese Tutsi to Rwanda. The UNHCR (United Nations High Commissioner for Refugees) estimates that, in 2011, approximately fifty thousand refugees – mostly Tutsi – were living in refugee camps in Rwanda. According to the Rwandan government, the number living outside of camps was about three times higher (Minority Rights Group International, 2011).

As they left the DRC, the Tutsi refugees either sold their land, abandoned it, or appointed a local caretaker (usually Bahavu, Batembo or Hutu). At the time of our research, however, many Tutsi were returning to the DRC. This gave rise to conflicts over the ownership of the plots of land they had previously vacated. So in effect, the returning Tutsi were reclaiming land that had been occupied by others for the past seventeen years. Moreover, in many cases the claimants were not the original occupants but had either bought the land in question or had been allocated the plot by the customary authorities.

In the course of our fieldwork, we came across several land conflicts involving Banyarwanda Tutsi. Among these conflicts, we identified three types of cases. First, there were cases involving Tutsi who were claiming back land they had never sold. A second type of conflict revolved around Tutsi who had sold their plots, but who – faced with the perceived threat of Hutu refugees arriving in Kalehe in 1994 – had done so at well below the market price. The third type concerned land that was being reclaimed after a legitimate sale, sometimes before the arrival of any Hutu refugees. In what follows, we discuss each category separately on the basis of some concrete examples.

A first group of Tutsi claimants had not sold their land before fleeing to Rwanda. Sometimes, they had appointed someone to manage the land on their behalf, often a friend or the local chief. Reclaiming their land after an absence of seventeen years often proved difficult.

We came across a land conflict in the *Hauts Plateaux* of Lemera in the village of Buzunga involving Majé, Freddy and Kirori. When Maje (Tutsi) left the DRC, he entrusted his cattle and land to Freddy

---

[4] The Rwandan Patriotic Front seized power in Rwanda after the genocide of 1994.

(Mushi). He also asked his friend and local chief Kirori to safeguard the documents that proved his ownership of the land. After Majé had left, however, Kirori used his absence to sell the land and the documents in question to Freddy. When Majé returned in 2011, Freddy refused to cede his rights, considering himself as the rightful owner after having paid Kirori.[5] At the time of our research (December 2011), the case was still being considered by the local tribunal.

Other Tutsi left their fields without appointing a caretaker. In several observed cases, this land had been redistributed by the customary authority to new landowners, who were now refusing to give back their plots to the returning Tutsi, arguing that they had become the rightful owners. One of our interviewees[5] explained: 'We thought they had left for good and that they wouldn't come back.'[6]

Other Tutsi sold their land before leaving, but below value. Many of them felt threatened by the sudden and massive influx of Hutu refugees, so that their sale was in effect a distress sale. However, it emerged during our research that opinions varied as to what would have been a fair price back in 1994. In quite a few cases, fleeing Tutsi considered the money they received for their land as *mpamba*, literally a provision for travelling; they saw it as a fee for the right to use the land in their absence rather than as a purchase fee. However, those who acquired the land in return for money regarded the exchange as a sale. The following case is an example of such a conflict, in which a local mediation initiative was working towards a consensus (CDM 'Comité de dialogue et de médiation'[7]):

> In 1994, a Tutsi sold 780 hectares of land to a Muhavu for $1500. The latter subsequently sold the land to seven Bahavu and Bahutu families. Recently, the original Tutsi owner returned and reclaimed his property. The CDM tried to reach a compromise by recognizing the needs of the present owners, while at once conceding that the price paid in 1994 did not reflect the true market value of the plot. The mediator proposed that the land should be divided between the former owner (Tutsi) and the present occupants. At the moment of our interview, the proposition had not been accepted yet by the present occupants.[8]

A third category of cases revolved around Banyarwanda Tutsi who had sold their land at the real market price. However, with growing land scarcity, the value had increased sharply in the decade prior to their return. We came across several such cases in the course of our research, including the following:

---

[5] To guarantee the anonymity of our informants, we used pseudonyms.

[6] Interview, Kasheke, 18 October 2011.

[7] These informal mediation offices were set up by the Congolese NGO 'Action pour la paix et la concorde' (APC) based in Bukavu.

[8] Interview with *animateur local,* office CDM, APC, 19 October 2011, Bushushu.

James, one of our interviewees, explained how his Muhavu family was involved in a land conflict with a Tutsi called Ndaro. Ndaro had sold his land to James's family and two other families in 1993. This transaction was concluded well before the influx of Hutu refugees in the region. According to James, a reasonable price had been paid ($1120 for 22 hectares). However, Ndaro had recently returned to sell one of his remaining plots. This time he obtained a much higher price than he got in 1993. According to James, this prompted Ndaro to resell the land he had previously sold to the three families to a Mushi called Ridego. This transaction was concluded in July 2010. The three families in question did not accept this transaction and refused to grant access to the contested fields. As an argument in their favour, James mentioned that Ridego was well aware of the illegitimate nature of the transaction, as the three families had announced on the radio that the land was already occupied and therefore not for sale.[9] At the time of our research, the case was in the hands of a local tribunal. Ridego, who lived in Bukavu, had never attempted to access the contested land.[10] James's family was continuing to farm the plot, even though Ridego frequently dropped by with prospective buyers. The two other families involved were no longer accessing the contested land.[11]

Another source of contestation and conflict is the fate of the land reclaimed by the returning refugees. Several Tutsi were being accused of reclaiming land simply to sell it on to third parties. In several cases, reclaimed land had subsequently been sold to Kinyarwanda-speaking families who had not lived in the region before but were attracted by its low land prices compared to prices in even more populated Rwanda. This was perceived as very problematic by the local population. One of our interviewees stated that 'nowadays everybody purports to be a refugee'.[12] Another respondent explained that the return of the refugees as such did not pose a problem, but that they were 'bringing along others. We are witnessing an influx of new residents [...]. Often they sell their land even if they say they will not. If they sell to indigenous folk, that's okay, but they should not sell their land to newly arriving Tutsi'.[13] Another interviewee agreed, stating that 'all ethnicities – Batembo, Bahutu, Bahavu and Batutsi – have the right to access land, but it has become difficult to distinguish between Congolese Tutsi and foreign Tutsi. 'Congolese Tutsi are bringing along "brothers" who are unknown in the area, and this is a big problem.'[14] Another respondent added that 'to claim a plot of land over here, one

---

[9]   Interview 18 October 2011, Kasheke.
[10] Interview 25 November 2011 Kasheke.
[11] Interview, 11 August 2012, Lemera.
[12] Interview, 18 October 2011, Kasheke.
[13] Interview, 19 October 2011, Chibanda.
[14] Interview with *animateur local*, office CDM, APC, 19 October 2011, Bushushu.

has to be the real owner or at least a descendant of the person who lived there before. Nobody should pretend to be the son of a local when in fact nobody in this area knows them.'[15]

On their return, Tutsi of all three categories rarely entered into direct negotiations with the new occupants of the land. Instead, they adopted more indirect strategies. One respondent claimed that 'most of them [i.e. returning refugees] do not pass through the "little door" [i.e. local authorities or mediators] but rather through the "big" one [i.e. authorities at a higher level]'.[16] In other cases, returning Tutsi reinforced their claims by calling on assistance from armed forces, particularly former CNDP[17] militiamen who had since integrated into the Congolese Army, FARDC. As one person explained: 'In some cases, we recognize that the land belongs to them. But why do they have to call on the army to assert their rights? This creates a negative impression.'[18] Another interviewee alleging that Tutsi actors relied on armed forces to (re)claim land said: 'When a Tutsi realizes he is failing [to get his land back], he will seek help from an armed group to combat civilians. This is why we often hear about confrontations between civilians and armed groups over land issues.'[19 and 20]

Indeed, Tutsi returnees' land claims seemed to provide an incentive for other population groups also to form armed groups to protect their interests. One such example comes from the bordering province of North Kivu and the APCLS ('Alliance patriote du Congo libre et souverain'). According to a 2011 report of a UN panel of experts, 'APCLS is the strongest Mai Mai in North Kivu, mobilizing its forces on the basis of popular resistance to Tutsi refugee returns, traditional land rights, and defence against the expansion of the Tutsi and Hutu dominance in the Masisi territory' (UN, 2011, para. 219: 65-66). In the province of South Kivu, and the territory of Kalehe in particular, there is the example of the aforementioned armed group of *Nyatura*. According to a report by the local NGO, 'Action pour la Paix et la Concorde' (APC), a land conflict between Hutu and Tutsi lay at the heart of the establishment of this armed movement. One of our respondents, a Hutu, felt it was not impossible that other armed groups would be formed: 'Within the Hutu community, there is a sense that we must defend our interests'. When asked if such groups already existed and, if they did, how they were organized, the respondent replied: 'We know each other.'[21]

---

[15] Interview, 19 October 2011, Kalehe.
[16] Interview with group of miners, 19 October 2011, Nyabibwe.
[17] 'Congrès national pour la défense du peuple', a rebel party founded by Laurent Nkunda and supported by Rwanda. The CNDP were integrated into the Congolese army in 2009.
[18] Interview, 19 October 2011, Chibanda.
[19] Interview, 12 November 2011, Numbi.
[20] It should be noted that, in Eastern DRC, there is a long history of rebel movements supported by Tutsi. Examples include the AFDL (1996), the RCD (1998-2003) the CNDP (2004) and more recently M23 (as from March 2012).
[21] Interview, 12 November 2011, Numbi.

We also recorded cases where customary authorities had been used to reinforce the land claims of returning refugees. One respondent explained how a Tutsi had called on the customary chief to confirm his ownership rights on a piece of land that had previously been sold to two different families. Our respondent described the customary chief in question as 'too young', 'he [the customary chief] is not familiar with our custom' and 'he is easily wooed with the smell of money'.[22] The perceived insincerity of some customary chiefs was cited during several of our interviews, with references to alleged instances of corruption and dishonesty. One respondent explained how some customary chiefs allocated the same plot of land to different persons. He added that this was 'the real problem with the customary chiefs: the sons of the original customary chiefs have to reposition themselves after the death of their fathers. Today they demand documents proving that our parents paid kalinzi which was unheard of in the old days. The young chief uses this "requirement" to reposition himself. He can dispossess people, mostly the poor, and reallocate the land to the rich and to members of the elite who often have no intention of living there.'[23]

The following case also illustrates how customary chiefs were trying to reposition themselves in order to retain their authority in a quickly changing institutional environment.

In Numbi, in the *Hauts Plateaux* of Kalehe, customary chiefs have played a pivotal role in a variety of land conflicts involving members of different ethnic communities. In many instances, the conflicts predate 1994. A Muhavu interviewee explained how the Kinyarwanda-speaking population entered Kalehe from Rwanda and from Masisi in North Kivu during the 1950s. They requested the customary chief, Hubert Sangara, to assign them land. At that time, there was still plenty of vacant land. But Sangara also granted concessions on land that had already been allocated to local families who subsequently had not been able to cultivate it. During this period, between 1950 and 1970, several Hutu and Tutsi families acquired land through the payment of the customary tribute or Kalinzi.

The real problems began, however, when Hubert Sangara was succeeded by his son Raymond Sangara in the 1980s. Demand for land had increased significantly and the new mwami applied a different strategy. He sought out vulnerable or poor individuals, grabbed (part of) their land and kept it for himself or sold it on to more powerful and rich newcomers, mostly Tutsi. The evictees were barely able to protest or put up resistance. One interviewee explained that 'Sangara wanted more space for his plantations [...] He drove away all those living there and just grabbed their land. [...] Sangara succeeded in his 'coup' because he was not just anybody. Who could bring to trial a big shot like Sangara? Hence the residents felt it was better to leave the area and to abandon their fields'.[24]

Then, in 1994, some of the original occupants who had obtained their land from Hubert Sangara – took advantage of the departure of most Tutsi to retake the land that used to be theirs. They argued that the transactions made by Raymond Sangara in the 1980s had been illegal, and that they were the legitimate owners of the land[25]. Further complications arose during the rebellion of the 'Rassemblement congolais pour la démocratie' (RCD) between 1998 and 2003. The customary chief, Raymond Sangara, maintained close relationships with this movement. He again played an important role in favouring Tutsi land claims (Namegabe, 2005). During the transition period (2003-2006), Raymond Sangara was involved in the policy of mass acquisition of land in the Hauts Plateaux of Kalehe. The most recent examples date from August 2011, when Sangara became involved in a conflict between Hutu families and a Tutsi family in the Numbi area and played an influential role in a village leadership challenge, where a Hutu leader was replaced with a Tutsi.

The aforementioned case studies illustrate how different strategic groups – often formed around a common ethnic identity – can become framed around land access issues. We have also highlighted the ambivalent role of different customary and military elites. Both groups are able to maintain their power base: customary authorities because of their historically acquired position in society and military actors through the violent enforcement of their claims. In some instances, customary chiefs appear to have instrumentalized their customary power in order to favour certain parties – in return for money – in the distribution of land. These dynamics indicate how conflicts over land (re)allocation and (re)distribution are rooted in local power relations. Although not all land conflicts can be reduced to ethnic cleavages, the cases described above certainly illustrate how ethnicity can play an important part in the mobilization and remobilization of strategic groups, often resulting in violence. The ethnic affiliation of a local military elite, for example, is often a decisive factor in whether or not access is gained to land resources. Or, as summarized in the following quote: 'When the army changes, the problems also change.'[26] The success of local actors in trying to access land depends in part on their ability to connect with the local military and customary authorities. Achieving such institutional connectedness makes them more likely to succeed in navigating the obstacles of a complex and plural institutional landscape.

---

[24] Interview, 12 November 2011, Numbi.
[25] Interview, 12 November 2011, Numbi.
[26] Interview, 12 November 2011, Numbi.

Access to mineral resources: economic interests and landownership at the mining sites of Nyabibwe

Competition over land can become even more fierce and complex if the land holds mineral wealth. Given the potentially high economic gains, it is perhaps not surprising that local elites tend to compete for access to such resources, so that a further amalgam of individual actors, strategic groups and institutions is added to an already complex situation. Again, though, one sees that competition over the mineral-rich land unfolds in an atmosphere of violence and the construction of implicit or explicit ethnic agendas.

In Nyabibwe, in the 'groupement' of Mbinga North, two cooperatives, each with their own legitimizing discourses and access strategies, were locked in dispute over access to the Kalimbi mining site. In the 1970s, the French company SEREMI ('Société d'études, de recherche et exploitation minière') discovered cassiterite on the Kalimbi hillside. By the early 1980s, the site was being exploited by the industrial mining company of SMDG ('Société minière de Goma). However, following a strong decline in the price of raw materials in the global market in 1986, SMDG terminated its exploitation at Kalimbi. All workers were dismissed, save for twenty-two security personnel who were to guard the site under the supervision of an engineer and geologist called Muteba.[27] In the early 1990s, the chief of Groupement Mbinga North, Jules Chirimwami, seized all of SMDG's local possessions. After Jules's subsequent death, these were passed on to his brother and businessman Placide Chirimwami. In 1993, Placide Chirimwami established a cooperative known as COMBECKA ('Coopérative minière pour le bien-être communautaire de Kalehe'). He made several attempts at expelling the artisanal diggers who had been occupying the mining shafts since the departure of Muteba. COMBECKA was formed of the different team leaders, each of which supervised a group of diggers. 10 per cent of production went straight to Chirimwami, 45 per cent went to the team leaders and 45 per cent to the diggers. However, the latter were obliged to sell their share to their team leader at a fixed price. In 1993, the provincial authorities of South-Kivu officially recognized COMBECKA and granted it the right to manage the goods left by SMDG (Cuvelier, 2010).

Since its foundation in 1993, the management of COMBECKA had been contested on several occasions by local and other actors. In response, COMBECKA resorted to a variety of strategies to maintain its control over the mining site. At the time of research, it was hard to establish which group had had control over the mine at which moments in time. Interestingly, different respondents provided divergent answers in this respect, depending largely on their own positions in the dispute over access to the site. Hence the time references in this case study are tentative.

---

[27] Interview, 15 November 2011, Kuweit mining site, Kalimbi, Nyabibwe.

First, the creation of competing cooperatives influenced the leadership structure of the mining site. Around 2005, a group of miners founded CMDK ('Coopérative minière pour le développement de Kalehe'). According to one of the founders of CMDK, they controlled the mine for a period of two years between 2005 and 2007. However, according to certain representatives of COMBECKA, these miners were only there for a period of three months, coinciding with the occupation of Nyabibwe and its surroundings by Laurent Nkunda's CNDP.[28] The representatives recalled how the executive staff of COMBECKA fled the area, after which the CMDK miners took control of the shafts.[29 and 30] COMBECKA claims that it regained control over the mine after a brief period of occupation.

In 2010, COMBECKA was challenged once more. Former members of CMDK, seeking to take advantage of general insecurity, established COMIKA ('Coopérative minière de Kalimbi'). Since COMIKA's creation, COMBECKA and COMIKA have been locked in dispute over access rights to the site, leading to violence on several occasions. According to a member of COMIKA, COMBECKA's exploitation of the mining sites lacked transparency. Moreover, he accused Chirimwami (the founder and coordinator of COMBECKA) of nepotism in appointing friends and relatives to key positions: '[Chirimwami] violated the rights of the members [of COMBECKA] [...]. He considers the cooperative as his private property.'[31] According to certain members of COMIKA, they took control of the site in 2008 after COMBECKA had abandoned it: 'They [COMBECKA] failed to organize the expenses. When they moved out, COMIKA took the opportunity to enter the site and to start exploitation because there was an economic crisis going on.'[32] COMBECKA – according to these interviewees – had failed to invest in essential equipment such as generators and motorized pumps. COMIKA then managed the mine for two years (between 2008 and 2010). According to its members, COMIKA obtained legal documents in September 2010 granting them official exploitation rights.[33]

An influential member of COMBECKA, however, had an entirely different recollection of events in 2008 and 2009. He linked the occupation by COMIKA to the presence of armed Hutu in the mine. In so doing, this interviewee framed the conflict between the two cooperatives in ethnic terms. According to this informant, PARECO (a movement born in 2008 from the Hutu militia *Bakobwa)* 'occupied the mine in 2009'; 'this seems to be the economic policy of our Hutu brothers: to grab all of our wealth, land and cattle'.[34] This statement should, however, be qualified. As a

---

[28] 'Congrès national pour la défense du peuple' (CNDP) is a Tutsi-based rebel group founded in 2004 by Laurent Nkunda.

[29] Interview with COMBECKA representatives, 15 November 2011, Nyabibwe.

[30] Interview with COMIKA representatives, 14 November 2011, Nyabibwe.

[31] Interview with COMIKA representatives, 14 November 2011, Nyabibwe.

[32] Interview with COMIKA representatives, 14 November 2011, Nyabibwe.

[33] Interview with COMIKA representatives, 14 November 2011, Nybibwe.

[34] Interview, 20 October 2011, Mukwidja.

matter of fact, PARECO never occupied the mine. Nonetheless, the armed group was indeed quite active in the mountains surrounding the mining site and may therefore have had a say in the transaction and in the trade in minerals. In 2008, after the Goma Conference, PARECO was officially integrated into the FARDC ('Forces armées de la République démocratique du Congo').[35] After this integration process, some of the former PARECO-FARDC officers seized control of mining shafts at Nyabibwe.

In 2010, SEASSCAM ('Service d'assistance et d'encadrement du *Small-Scale Mining*')[36] organized a meeting with representatives of the two different cooperatives (COMBECKA and COMIKA) to inform them that neither met the legal requirements to claim exclusive rights to the mine. After this meeting, a group of armed miners attempted to occupy the shafts, but they were stopped by members of COMIKA, who had control over the site at the time (our research; see also Cuvelier, 2010 and UN, 2011). The violent confrontations resulted in one death and several injuries. According to certain members of COMIKA, the violence had been initiated by Chirimwami (founder and coordinator of COMBECKA), who recruited labourers from his plantation to occupy the mining shafts.[37] According to COMBECKA, however, it was COMIKA who had violated COMBECKA's rights by exploiting the contested site. On 31 August 2010, the administrator of the territory of Kalehe granted temporary management rights over the site to COMIKA until the installation of a neutral management committee (Cuvelier, 2010). This committee, made up of members of the two cooperatives, was appointed by the public authorities the following year, in July 2011. Two persons were assigned to each position: one representing COMIKA, the other COMBECKA. According to several members of COMIKA, this structure proved to be rather unproductive, due largely to the enduring distrust between the two cooperatives. A representative of COMBECKA described the situation as 'provisional': 'The province asked us to cooperate with the others, but we drive them out later [...] I have capable children and I know that one day [we] will regain control.'[38]

The introduction of yet another actor led to further complications. In 2007, Shamika Resources, a Canadian mining company started its exploration phase in Kalimbi. One of the four exploration permits held by Shamika Resources covers the area of the mining site of Kalimbi in Nyabibwe. The presence of this industrial mining company caused concern among the artisanal miners, who feared they might lose their jobs (Cuvelier, 2010). Local civil society and the provincial minister in charge of mining called the firm's exploitation of the mine illegal. Shamika Resources dismis-

---

[35] These former PARECO soldiers were under the command of FARDC colonel Guigui, who would be arrested in Bukavu in 2011 after being caught transporting minerals in an FARDC vehicle.

[36] The 'Service d'assistance et d'encadrement du *Small-Scale Mining*' (SEASSCAM) was founded in 2003 to support artisanal miners.

[37] Interview with representatives COMIKA, 14 November 2011, Nyabibwe.

[38] Interview with a member of COMBECKA, 20 October 2011, Mukwidja.

sed these allegations: 'We are legally authorized to do this [exploring the resources] and are not exploiting yet. We have not arrived at the exploitation phase, but are still in the exploration phase.'[39] At the time of our research, the exploitation phase has not taken off. According to the president of Shamika Resources, there have been contacts between the company and Chirimwami, who claims to be the legal landowner and the manager of the cooperative that exploits the site (COMBECKA). Shamika have offered to pay him compensation on condition that he can demonstrate his rightful ownership of the site (Cuvelier, 2010).

These three contestations – the presence and influence of armed groups, the establishment of competing cooperative and the presence of an industrial mining company – have weakened the bargaining power of Chirimwami. In order to maintain his control over the mining site, Chirimwami would appear to have resorted to a military strategy. According to some sources, Chirimwami has close ties with members of FARDC, particularly with a group with former CNDP affiliations, one of whose members he appointed as supervisor of the mining site (see also Cuvelier, 2010).

Despite the divergent interests of the different actors involved and the various phases of contestation, at the time of our research Chirimwami seemed to be in control of the mine. According to some members of COMIKA, Chirimwami was also the principal buyer of cassiterite in the region and maintained strong commercial links with Rwanda: 'Placide draws his money straight out of Rwanda. He takes money and he gives it to the members of COMBECKA. He asks his compliers to buy and to bring him all the cassiterite to take to Rwanda to sell it over there.' Furthermore, the UN panel of experts has stated that, according to local businessmen, Chirimwami held meetings with Bosco Ntaganda[40] in Goma in March 2011 to discuss the organization of a military intervention by the former CNDP Colonel Saddam Ringo,[41] a close ally of Ntaganda's. The UN report states that, through the Ringo connection, COMBECKA was able to transport the minerals across Lake Kivu to Rwanda. [42] It is interesting to note that during the suspension of mining activities, that same Colonel Ringo protected the trading activities of Chirimwami's protagonist COMIKA.

---

[39] Radio Okapi, 13 July 2007: *Bukavu: exploitation illégale de minerais, le ministre provincial dénonce.*

[40] Bosco Ntaganda was the deputy leader of the CNDP movement and the leadership of General Laurent Nkunda. The latter was defeated in 2008 and was replaced by Bosco Ntaganda, who joined the Congolese peace process in 2009. The CNDP was a Tutsi-dominated armed militia that operated in the Kivu region from 2004 to 2009. Following the peace agreement of March 2009, the CNDP was integrated in the FARDC, where Ntaganda was appointed as a General. The International Criminal Court has issued an arrest warrant for Ntaganda for crimes against humanity. The UN Group of Experts reported in November 2012 that Bosco Ntaganda was involved in the M23 rebel movement.

[41] Edmond 'Saddam' Ringo was a former PARECO commander who integrated in the FARDC. He joined the M23 movement but subsequently deserted and rejoined the FARDC.

[42] Group of Experts on the DRC (S/2011/738), para. 465, pp. 119-120.

This demonstrates very clearly the volatility of the strategic groups involved. Moreover, local authorities have confirmed that, in June 2011, Chirimwami arranged a meeting with Colonel Nsabimana Mwandagabo, an FARDC brigade commander in Kalehe, to discuss the reinstallation of COMBECKA.[44]

The case study of the Nyabibwe mining site illustrates how access to and control over resources is secured through alliances and counteralliances involving a variety of actors, different levels of governance and divergent strategies. As is the case with land conflicts, the legitimacy and the power of each actor to access and exploit the resources concerned is rooted in their economic and political capacity to manipulate or to mobilize armed groups (i.e. the army or militia) and to use state and customary services to obtain legitimization. The relationships between the various actors are determined mainly by economic factors, but ethnicity also comes into play in the competition over resources between the two cooperatives. For example, economic life in Nyabibwe is dominated by the Hutu, while the Havu primarily run the administration. The deployment in the area of former PARECO militiamen (mostly Hutu) in 2008-2009 reinforced the position of a specific group of miners linked to COMIKA. COMIKA is indeed essentially Hutu dominated, whereas the COMBECKA leadership is more closely associated with the Tutsi and their strong ties with Rwanda. This shows how the antagonism at the mining site is, to some extent at least, determined by identity cleavages and interethnic competition over resources.

Conclusion

In this chapter, we have analysed specific land ownership disputes and cases of land grabbing that have unfolded in an atmosphere of conflict and ethnic cleavages in Kalehe in Eastern DRC. We have highlighted the roles of local elites in negotiation processes, and have identified their chosen strategies for obtaining and maintaining control over land, mines and associated rents in a context of competition over resources and institutional complexity. The lessons drawn from the case studies lead us to four main conclusions.

First, the various case studies illustrate quite clearly how negotiations over access to and control over land do not unfold in a political or historical vacuum. In fact, they take shape in a highly politicized and historically determined context. The cases studied in this chapter were mainly examples of local disputes over land and mining sites, yet they were clearly linked to the wider dynamics at the national and regional levels. Indeed, interethnic competition over land is a regional issue, rooted in the history of the Great Lakes Region, including its cross-border migration patterns and interethnic conflicts. Hence it is clearly important that due attention be paid in the debate on land grabbing to the specific political and historical settings.

Second, struggles over resources are shaped by the local institutional context. In the DRC, the malfunctioning state apparatus contributes significantly to the complexity of land conflicts. In the case of the Nyabibwe mining sites, the two rival cooperatives both legitimize their claim to the lawful exploitation of the mines by means official, yet incompatible, documents. In the case study concerning the returning refugees, the land issue is intertwined with instances of corruption and the incapacity of the State to control its territory and its armed forces. The nature of the land conflicts changes with the deployment of military or militias that are aligned along ethnic lines. This fluctuating and volatile institutional context creates opportunities for the more powerful actors involved.

Third, our cases demonstrate quite clearly that the land issue and conflict are closely associated. The impact of conflict on the access patterns of local actors is twofold. First and foremost, conflict and violence may alter the institutional landscape, as new rules and norms take shape. This new institutional context can create further opportunities for the most powerful actors, as they try to bend the prevailing rules to their advantage. Furthermore, instances of land grabbing that predate the conflict, for example as a result of displacement, can become a source of new conflict. In both of our cases, this duality is quite apparent. The case of the returning Tutsi refugees again demonstrates how complex and conflict-induced patterns of displacement and return can create opportunities for certain actors. For one thing, some customary chiefs appear to have taken advantage of the departure of the Tutsi to sell or reoccupy their land, thereby sowing the seeds of further conflict. Subsequently, the returnees relied on assistance from certain actors in the newly shaped institutional environment, i.e. the integrated former CNDP, in order to reinforce their own land claims. In Nyabibwe, the ensuing presence of opposing armed groups again created opportunities for certain economic actors to seize control over the mine, inducing contestation on the part of other groups.

Finally, the seemingly less powerful individuals and groups affected by processes of land grabbing are not necessarily passive victims in such land-related conflicts. Quite the contrary: in our research, they were found to act quite deliberately with the aim of improving their livelihoods. Our cases show how various seemingly weaker actors managed to invent and reinvent strategies for gaining access to resources. For example, in Nyabibwe, independent miners founded a cooperative (CMDK – later COMIKA) in order to compete with the interests of the local elites. Another example of the agency of 'victims' in land conflicts is provided through the case study of a conflict involving three Bahavu families and one Tutsi family. These three families broadcast a radio message, warning people for potentially 'illegitimate' sales. This constitutes an example of how the power of the elites may be contested at the local level. It should however be noted that, despite such acts of resistance and protest, there is limited room for manoeuvre and contestation. Two of the three families involved in the previously mentioned case study lost their land and the third has been threatened and even imprisoned on several occasions.

In general terms, this chapter has demonstrated that land conflicts and cases of land grabbing should not be separated from the local, national and even regional, historical, political and institutional context. We have shown how, in a context of plurality of norms and rules in the landownership arena, the rights of the 'strongest' tend to prevail. These 'stronger actors' are not only financially more resilient, but also, and arguably more importantly, stronger in terms of their formal and informal institutional connectedness. Success or failure in acquiring land rights depends upon actors' capacity to strategically use and, as the case may be, manipulate the Congolese army, official state agents, and/or the local customary authorities in their efforts to maintain or regain control over the targeted resources. These local practices of land grabbing deserve academic attention, because they are an important source of information on local practices of land governance and their political, historical and institutional context. Furthermore, in the specific case of Eastern DRC, where land is a source of wealth as well as conflict, local practices of land grabbing have the potential to fuel smouldering conflicts or to spark new ones.

Bibliography

Action pour la paix et la concorde (APC), 2009. 'Analyse du contexte socio-sécuritaire du territoire de Kalehe'. *APC Series*, Bukavu, DRC.

Action pour la paix et la concorde (APC), 2011. 'Flash info sur les dynamiques autour de la formation du groupe armé Nyatura dans les Hauts Plateaux entre le territoire de Kalehe et Masisi. *APC Series*, Bukavu, DRC.

Action pour la paix et la concorde (APC) 2012. Groupes armés et populations locales: une coexistence difficile en territoires de Kalehe et Walikale. *APC Series*, Bukavu, DRC.

Anseeuw, W., Alden Wily, L., Cotula, L., and Taylor, M., 2012. *Land Rights and the Rush for Land: Findings of the Global Commercial Pressures on Land Research Project.* International Land Coalition, Rome.

Bastiaensen, J., De Herdt, T. and D'Exelle, B., 2005. 'Poverty Reduction as a Local Institutional Process'. *World Development,* vol. 33, no. 6, pp. 979-993.

Berry, S., 2002. 'Debating the Land Question in Africa'. *Comparative Studies in Society and History,* vol. 44, no. 4, pp. 368-668.

——, 2009. 'Property, Authority and Citizenship: Land Claims, Politics and the Dynamics of Social Division in West Africa'. *Development and*

Change, vol. 10, no. 1, pp. 23-45.

Borras, S. M. and Franco, J., 2010. 'Towards a Broader View of the Politics of Global Land Grab: Rethinking Land Issues, Reframing Resistance'. *ICAS Working Paper Series*, no. 1.

Conflict Research Group (CRG), 2012. *Dealing with Land Issues and Conflict in Eastern DRC: Towards an Integrated and Participatory Approach*. Report presented on a seminar held in Brussels on 20-21 September 2012.

Cuvelier, J., 2010. 'The Complexity of Conflict Dynamics in Kalehe's Nyabibwe Mines'. *International Alert: The Complexity of Resource Governance in a Context of State Fragility: The Case of Eastern Congo*.

De Schutter, O., 2011. 'How Not to Think of Land Grabbing: Three Critiques of Large-Scale Investments in Farmland'. *Journal of Peasant Studies*, vol. 28, no. 2, pp. 249-279.

Griffiths, J., 1986. 'What is Legal pluralism?' *Journal of Legal Pluralism and Unofficial Law*, no. 24, pp. 1-55.

Hall, R., 2011. 'Land Grabbing in Southern Africa: The Many Faces of the Investors Rush'. *Review of African Political Economy*, vol. 38, no. 128, pp. 93-214.

Hilhorst, T., Nelen, J. and Traoré, N., 2011. 'Agrarian Change Below the Radar Screen: Rising Farmland Acquisitions by Domestic Investors in West Africa'. *Results from a Survey in Benin, Burkina Faso and Niger*.

Minority Rights Group International, 2011. *State of the World's Minorities and Indigenous Peoples 2011 – Democratic Republic of Congo (DRC)*.

Moore, S. F., 1978. *Law as a Process: An Anthropological Approach*. Routledge and Kegan Paul, London.

Mugangu Matabaro, S., 2008. 'La crise foncière à L'Est de la RDC'. In: *L'Afrique Des Grands Lacs. Annuaire 2007-2008*, eds, Marysse, S., Reyntjens, F. and Vandeginste, S., L'Harmattan, Paris, pp. 385-414.

Namegabe, P. R., 2005. 'Le pouvoir traditionnel au Sud-Kivu de 1998-2003: rôle et perspectives'. *L'Afrique Des Grands Lacs. Annuaire 2004-2005*, eds, Reyntjens, F. and Marysse, S., L'Harmattan, Paris, pp. 193-228.

Olivier de Sardan, J.-P., 2005. *Anthropology and Development, Understanding Contemporary Social Change*. Zed Books, London.

Stearns, J., 2012. *From CNDP to M23: The Evolution of an Armed Movement in Eastern Congo*. Usalama Project, Rift Valley Institute.

Stearns, J., 2013. *PARECO: Land Local Strongmen and the Roots of Militia Politics in North Kivu*. Usalama Project, Rift Valley Institute.

UN (2011) *Final Report of the Group of Experts on the DRC* (S/2011/738). Security Council, New York, UN.

Utshudi Ona, I. and Ansoms, A., 2011. 'Reconciling Custom, State and Local Livelihoods: Decentralized Land Management in South-Kivu (DRC)'. *Natural Resources and Local Livelihoods in the Great Lakes Region of Africa*, eds, Marysse, S. and Ansoms, A., Palgrave Macmillan, Basingstoke (UK), pp. 26-47.

Van Acker, F., 2005. 'Where did all the Land Go? Enclosure and Social Struggle in Kivu (DRCongo)'. *Review of African Political Economy*, vol. 32, no. 103, pp. 79-98.

Vlassenroot, K. and Huggins, C., 2005. 'Land, Migration and Conflict in Eastern DRC'. *From the Ground up: Land Rights, Conflict and Peace in Sub-Saharan Africa*, eds, Huggins, C. and Clover J., African Centre for Technology Studies/Institute of Security Studies, Nairobi/Pretoria. pp. 116-194.

World Bank, 2010, *Rising Global Interest in Farmland: Can It Yield Equitable and Sustainable Benefits?* World Bank, Washington, D.C.

6

The Continuities in Contested Land Acquisitions in Uganda

MATHIJS VAN LEEUWEN, ILSE ZEEMEIJER, DOREEN KOBUSINGYE
CHARLES MUCHUNGUZI. LINDA HAARTSEN & CLAUDIA PIACENZA

Introduction

Land grabbing is a 'hot' issue in Uganda. In late 2011, NGO-activists raised the alarm bell, accusing local elites, army generals, and high-level politicians – including the president – to be at the centre of a series of contested large-scale land acquisitions and condemning the violence accompanying the evictions of land occupants. The debate on those acquisitions is complex not only because of the questionable roles of government and investors, but also because of the contested contributions of the deals to development. In that sense, the debate resonates with global discussions between those propagating the need for up-scaling and modernizing land use and those concerned about the fate of the original users of the lands acquired (Oxfam, 2011, Peluso and Lund, 2011; Borras and Franco, 2012; Cotula, 2012; White, et al., 2012). As in the global discussion, the details of the deals, their implementation, and their consequences often remain unknown, and the debate between opponents and supporters is frequently a mix of verifiable facts, unverifiable opinions and anger. Moreover, as often happens with catchwords, in Uganda, 'land grabbing' has become a label that covers a diversity of issues. While the common denominator is a sense of irregularity or injustice in the acquisition of land, Ugandan media, academics, civil-society activists and government use the term for multiple types of land acquisitions. 'Land grabbing' may range from the contested allocation of vast expanses of land at national level to 'everyday' land grabs between neighbours and relatives. Accordingly, many 'land grabs' involve not just (inter)national investors but also national and local elites and include contemporary as well as historical cases of 'unjust' land acquisitions.

In this chapter, we sketch the diversity and complexity of what is understood as 'land grabbing' in Uganda. We consider land grabbing as acquisitions that are contested because in the process human rights were violated, transparency was lacking, or affected land users were not consulted in the deals.[1] From such a definition, however, it becomes clear that land grabbing in Uganda is not as 'new' and externally driven as is often assumed. Instead, there are important continuities between past and present practices of land grabbing. Even if land grabbing is externally driven, it remains strongly connected to local and national socio-political dynamics. The case of Uganda suggests that to better understand the 'new' wave of global land acquisitions we need to take account of such continuities.

This is important because contemporary international discussions on land grabbing rather tend to focus on discontinuities between past and present large-scale land acquisitions. They explore new 'drivers' of land grabbing, such as the search for land for investment, food, bio-fuels or carbon credits (Cotula, et al., 2009; Zoomers, 2010; White et al., 2012). Media underscore the involvement of (government-backed) investment agencies from the Gulf, East Asia, and the West and emphasize the size of the agricultural areas involved. The picture presented is one of a radical transformation of agricultural production, and dramatic shifts in ownership relations. 'New' features of these large-scale acquisitions are their unprecedented scale and pace (Oxfam, 2011; Cotula, 2012); their unprecedented impact in restructuring agrarian economies and expelling people from agriculture without employing them elsewhere in the economy (White et al., 2012); and, the new ways in which they are justified, with reference to a neoliberal logic of agribusiness accumulation (Peluso and Lund, 2011).

However, as authors before us have also pointed out, large-scale acquisitions often have a long history and are sometimes seen as the latest stage of a neo-colonial project of ensuring continued supply of agricultural commodities to northern markets (Cotula, 2012). Moreover, it is increasingly clear that regional and national factors, such as domestic political concerns for food and energy security, or domestic interests in export-production and investment in land, also play a role as drivers of land acquisition. National elites – politicians, senior civil servants, and business people – play key roles, both as investors and facilitators of land acquisitions (see e.g. Anseeuw and Alden, 2010), and the aggregate land area of such national deals may be larger than that of international deals (Cotula, 2012: 655-656, 659). The involvement of such domestic players should be understood from the political economy of the African State. When the State enables national elites to control resources, resources enable them to keep their grip on the State 'by using resource allocation as a tool for political patronage' (ibid.: 671).

This chapter acknowledges that the global rush for land implies new complexities in terms of new actors, contexts, and dynamics (Peluso and Lund, 2011: 669). At the same time, it argues that our understanding of

---

[1] The 2011 Tirana Declaration contains such a definition of land grabbing. Online at: http://www.landcoalition.org/fr/node/1109 [date of last access: 19 June 2014].

contemporary large-scale land deals will remain incomplete if we fail to acknowledge the continuities involved. Through exploring the Uganda case, the chapter demonstrates that contemporary land acquisitions still need to be interpreted as part of longer-term, domestic processes of inclusion and exclusion, patronage politics, and elite appropriation of resources and state institutions. It also points out how local assessments of tenure insecurity and land acquisitions strongly relate to collective memories of past irregular acquisitions, and government's track-record of reorganizing agricultural production and protecting tenure security.

To make our argument, we first revisit the debate on land grabbing in Uganda, sketching how land grabbing is currently understood by NGOs, media, academia, and government actors, and the major issues of contention. We then present four case studies of contested land acquisitions based on field work by the authors. Although information was collected as part of different research projects, all the case studies are based on (extended) ethnographic field research, including substantial numbers of interviews and focus-group discussions, and perusal of the (grey) literature on those cases. Details on those projects and their respective methodologies are provided in footnotes at the beginning of each case study. Finally, the conclusion emphasizes the continuities between large-scale and 'everyday' land grabbing, as well as between contemporary and past practices of land acquisition.

Debates on land grabbing in Uganda

In national media and NGO reporting on land grabbing in Uganda, the cases most often discussed are the contested acquisitions of land in Mubende District, in which people have been displaced for the establishment of a coffee plantation, and the resettlement of people and acquisitions of communal land in Buliisa and Hoima Districts, purportedly because of the discovery of oil in the region. Other cases are in the North, where army officials took advantage of the conflict-induced displacement of landowners to acquire properties for speculation (see e.g. Mabikke, 2011).

To a certain extent, the debates in Uganda reflect global discussions on 'new' land deals. For instance, there is intense discussion on whether large-scale acquisitions may benefit economic development, and at the same time may ensure the livelihoods of local communities and protect the rights of local landowners. The Ugandan Government underscores the need for investment in the agricultural sector, to increase productivity and bring unused lands into production, to enhance local economic growth and the creation of jobs and infrastructure (GOU – Government of Uganda, 2010). However, representatives of Uganda civil society we interviewed pointed out that in many instances land is simply sold or leased to new owners by the government. Out-grower contracts are not often drawn up, and when they are, the conditions of the contracts are deplorable. They observe further that lands acquired may have been underused but were rarely vacant, or point out that large-scale agricultural production negatively impacts local food production and contributes to soil depletion. As already mentioned, suspicions are voiced about the private interests of high level politicians. Various civil-society organizations emphasized the deals made by government officials without properly consulting the affected people (see also Oxfam, 2011).

Nonetheless, land grabbing in Uganda cannot be understood separately from ongoing debates on tenure insecurity and changes in the land law. Tenure insecurity is a historical problem in Uganda, and the legacy of policies of previous regimes. First of all, while customary land may account for roughly 85 per cent of land in the country (GOU, 2001: 34), for long, it was not taken into account in written legislation. While the British colonizers introduced freehold tenure, customary land belonged to the Crown. In exchange for their loyalty, the colonizers also awarded kingdom representatives and chiefs ownership over large tracts of land, thereby turning the occupiers into tenants. This customary system of freehold tenure became known as *mailo*. The British further transferred estates of the western Bunyoro Kingdom to the central Buganda Kingdom. After decolonization, the first Obote government (1966-1971) officially abolished the mailo land system, although little changed in practice, and tenants' claims remained unacknowledged. Under the Amin dictatorship (1971-1979), the 1975 Land Reform Decree vested all land in the hands of the State, resulting in large-scale misappropriation (MLHUD, 2011: 4-5). The repressive second regime of Obote (1980-1985) again resulted in various contested acquisitions of land.

After a five-year bush war against Obote and his successor Lieutenant-General Okello, President Museveni came into power in 1986. Stability gradually returned in the south and central parts of Uganda, although civil war in the North between the Lord's Resistance Army (LRA) and the National Resistance Movement (NRM) government continued until recently. Over the last two decades, Museveni's government introduced a series of reforms to increase tenure security, and prevent irregular appropriation of land. The 1995 Constitution presented a radical break with the past in stating that land belongs to the citizens of Uganda, thereby reversing the 1975 Land Reform Decree. Further, the Land Act of 1998 recognized customary claims on land, and made it possible to record customary land through a simplified procedure at the local level. This would reduce chances that land would be titled without the actual occupants being aware of it. The legislators also addressed the insecurity of tenants on mailo land, by recognizing mailo as one of the four tenure systems in the country.[2] Later amendments in the Land Act aimed

---

[2] The other three are: freehold, leasehold, and customary tenure.

to strengthen the claims of tenants on mailo land, granting formal status to long-term occupancy, and reducing possibilities for evicting tenants.

The question remains whether the reforms introduced by the NRM-government have indeed contributed to more tenure security and reduced irregular acquisition of land (see e.g. Bosworth, 2003; Francis and James, 2003; McAuslan, 2003; Hunt, 2004; Rugadya et al., 2004; Harrtera and Ryan, 2010; GOU, 2010). A recurring question among civil society representatives is to what extent there is political will to realize those reforms. Questions are also raised as to whether the policies effectively deal with the diverse sources of tenure insecurity and with a series of so-called 'historical injustices', through which some communities lost their ancestral lands, such as the Bunyoro issue. The Uganda National Land Policy (MLHUD, 2011) points out that tenure regimes will be harmonized to prevent double claims, protect vulnerable people, and solve the mailo issue and other 'historical injustices'. Yet, the document remains silent about contested land acquisitions under the Amin and second Obote regimes. Questions remain also about the juridical value of certificates *vis-à-vis* titles,[3] or about the status of unregistered customary land.

In particular, there is debate about the extent to which the new legislation protects against irregular large-scale acquisition of land. Questions are posed about the possibilities it provides to the government to expropriate landowners for the sake of development. While the Land Policy emphasizes the importance of (securing) ownership of land, at the same time, it promotes 'sustainable and optimal use of land and land-based resources for [the] transformation of Ugandan society and economy' (MLHUD, 2011: 2). The document starts from the assumption that the system of peasant farming needs to change, to free the land for large-scale agricultural production, while the government considers to have 'a duty to attract private investment [...] This duty includes creating an enabling investment climate, as well as facilitating investors to access land' (ibid.: 7). If this is in the public interest, the State – as a trustee for the citizens of Uganda – has the power of compulsory acquisition (ibid.: 13).

There is thus the risk that such government attributes will override the land rights of local landowners. Different statements from government demonstrate the low esteem small scale farming is held in. The National Development Plan (GOU, 2010), for instance, considers that '[t]he majority of landowners in rural areas [...] have continued to practice primitive and peasantry methods of production, utilizing very small proportions of their land holdings' (GOU, 2010: 160). Noticeable are also diverse efforts by the government to reform traditional pastoralist production. Janet Museveni,

---

[3] See e.g. LEMU (Land and Equity Movement of Uganda), *What Happens if I Get a Certificate of Customary Ownership?*
Online at: http://www.land-in-uganda.org/lemu/documents/ [date of last access: 19 June 2014].

the president's wife, and minister in charge of Karamoja affairs, reportedly wrote to the EU delegation in Kampala: 'We cannot romanticise about nomadism as a way of life [...] it is a danger we have to fight like we fight all other social ills'.[4] Such limited appreciation by the government of small-scale or traditional farmers puts into doubt government's commitment to protect their land claims. Moreover, the government's discourses on the need to modernize and up-scale agricultural production legitimize expropriation for large-scale, market-oriented production.

Then, despite the extensive debates, detailed information on current land acquisitions is lacking, and sentiments seem to play an important role in the positions taken. At first sight, large-scale land acquisitions concern a substantial part of Uganda's rural area. According to the Global Land Project, there have been seven large land deals from 2007 to 2010, covering about 1,9 million hectares, or 14.6 per cent of the country's agricultural area (Friis and Reenberg, 2010: 11). A survey of media and international reports by one of the authors of this chapter identified twenty-one land acquisitions in the same period. While various deals involved foreign investors from countries like China, Russia, Germany and Kenya, many of the deals involve Ugandan companies (Zeemeijer, 2012: 99). Yet, consistent information about those deals is lacking. In an attempt to verify these land deals, only fourteen of these twenty-one deals could be confirmed with relevant authorities in Uganda and representatives of the home country of the investors. For instance, a deal with an Egyptian investor involving over 800,000 hectares – thus representing almost half of the above mentioned acreage – could not be verified (ibid.: 102-112). Moreover, several of the deals might have been proposed but were never realized.

Debate is further complicated by the fact that the term 'land grabbing' is used to refer to a variety of practices, at different levels and scales, and involving different actors. Exemplary are the publications of the Land and Equity Movement of Uganda (LEMU), that see land grabbing taking place within families, for instance when relatives take advantage of the vulnerability of widows or orphans; between individuals and the State, for instance when people encroach on public land; between communities that disagree about the use of communal land; or involving people that manage to get powerful backing from military, the church, or government representatives (LEMU, 2011). In contrast to the image of powerful outsiders intruding into local communities, their inventory emphasizes the small scale, localized, often intra-family character of everyday land grabbing. Various people interviewed in our various research projects pointed to the role of local elites in such 'everyday' cases of land grabbing.

Not unimportantly, the label of 'land grabbing' has become politicized, and is easily used to delegitimize any intervention in land tenure. This is

---

[4] John Vidal, 'Uganda: Nomads Face an Attack on their Way of Life'. *The Observer*, Sunday 27 November 2011.

particularly the case in the power struggle between the government and the central Buganda Kingdom, a sub-national kingdom that comprises Uganda's central region including the capital Kampala. Under the first Obote government, all Ugandan kingdoms were abolished. In 1993, however, the Buganda kingdom was restored as a monarchy with a large degree of autonomy from the central State. It is here that the system of mailo tenure (see above) is very common. The awarding of mailo properties by the British is often interpreted as a historical instance of land grabbing that turned customary owners into tenants. Ironically, current government efforts to increase tenure security of tenants on mailo land are interpreted as land grabbing from the Buganda chiefs, and as a deliberate strategy to decrease the power of the Buganda Kingdom (see e.g. Hunt, 2004).

It is clear that land grabbing in Uganda is a complex phenomenon, involving diverse practices in terms of scale and the actors concerned, and strongly embedded in existing long-term tenure insecurity and historically disputed acquisitions of land. The following four case-studies delve deeper into those continuities between large-scale and 'everyday' land grabbing, and assumedly 'new' land acquisitions and irregular acquisitions in the past.

The diversity of practices of land grabbing in Uganda

Our first case study of Mbarara District brings out the diverse practices local people consider as land grabbing. While locally there are many fears for land grabbers from outside, the case underscores the importance of local elites in those practices. A historical continuity is found in the communities' persistent lack of confidence in the government as protector of land tenure. The second case study of Ruhunga hill in Mbarara District delves deeper into both themes. It demonstrates the persistent failure of the government to take charge for irregular acquisitions under previous regimes, and exemplifies how land grabbing is a matter of local, yet politically well-connected elites. The third case study of rearrangements of pastoral lands around Lake Mburo demonstrates how both past and present programmes to develop pastoralists have effectively resulted in the appropriation of their lands by elites from other regions in Uganda. Past discourses on economic progress to legitimize such arrangements show similarities with contemporary ways of promoting large-scale agriculture. Another continuity is that land grabbing both past and present has been interpreted in terms of ethnic favouritism by the government. The fourth case study concerns a well-known 'recent' case of contested land acquisition in Amuru District. At first sight, the case conforms to the global imaginary of those 'new' deals: as being driven by commercial investors, aiming at producing for the global market, and suspected to disenfranchise customary owners. Yet, upon further scrutiny, this 'new' acquisition represents only the latest episode in a longer history of contested changes in ownership over the land. Continuity is found in the important role played by elites and (political) representatives from the region as 'grabbers' of land.

Local notions and perceptions of land grabbing in Mbarara District [5]
Development practitioners and academics from other parts of the country tend to believe that most land in Mbarara District in Southwestern Uganda is registered and privately owned. In practice, however, while there are some extensive, titled properties in the district, few small cultivators possess titles. An inventory of land tenure insecurity in the district identified various practices that are locally understood as 'land grabbing' (for more details, see van Leeuwen, 2012).

First, there are many rumours about people who have been chased away from land they considered their property. They only found out that somebody else had acquired a title on their land when the registered owner arrived to install himself there. When tracing such rumours to particular cases, it turned out that their number is limited. Further, most cases in which titles were acquired on somebody else's land occurred in the 1970s and early 1980s, and mainly affected communal land or land on which government buildings were located. Under Amin, military personnel were stimulated to cater for themselves and acquire land. In the Obote-II period, land governance was in disarray, providing opportunities to manipulate ownership. For instance, powerful community members, such as the (sub-)parish chief, would include stretches of land belonging to their neighbours in their leasehold titles.

Few examples of such irregular titling of land of more recent date could be identified. It is likely that decentralization of land registration has made the titling of other people's land more difficult. Still, several people interviewed told that space remains for manipulating the registration of land as freehold, as witnesses may not know what they are witnessing, neighbours' signatures can be bought, and not all Area Land Committees consistently follow the procedures. Also government land continues to be vulnerable to land grabbing. For instance, in one community visited by the researcher, public land that the local government had wanted to turn into a shopping-centre turned out registered as freehold in the name of private investors.

In fact, most cases of what people refer to as 'land grabbing' involve small-scale grabs of customarily owned land by other customary owners. For instance, customary land may be sold by another than the owner to

---

[5] This case study was conducted by Mathijs van Leeuwen, as part of 'Grounding Land Governance', a NWO-Wotro funded research project on land governance reform in post-conflict settings. Fieldwork in Mbarara District (March 2011–March 2012) included ten focus-group discussions and seventy semi-structured interviews with local members of Mbarara District Farmers' Association, representatives of local government, elders from the communities, and church representatives. Linda Haartsen participated in the fieldwork.

people migrating into the community, who are unaware of the actual ownership. Interviewees also pointed out how some rich people shift the vegetation used as border-demarcation to slowly move onto the land of their poor neighbours, speculating that the latter lack the money to begin a court case. In some cases, rich men openly threaten the neighbours on whose land they encroach with the fact that they have enough money to overrule them in court. In particular, single women, like widows, are vulnerable to such land grabbing, as they have limited access to authorities, may lack support from their family, and often lack financial resources. Furthermore, women are more often threatened with violence. In such cases, land grabbing is not caused by 'outsiders' such as migrants or rich people from town, but happens within the family.

Finally, although they did not label this as land grabbing, participants to various focus-groups highlighted what were, in their eyes, irregular or illegitimate ways in which (local) government acquires land in their communities. In one locality, several families lost land when a road was reconstructed, and did not get market-conform compensation. Such irregular dispossessions fuel a more general perception that the government cannot be trusted as protector of local landownership. Even if according to the 1995 Constitution 'land in Uganda belongs to the citizens of Uganda', many rural dwellers interviewed had the feeling that land belongs to the State, and can be taken away from them any time. In one locality, people were referring to themselves as 'squatters' on the land, even while their land was customarily owned. In some communities, violent evictions in the past, involving government forces, have reduced local confidence that government will protect local claims on land. In other communities, distrust is fuelled by government's failure to deal with disputed acquisitions that took place during the Amin and Obote-II governments (see the second case study), or by incidents in other communities, like the reordering of pastoral land elsewhere in the district (see the third case study).

This case study makes clear that there is large diversity in what local people consider as land grabbing, and a lot of fear of it. A common idea is that land grabbing is an externally-driven affair: many people in Mbarara District fear land grabs by people from outside the community. In practice, however, small-scale land grabbing by neighbours and relatives is a more real threat, putting single women in particular at risk. Rather than outsiders, local elites have been key actors in those practices, taking advantage of ineffective state institutions. Striking is also the continuing lack of confidence of community members in the government as protector of local ownership. Distrust has been fuelled by past experiences in which the government appropriated land in ways that are locally perceived as arbitrary. Distrust also results from government's failures to deal adequately with contested acquisitions from the past, a point further elaborated upon in the following case-study.

The disputed acquisition of Ruhunga Hill[6]

Over the last twenty-six years, there has been contestation over a stretch of 183 hectares of land on Ruhunga hill in Mbarara District. Land belonging to thirty-five families was irregularly acquired by a military commander under the Amin government, and its ownership is still disputed.

Under Amin's regime, after the 1975 Land Reform Decree, some families cultivating bananas at the bottom of Ruhunga hill applied at the Uganda Land Commission for leasehold for their up-hill communal meadows. However, in 1976, an army captain settled in the area and claimed that the land on the hill was his. People have vivid memories of how this military commander threatened to kill them if they did not accept his claims on the land, while youth from the community were forced to fence the land at gunpoint. Under the Obote-II government, shortly before the take-over of power by Museveni in 1986, the commander in question sold the land to the current owner, who was a staunch supporter of Obote, and treasurer and vice-mayor of Mbarara town.

After Museveni took over power, neighbours started reoccupying the land. In 1988, however, the current owner went to the Magistrate Court, and his neighbours were convicted for encroachment and imprisoned. After their release, these neighbours contacted the Permanent Secretary of the Ministry of Lands, who originated from Mbarara District. Curiously enough, he had been an advisor to the Uganda Land Commission at the time the commander claimed to have acquired a leasehold title. The Permanent Secretary assured that the Ministry of Lands sent its Vice-Minister to the community to mediate in the case. The Vice-Ministers' written report of the mediation describes that while the commander claimed to have bought the land from the neighbours, the Vice-Minister considered that there was enough evidence that the neighbours had never genuinely sold their land. For instance, the 1977 leasehold paperwork showed the thumbprint of a neighbour who had died two years earlier. The Vice-Minister also considered that it was not good practice that one person should dispose of so much land. He concluded that the current owner had to surrender the whole of Ruhunga hill to the community members.

The current owner, however, approached the Ministry of Justice, who then reproached the Ministry of Lands that it had no jurisdiction to intervene in land disputes, and that its mediation interfered with a case in court. The Ministry of Justice pointed out that compensation would have to be paid if the current owner would lose his land. However, the Ministry of Justice took no action to remove the community members of the land. Thus, in January 1990, the current owner

---

[6] This case study was also conducted by Mathijs van Leeuwen, as part of fieldwork in Mbarara District, (see previous footnote). Fieldwork included two focus-group discussions with members of Mbadifa, and ten extended, open-ended interviews in Rubaya Sub-county with affected community members (including the LC1 chairperson), the current owner of the land, and the chief of Ruhanga parish and acting chief of Rubaya sub-county.

started a court case in the High Court in Mbarara against the attorney general, in his own words 'to discipline the Ministry of Lands', and to get compensation for the damage done on his land by his neighbours. By the end of fieldwork there had been no judgement, only a statement from the Court prohibiting the cultivation of the land awaiting the verdict.

The current owner is convinced that the land has been sold to him in a legal way, and that documents exist to prove this.[7] He also argues that the preceding acquisition of the title had been sanctioned by the then government, and is thus 'legal'. 'Until 1986, nobody from the community complained', he argues: 'if the government knew the land was communal, how could they have given a leasehold title to an individual?' He sees his neighbours as opportunistic encroachers on his land. 'They had leasehold titles on the surrounding land. Why hadn't they earlier [included] the land higher on the slope [when registering their land]?' He suspects that the surrounding landowners never realized the value of the land. Only after the commander applied for leasehold, they understood they had made a miscalculation, which they hoped to undo with the arrival of a new government in 1986.

The case of Ruhunga hill exemplifies the persistent doubts among community members that the government will protect their claims on land, being incapable to address irregular acquisitions under previous regimes. To many people, the fact that the case is in court since 1990 exemplifies that the judicial system is ineffective: judges lack a juridical basis to unequivocally solve land issues, and progress is dragged down by corruption. Different representatives from the government tried to solve the case in ad hoc and contradictory ways, and these solutions were later contested again. People were particularly disappointed that the government did not want to take responsibility for the actions of its predecessors, for instance by acknowledging that both parties hold legitimate claims. A crucial problem here is that government intervention has been merely a personal affair of district and national level politicians that seek to establish their reputation by showing that they act to protect the interests of their constituents. Unfortunately, this has complicated rather than resolved the dispute.

Further, the case raises questions about ideal-typical images of 'land grabbing' that focus on local communities being victimised by powerful outsiders. Indeed, the military commander was an outsider and influential military, while the current owner of the land was a powerful government representative under the Obote-II government. Still, the people that claim to be victims are the richer and most influential members of the community. It is for instance revealing that most of them tried to acquire leasehold titles on the up-hill lands in the 1970s. Considering the small number of leasehold titles in the district, the occupants of Ruhunga hill were likely well-connected themselves, but out of favour with the regimes

---

[7] Interview Ruhunga Parish, 19 January 2012.

at that time. Political connections seem to play an important role in whose reading of events is acknowledged. The current owner's portrayal of his neighbours as 'encroachers', as well as his alleged delaying of the court case awaiting a regime-change should be seen in this light. In this case, land grabbing, as well as efforts to deal with contested acquisitions from the past, are clearly part of patronage politics. More in general, the case underscores again the importance of local elites, rather than outsiders, in land grabbing.

The rearrangements of pastoral lands around Lake Mburo[8]
Little-discussed but contested acquisitions of land in Uganda are those in the so-called 'cattle-corridor', an area mainly inhabited by pastoralists which extends roughly from the southwestern border with Tanzania to the northeastern borders with Kenya and South Sudan. Several rearrangements of grazing land by government to improve pastoralists' livelihoods have been seen as bolstering the interests of political elites or particular ethnic groups. As an example, we here discuss consecutive rearrangements of pastoralist land in the southwestern part of the country, and how these provided opportunities for outside elites to acquire the land (for more details, see Muchunguzi, 2013).

The semi-arid area close to Lake Mburo used to be sparsely inhabited, and was deserted even further due to outbreaks of rinderpest and sleeping-sickness in the beginning of the twentieth century. In 1935, the colonial government turned part of the area into a controlled hunting area. In the 1950s, a series of radical measures were taken to eradicate the tse-tse flies: the killing of the entire wildlife population, the burning of large tracts of land, and finally, the spraying of the complete area with insecticides. In the early 1960s, Bahima pastoralists started returning to the area (UWA – Uganda Wildlife Authority, 1998; Zwick and Lloyd, 1998; Musinguzi, 2002). In 1964 the first Obote government degazetted a large portion of the controlled hunting area for settlement of subsistence farmers and herders. Yet, many of the original inhabitants could not return as the government only allowed sedentary livestock keepers.

Between 1964 and 1974, the government allocated 650 squares kilometres of previously communal grazing land, next to the boundary of the then Lake Mburo Game Reserve, to the Ankole Ranching Scheme (IPDP/GTZ – Integrated Pastoral Development Project/GTZ, 1997). This scheme, sponsored by USAid and World Bank, aimed to replace traditional (nomadic) pastoralism – considered to contribute little to economic growth – with commercial, intensive livestock farms. The land was demarcated into 50 ranches of 5 square miles each, which were then

---

[8] This case study was conducted by Charles Muchunguzi, who over the last decade carried out research on the dynamics of landownership in the Uganda cattle corridor. The case is based on one hundred and fifty interviews, mainly in the 2008-2011 period, including interviews with pastoralists still residing in the area, pastoralists who migrated outside Ankole region, receiving communities, and local government officials.

allocated to 'progressive farmers' as commercial ranchers. These ranches were heavily subsidized by the government, receiving free services and infrastructural development, in order to promote the beef industry in Uganda (Pulkol, 1991).

A large part of the ranches ended up in the ownership of influential personalities from outside, who had no skills in cattle keeping, and failed to stock and maintain their ranches, but were in favour with government (Busenene, 1993; Mamdani, 2001). So, in practice, the scheme did not make livestock production more efficient, and some of the ranches were never used by their new owners at all. Left without alternative grazing grounds, the original pastoralists ended up as 'squatters' with their herds in Lake Mburo Game Reserve, or had to pay the new owners of the adjacent ranches to allow them to graze their cattle and use water facilities (Pulkol, 1991; Namara and Kimbowa, 1999). Then, in 1983, the second Obote government gazetted Lake Mburo as a national park, following the boundaries of the original game reserve. In the process some four thousand five hundred families were evicted without compensation. This further exacerbated the hatred and suspicion between ranchers and pastoralist squatters. According to Pulkol (1991), it made squatters support the armed struggle of the National Resistance Movement (NRM) against the Obote II regime, hoping that – once in power – the NRM might redress the unjust appropriation of their lands.

When the NRM government came to power, several measures were indeed taken to redress the loss of land by the pastoralists in the Lake Mburo area. Unfortunately, original occupants still fell out in the process. First, in 1987 the government reduced the area of the national park by 60 per cent, but this only benefitted war displaced people coming from elsewhere. Regarding the Ankole Ranching Scheme, the government issued a proclamation telling squatters to stop paying dues to the ranchers, since these dues were illegal under the original terms of ranch occupancy. To find a definitive solution to the rancher-squatter conflict, a 1988 Commission of Inquiry recommended to investigate which of the commercial ranches were actually used for livestock production, and allocate the vacant ranches to the pastoralists. Due to lobby by the ranchers, no action was taken until the second half of 1990. Tensions exploded into a month-long squatter uprising in August 1990 (Mamdani, 2001: 176).

This led to the establishment of a Ranch Restructuring Board in 1991, which had to arrange resettlement for all the landless pastoralist families and recommend a long-term policy on livestock development in Uganda (Pulkol, 1991; Namara and Kimbowa, 1999; Musinguzi, 2002; Muchunguzi, 2003). The board subdivided the ranches of the Ankole ranching scheme and established seven hundred and ten families of landless pastoralists there. Again, the exercise ended up being hijacked: part of the land was allocated to wealthy pastoralists having land elsewhere, as well as local politicians, army officers, and even an officer of the committee in charge of allocation.

Several consecutive government interventions have thus resulted in the appropriation of pastoralist land by (national) elites from outside the community. Nowadays, many of the pastoralists still feel aggrieved about the diverse government interventions that effectively took away their land. They still demand that the land, including the park, should return to them.

Unfortunately, the contested rearrangements also have an ethnic element. Formerly, the Ankole Kingdom – in which Lake Mburo was located – manifested a social division between two groups: the Bahima (including the royal clans) and the Bairu, which were associated with cattle keeping and sedentary agriculture respectively. In colonial times, the system of indirect rule strengthened powers of the Ankole Kingdom, and prioritized Bahima to become chiefs, at the disadvantage of the Bairu. The newly bestowed positions, benefits and privileges contributed to feelings of superiority and inferiority, but also to economic differentiation. Important in this respect was land: large chunks of mailo land were allotted to Bahima chiefs (Doornbos, 1978). After decolonization those divisions lost their sharp edges. Yet, under the Obote-II government (1981-1985), divisions grew significant again, not in the least because the guerrilla fighter Museveni was a Muhima. Some Bahima claim that Lake Mburo National Park was created in 1983 as revenge for their support to Museveni's war (Muchunguzi, 2003). When Bahima pastoralists later reoccupied the park, this was interpreted by both groups as a victory over the Bairu. And while the political and economic gap between the Bahima and Bairu has greatly reduced, mutual resentment increased during the Museveni regime.[9] Bahima interpret regular land acquisitions by Bairu as displacing and impoverishing Bahima, while Bairu consider the current government to be more in favour of Bahima.

Another complication is that the ranching scheme and the restructuring exercise made Bahima pastoralists from the Lake Mburo area move to other parts of the Uganda cattle corridor, fuelling competition over land over there. In Teso, Lango and Bunyoro Districts, Bahima pastoralists from Lake Mburo have either by intent or in dire need of livelihood resources, marginalized other communities by taking over their land through illegal purchases or by force. Furthermore, politically well-connected pastoralists from those areas have contracted Bahima immigrants to herd their cattle and invade other people's lands. This has given the Bahima pastoralists the reputation of 'land grabbers'. What is critical is that local inhabitants associate these immigrant Bahima with the government of Museveni, a Muhima. In several districts, stories circulate about large-scale land acquisitions by Bahima from the government, military and economic elite. This has reflected on common Bahima pastoralists, who are now seen as privileged, even if in practice they have consistently been marginalized by government.

---

[9] See e.g. Eric Kashambuzi, 'Why Bahima Men will Never Marry Bairu Women'. *The Observer*, 1 April 2010.

To conclude, in relation to our wider argument on land grabbing in Uganda, this case study illustrates three continuities. First, several episodes of gazetting land for the park, and programmes to transform pastoralist ways of living have effectively resulted in the appropriation of pastoralist land by (elite) cattle keepers from outside. As such, the case study underscores the fact that appropriation of customarily held land by elites has a longer history in Uganda. A second continuity is that both the Ankole ranching scheme and the restructuring exercise were legitimized by the notion that pastoral areas were idle and unproductive. Such rationalizations predate contemporary discourses to legitimize expropriation, which promote large-scale intensive agriculture and the need to create an enabling investment climate. Third, the case study shows continuity in that local community members both in the past and the present interpret land grabbing in terms of political patronage and ethnic favouritism. Large acquisitions of land, even if done in a legal way, are perceived to be facilitated by connections to the government in power, evidenced by the ethnic identity of those acquiring the land.

Competing claims on land in Amuru District[10]
Since relative peace returned to Northern Uganda in 2006, there is much discussion on the repossession of lands of which owners were displaced by the violence from the Lord's Resistance Army. The process is complicated due to contested land acquisitions by investors, both from within and from outside the community. A prominent case is that of the allocation of land to Amuru Sugar Ltd., which resulted in a huge controversy (for more details, see Zeemeijer, 2012).

In February 2008, cabinet ministers approved an investment proposal by Amuru Sugar Works Ltd. for sugar production and processing in Amuru District, and suggested that the 'relevant authority' should allocate the necessary land. Amuru Sugar Works is owned by Madhvani Group, the largest private-sector investor in agriculture and agro-processing industry in Uganda. The company requested 20,000 hectares for growing sugarcane and establishing a processing plant, and 10,000 hectares to sublease to out-grower farmers. The project promised to provide employment for 1,175 semi-skilled local employees and six thousand casual labourers, as well as free housing, subsidized primary education and free medical

---

[10] This case study is based on research by Doreen Kobusingye, who from late 2011 to early 2013 conducted ethnographic fieldwork in Northern Uganda on land conflicts and decentralized land governance, also as part of 'Grounding Land Governance'. The case presented here is constructed on data collected in eight focus group discussions, five community dialogues, and thirty-five interviews with members of parliament from the region, Area Land committees, Local Council leaders, District officials, traditional leaders, and other community members. Ilse Zeemeijer also contributed to this case. She conducted six months of field research in 2011, in collaboration with the Uganda Land Alliance, exploring how land was actually acquired in a series of six contested commercial acquisitions. For the Amuru case, she conducted seven interviews with NGO and local government representatives, community members in Amuru and Gulu, and a representative of Madhvani Group.

treatment for the employees (Zeemeijer, 2012:157). The government of Uganda would hold a 40 per cent share in the project.

After this go-ahead, Madhvani went to Amuru District Land Board, who then allocated the first 10,000 hectares for a forty-nine year lease. However, by the time formalities were completed, the Acholi Parliamentary Group, a group including three former members of parliament from the region, filed a case in the high court of Gulu, suing the Amuru District Land Board and Amuru Sugar Works for wrongful allocation of land and depriving the customary owners. Early in 2012, the High Court in Gulu dismissed the case, judging that the land was public rather than customary, and that Amuru District Land Board had acted in the interests of development. In September 2012, the Court of Appeal however ruled that Madhvani should not start any activity on the land. In October, President Museveni urged the Attorney General and the lawyer of the Amuru residents to resolve the matter.

The conflict about the deal concerns different issues. First, there is the question whether the land allocated was already occupied and whether the District Land Board had the authority to give out the lease on this land. The joint manager of the Mahdvani group argues that the project was intended to bring development to conflict-affected Northern Uganda, and that the land was very suitable considering that it was 'totally free of inhabitants and in an extremely isolated area'.[11] A representative of the Madhvani Group, interviewed by one of the authors of this chapter, argued that they had followed the proper procedures at the District, who welcomed the initiative, and that several members of the District Council had expressed their support, as well as the Acholi Parliamentary Group. Mahdvani assumed the land was owned by the Amuru District Land Board.[12] According to the community, however, 'the contested land is customary land. The idea of Madhvani coming is a game by high government officials to grab our land and sell it to investors' (ARLPI – Acholi Religious Leaders Peace Initiative, 2011).

In that respect, the acquisition is just the latest in a series of contested changes in ownership of the land concerned. Before colonization, the land in question was utilized by the local Acholi people for hunting and grazing. During colonial rule, a conservation sanctuary was established, as a result of which the original inhabitants were displaced. In later years, the original inhabitants gradually started to return (Serwajja, 2012: 14-15). Yet, the contested land was gazetted as part of Aswa-Lolim game reserve in 1959 by the colonial government,[13] while the post-colonial government maintained its status of a conservation area. In 1972, the

---

[11] Mayur Madhvani, Amuru sugar project will bring development to Northern Uganda. *Daily Monitor*, Thursday, 9 February 2012. Online at: http://mobile.monitor.co.ug/Oped/-/691272/1322852/-/format/xhtml/-/5dl0mtz/-/index.html [date of last access: 13 June 2014].

[12] Interview IZ, Director of Corporate Affairs Madhvani Group of Companies, 14 July 2011.

[13] Legal notice no. 217 of 1959.

land was de-gazetted by president Amin, enabling the return of some of the displaced to their ancestral lands. However, the de-gazetting also provided chances for ministers, military elites and other members of Amin's government to acquire titles for large tracts of land in the area through the Uganda Land Commission. Amin also rewarded some of his allies with large tracts of land (Serwajja, 2012: 17-18). With the outbreak of the LRA conflict in 1986, those few original occupants that had managed to return to their land had to flee again.

As a result of these multiple shifts in ownership rights, five categories of people currently claim ownership on the land: the 'original' customary occupants, the Uganda Wildlife Authority, people who acquired properties in the time of Amin, various individuals – including members of parliament and local chiefs – who got land after the LRA war, and finally the Madhvani Group. Key problem for the remaining 'original' occupants (local Acholi people) is that there is no written evidence of their claims on the land. Although Uganda legislation acknowledges customary tenure as one of four tenure systems in the country, as long as customary claims are not registered, their status remains weak. The judge in the court case considered the land to be 'public',[14] being not owned by any person or authority, and thus subject to allocation and management by the District Land Board. In this respect, the case illustrates a caveat in land legislation, which does not define the status of unregistered customary land. At the same time, due to all the diverse expropriations and population movements it has become extremely difficult to establish who are the 'original' occupants. While the Acholi Parliamentary Group claims to represent 'the original occupants', it has distanced itself from other groups that do the same, like the local cultural institution Ker Kwalo Acholi. Both now negotiate independently with the sugar company about the interests of the local community.

Next to this question about who is the actual owner of the land, the Amuru controversy is about the procedure through which Amuru Sugar Works acquired the land, and the involvement of local communities in this. For instance, the Acholi Religious Leaders Peace Initiative argues that people in Amuru District were not against sugarcane growing, but 'want Madhvani to dialogue with them, and then they will give Madhvani land to put his factory and piloting while they remain outgrowers and sell to Madhvani' (ARLPI, 2011). People in the community have the feeling that decisions on the land are taken over their heads. 'Why should the authority bypass [us] and arrange giving away of land for development without [our] consent?'.[15] Community members also fear that their leaders are lured into the programme by the government and the company. They observe how various traditional leaders and councillors were invited by

---

[14] In 1972, the land was degazetted by President Amin and went to Uganda Land Commission, and later to District Land Board as 'public land' under the 1998 Land Act.

[15] Focus group discussion DK with youth in Lakang, 21 June 2012.

Madhvani to visit their sugar factory in Jinja, after which they supported the project.

Debate also concerns whether the project contributes to development and for whom. Some local people are fairly positive about the sugar project, and the infrastructure and employment it will bring.[16] Others doubt the benefits of the project. A report of the local cultural institution Ker Kwalo Acholi argued that the project would not benefit the farmers, but only the government and Madhvani (Ker Kwalo Acholi, 2008). Some people see the deal as a way of appropriating community land, after which the land will be subleased to them as out-growers.[17] Local people fear that the project sets a precedent for other investors. 'All the investors in the world are watching and waiting to see what happens to Amuru sugar'.[18] Unwavering support to the project by President Museveni has further raised questions about the integrity and real intentions of the project (Serwajja, 2012).

The contested land acquisition by Amuru Sugar Works in Amuru District is often considered as a prime example of the 'new' land grabs taking place in Uganda, involving a large commercial investor who aims to produce for the global market at the risk of infringing on the rights of local landowners. Yet, as the above case-study exemplifies, there are diverse parallels with past or more localized practices of land acquisition that featured in the previous cases. Similar to the other cases, the contested allocation of land to the company represents only the latest in a series of contested appropriations in the area, which now results in a series of claims on the land by diverse groups. Again, as in the cattle corridor, claims about improving productivity and enhancing development have been used to legitimize the allocation. Both in past and present acquisitions, elites and (political) representatives from the region have played important roles in facilitating the deal, and have profited from the ambiguities of land legislation and in the division of land governing roles.

Conclusion

In this chapter, we have explored different manifestations of land grabbing in Uganda. The cases discussed challenge the image of land grabbing as a largely externally-driven and 'new' phenomenon. Irregular land acquisitions have a long history in the country. And, while global influences may play a role, land grabbing continues to be very much part of local and national socio-political dynamics.

When exploring actual practices of land grabbing, several continuities stand out. First, customary land and the tenure security of small landowners

---

[16] Focus group discussion DK with Amuru Area Land Committee, 23 March 2012.
[17] Interview DK with an elder in Otwee, Amuru district 28 May 2012.
[18] Meeting of Acholi leaders at Bomah hotel, Gulu, fieldnotes DK 17 June 2012.

remain ineffectively protected, which enables land grabbing. Both in the past and present, civil violence and authoritarian rule have weakened land governing institutions and their ability to protect tenure. The case of Amuru District suggests that post-conflict settings provide a window of opportunity for irregular acquisition (cf. van der Haar and van Leeuwen, 2013). The case of Ruhunga hill points out how past episodes of civil violence can leave a long legacy in terms of contestation about land. Both the Amuru District case and the Lake Mburo case underscore how such past irregularities may result in multiple, contested claims on the same property. Despite new legislation and policies over the last fifteen years, local people continue to have limited confidence in the government as a protector of their land. Instead they see a continuation of contested acquisitions and observe how the government continues to fail to deal effectively with past injustices, denying responsibility for practices of its predecessors.

A second continuity is the repeated efforts from governments in different periods to reorganize and modernize agriculture and to appropriate land in the name of development. This has effectively threatened tenure security of customary landowners (see also Huggins on Rwanda in Chapter 8). This was strongly the case in the cattle corridor, where dispossession of pastoralist land by outside elites was and continues to be legitimized by reference to modernization. A collective memory of the contested reordering of land by the government influences how current practices of land acquisition in the name of 'development' are locally perceived and resisted.

Third, in all instances, local and national elites played important roles in land grabbing. In different periods, those elites have taken advantage of ambiguities in regulation, weak land governing institutions, and a faltering justice system to expand their property. On Ruhunga hill, different elites that at different times were politically well-connected disputed the transfer of land. In the lake Mburo area, well-connected local elites have profitted from the diverse reform programmes to appropriate lands.

Finally, the case studies highlight the fact that contemporary land grabbing in Uganda is just another episode in longer national and local processes of exclusion, patronage politics, and elite appropriation of the State, its institutions, and natural resources. After all, the idea that those in power offer favours to their followers (Chabal and Daloz, 1999) is a feature of Uganda politics, where land has frequently served as 'one of the currencies of patronage' (Huggins, 2004: 3). The examples of Ruhunga hill, the Ankole Ranching Scheme, and Amuru District demonstrate that this was certainly the case under the Amin and Obote-II governments, when land was given away to allies of the government and misappropriation was ignored. More recent examples are those cases in which District Land Boards are used by office holders to favour their political allies. The personal involvement of politicians in dealing with the land disputes in Ruhunga and Amuru demonstrates how dealing with land issues is a way for politicians to assert their power and authority (see also Chapter 7, Aymar and Ansoms for Burundi; and Chapter 5, Claessens et al. for Eastern DRC, in this book). It is also from a perspective on exclusion and patronage politics that we may understand local perceptions that government privileges or disadvantages certain ethnic groups or regions. Whether justified or not, such perceptions fuel distrust in government's stated intentions to promote economic development and secure tenure for all. Although we cannot supply data on whether land grabbing is indeed ethnically motivated, practices are clearly perceived to promote the interests of certain ethnic groups, which poses risks for societal stability.

To conclude, there is currently much debate on how to avert the irregularities and injustices that might accompany large-scale land acquisition. Some promote 'responsible' entrepreneurship, facilitated by codes of conduct. Others suggest that we need to shift the discourse on land investment from its biased focus on large-scale corporate investment to the search for alternatives like public investment in land or the intensification of small farmer production (White et al., 2012). The findings in this chapter suggest that neither of these solutions will work if they fail to take account of the continuing importance of local power dynamics that render rural dwellers vulnerable to land grabbing.

Bibliography

Anseeuw, W. and Alden, C., 2010. 'Introduction'. *The Struggle over Land in Africa: Conflicts, Politics and Change*, eds, Anseeuw, W. and Alden, C., HSRC Press, Cape Town. pp. 1-15.

Acholi Religious Leaders Peace Initiative (ARLPI), 2011. *Consultation Meeting at Lakang Village, Pailyech Parish in Amuru Sub-county in Amuru District*. ARLPI, Gulu.

Borras Jr., S. M. and Franco, J. C., 2012. 'Global Land Grabbing and Trajectories of Agrarian Change: A preliminary Analysis'. *Journal of Agrarian Change*, vol. 12, no. 1, pp. 34-59.

Bosworth, J., 2003. 'Integrating Land Issues into the Broader Development Agenda: Uganda'. *Land Reform*, no. 2003/3, pp. 233-248.

Busenene, F., 1993. *The Management of Lake Mburo National Park Rangeland*. Unpublished mimeo.

Chabal, P. and Daloz, J.-P., 1999. *Africa Works: Disorder as Political Instrument*. International African Institute/Indiana University Press, James Currey (UK)/Bloomington (IN).

Cotula, L., Vermeulen, S., Leonard, R. and Keeley, J., 2009. *Land Grab or Development Opportunity? Agricultural Investment and International Land Deals in Africa*. IIED, FAO, IFAD, London/Rome.

Cotula, L., 2012. 'The International Political Economy of the Global Land Rush: A Critical Appraisal of Trends, Scale, Geography and Drivers'. *Journal of Peasant Studies*, vol. 39, no. 3-4, pp. 649-680.

Doornbos, M. R., 1978. *Not All The King's Men: Inequality as a Political Instrument in Ankole, Uganda.* Mouton Publishers, The Hague.

Francis, P. and James, R., 2003. 'Balancing Rural Poverty Reduction and Citizen Participation: The Contradictions of Uganda's Decentralization Programme'. *World Development*, vol. 31, no. 2, pp. 325-337.

Friis, C. and Reenberg, A., 2010. *Land Grab in Africa: Emerging Land System Drivers in a Teleconnected World.* Global Land Project, University of Copenhagen, Copenhagen.

Government of Uganda (GOU), 2001. *Land Sector Strategic Plan. Utilising Uganda's Land Resources for Sustainable Development.* GOU, Kampala.

Government of Uganda (GOU), 2010. *National Development Plan (2010/11–2014/15).* GOU, Kampala.

Harrtera, J. and Ryan, S. J., 2010. 'Top-down or Bottom-up? Decentralization, Natural Resource Management, and Usufruct Rights in the Forests and Wetlands of Western Uganda'. *Land Use Policy*, no. 2010/27, pp. 815-826.

Huggins, C., 2004. *Preventing Conflict through Improved Policies on Land Tenure, Natural Resource Rights, and Migration in the Great Lakes Region. An Applied Research.* African Centre for Technology Studies, Nairobi.

Hunt, D., 2004. 'Unintended Consequences of Land Rights Reform: The Case of the 1998 Uganda Land Act'. *Development Policy Review*, vol. 22, no. 2: pp. 173-191.

Integrated Pastoral Development Project/GTZ (IPDP/GTZ), 1997. *Monitoring and Evaluation Systems: A Household Survey Report.* IPDP/GTZ, Mbarara.

Ker Kwalo Acholi, 2008. *Technical Committee Report on Madhvani Land Proposal for Sugar Works in Amuru.* Ker Kwalo Acholi, Gulu.

Land and Equity Movement of Uganda (LEMU), 2011. *Let's Face up to Land Grabbing.* LEMU, Kampala.

Mabikke, S., 2011. 'Escalating Land Grabbing in Post-conflict Regions of Northern Uganda: A Need for Strengthening Good Land Governance in Acholi Region'. Paper presented at the *International Conference on Global Land Grabbing. Institute of Development Studies*, University of Sussex, Brighton.

Mamdani, M., 2001. *When Victims Become Killers.* Princeton University Press, Princeton.

McAuslan, P., 2003. 'A Narrative on Land Law Reform in Uganda'. *Working paper.* Lincoln Institute of Land Policy, Cambridge.

Ministry of Lands, Housing and Urban Development (MLHUD), 2011. *The Uganda National Land Policy. Final Draft.* MLHUD, Kampala.

Muchunguzi, C., 2003. *The Challenges of Integrating Indigenous People in Protected Area Management: A Case of Bahima Pastoralists and Lake Mburo National Park Nyabushozi Uganda.* Unpublished MA-thesis. Mbarara University of Science and Technology, Mbarara.

———. 2013. *Responding to Crisis: Adaptive Responses of Bahima Pasto-

ralists Searching a Livelihood Resource along the Uganda Cattle Corridor. Unpublished PhD thesis. Mbarara University of Science and Technology, Mbarara.

Musinguzi, C., 2002. *Self-help Initiatives for Water Security: A Case Study of Settlers in Ankole Ranching Scheme.* Unpublished Thesis. Mbarara University of Science and Technology, Mbarara.

Namara, A. and Kimbowa, E., 1999. 'The Fate of a Pastoralist in a State of Resource (Land Tenure) Insecurity: A Case Ctudy of Nybushozi County'. *Working Paper,* no. 6. ALARM, Kampala.

Oxfam, 2011. 'Land and Power. The Growing Scandal Surrounding the New Wave of Investments in Land'. *Oxfam Briefing Paper,* no. 22. Oxfam, Oxford.

Peluso, N. L. and Lund C., 2011. 'New Frontiers of Land Control: Introduction'. *Journal of Peasant Studies,* vol. 38, no. 4, pp. 667-681.

Pulkol, D., 1991. 'Resettlement and Integration of Pastoralists in the National Economy: The Case of Ranches Restructuring in Southwestern Uganda'. Paper presented at *The African Conference on Settlement and Environment.* World Bank, ISR, Kampala.

Rugadya, M., Obaikol, E. and Kamusiime, H., 2004. *Gender and the Land Reform Process in Uganda. Assessing Gains and Losses for Women.* Associates for Development, Kampala.

Serwajja, E., 2012. 'The Quest for Development through Dispossession: Examining Amuru Sugar Works in Lakang-Amurur District of Northern Uganda'. Paper presented at *The African Conference on Global Land Grabbing II.* LDPI, Ithaca (NY).

Uganda Wildlife Authority (UWA), 1998. *Lake Mburo National Park Guide Book.* UWA, Kampala.

van der Haar, G. and van Leeuwen, M., 2013. 'Land Grabbing: Governance Challenges'. Paper presented at *the Annual World Bank Conference on Land and Poverty,* Washington.

van Leeuwen, M. 2012. *Tenure Insecurity & Land Disputes Affecting Members of Mbarara District Farmers Association.* MBADIFA, Mbarara.

White, B., Borras Jr., S. M., Hall, R., Scoones, I. and Wolford, W., 2012. 'The New Enclosures: Critical Perspectives on Corporate Land Deals'. *Journal of Peasant Studies,* vol. 39, no. 3-4, pp. 619-47.

Zeemeijer, I., 2012. *Who gets What, When and How? New Corporate Land Acquisitions and the Impact on Local Livelihoods in Uganda.* Unpublished MA Thesis. Faculty of Geosciences, Utrecht University, Utrecht.

Zoomers, A., 2010. 'Globalisation and the Foreignisation of Space. Seven Processes Driving the Current Global Land Grab'. *Journal of Peasant Studies,* vol. 37, no. 2, pp. 429-447.

Zwick, K. and Lloyd, J., 1998. *Ankole Ranching Scheme 48a, Mbarara District: Biological Survey. The Society for Environmental Exploration,* Frontier-Uganda. Kampala, London.

7

Land Grabbing & Power Relations in Burundi

Practical Norms & Real Governance

AYMAR NYENYEZI BISOKA
& AN ANSOMS

Introduction: land grabbing and 'real governance' in Burundi

Since the 1960s, Burundi has known several cycles of conflict – partly motivated by ethnic cleavages – with particularly violent escalations in 1968, 1972, 1973, 1988 and 1993 (Buyoya, 2011). These events lay at the base of massive refugee fluxes, with farmers leaving their place of origin and (temporarily) settling in neighbouring countries or elsewhere in Burundi, while leaving behind their land. Particularly following the 1972 flux, a large number of such properties were confiscated by the State or by individuals (see ibid.). Indeed, after the departure of these refugees, the reaction of local administrative authorities, from *chefs de collines* up to provincial governors, was often to redistribute this land as if it was vacant.

While most 1993 refugees and internally displaced persons (IDPs) could still recover their properties and reinstall themselves upon return to Burundi after 2000, this was not the case for the 1972 refugees (CNTB – Commission nationale des terres et autres biens, 2010: 1-3; for statistics, see UNHCR – United Nations High Commission for Refugees, 2009). After having spent more than thirty years in exile before their return, they were often confronted with fierce contestation over their old properties by those who now occupied them. The southern provinces were most affected by this problem, namely Bururi, Makamba and Rutana. The various governments that had ruled the country since the end of the civil war in 2000, made attempts to offer some solutions to this situation by setting up specialized commissions responsible for dealing with land conflicts related to the reinstallment of returnees and IDPs on their land (Manirumva, 2005). The most recent 'Commission nationale des terres et autres biens' (CNTB) has taken up its responsibilities since 2006.

However, conflicts over land in Burundi do not only concern (ex-) refugees or internally displaced population groups. Since independence, local Burundian officials have grabbed land. Elites often used their official positions to enforce their grip on particular landholdings. Moreover, these forms of land acquisition were often legitimized through the formal regulatory framework, defined by those in power at that particular moment in time. Land grabbing by local elites did not stop at the end of the civil war in 2000, even after the CNTB was established. A variety of political elites have grabbed vast tracks of land ever since (RCN – Réseau citoyens/Citizens Network 'Justice et Démocratie', 2004). The study of land issues in Burundi therefore requires a detailed examination of the normative framework with regards to land matters, of the institutions that are responsible for translating this framework into practice, and of the structural, political, social and economic factors that impact upon the implementation of the normative framework.

There is an enormous amount of legislative material with relevance to land matters in Burundi. The land code of 1986 – which was a major reference point for over twenty-five years – aimed to make all legislation with regards to land matters uniform, including all written procedures, but also including prevailing customary arrangements. Other juridical texts, produced since 1986, were partially based upon the original land code but sought to modify certain arrangements. This was the case for the forest legislation, the legislation with regards to the protection of the environment, the water legislation, etc. But in day-to-day land arrangements, traditional customary practices persisted. It seems that the 2011 land code has not resolved this. First of all, the code is very voluminous, which does not facilitate its popularisation. Furthermore, its ambition to formally register landholdings does not seem to align to the priorities of rural farmers in Burundi. In addition, the code has not foreseen any role for the *Bashingantahe*, traditional leaders that often mediate in land conflicts in line with customary traditions.[1]

As well as formal legislation that explicitly deals with land issues, the Arusha Agreement contains important land conflict resolution principles regarding refugees. It foresees in the provision of land rights for returnees, but also in the protection of actual owners; it pleads in favour of equity in the distribution of resources between different ethnic groups; it spells out some general principles that should be applied during land reforms; it foresees juridical reform, and in the rehabilitation of the traditional institution of bashingantahe at the level of each hill. However, whereas the principles of the agreement are recommendable, their translation into practice is again problematic (ICG – International Crisis Group, 2003). They should be included in the Constitution, translated into laws, and be

---

[1] The *bashingantahe* (singular: *mushingantahe*) are customary leaders who operate at the level of each hill. Traditionally, they mediate in case of local level conflicts, for example within families or between neighbours. Since the promulgation of the Constitution in 2005, the CNDD-FDD ('Conseil national pour la défense de la démocratie – Forces de défense de la démocratie') aims to limit the power of the Bashingatahe as much as possible. However, in practice, these customary mechanisms continue to function very frequently at the local level.

put into practice by the administration and judiciary. But in reality, this is far from the case.

In Burundi land conflicts are frequent and may take multiple forms. Most reports and analyses in relation to land conflicts in Burundi focus on bad governance, referring to overall disorder (ICG, 2003; Gatunange, 2005; Hatungimana and Ndayishimiye, 2005; Manirumva, 2005, Ntampaka, 2008; Kohlhagen, 2010, 2011). In this chapter, however, we will argue that challenges to governance in the land arena also result from the discretionary space that mediators have when applying the rules responding to specific logics. Their actions may be identified and analysed on the basis of the discursive practices of public actors. According to Olivier de Sardan, 'all researchers in the social sciences admit the existence of a particularly important gap, in Africa, between official norms issued by the state and public services on the one hand, and the behaviour of political elites and officials on the other hand' (Olivier de Sardan, 2008: 3). But these behaviours do respond to certain logics, and this has inspired Olivier de Sardan to reflect upon the 'practical norms'[2] that regulate these elites' everyday actions. For this author, 'real governance' is not homogeneous. It is 'composed of a multitude of dimensions that sometimes converge, sometimes conflict; it is also the product of local, sectoral, and individual micro-dynamics; and finally, it is everywhere confronted with the pluralism in action models' (ibid: 6). Olivier de Sardan therefore proposes to analyse such forms of 'real governance' on the basis of empirical case studies in order to identify the practical norms that regulate the actions of public actors in Africa.

The notion of 'practical norms' is, in our opinion, closely linked with the concept of legal pluralism that refers to the existence of multiple normative frameworks that partly overlap, partly reinforce and partly compete with each other. This theoretical concept highlights the importance of social relations and power play in the implementation of particular normative frameworks (Meinzen-Dick and Pradhan, 2002; Merlet, 2010: 4). The concept also points to the importance of other normative institutions besides those enforced by formal authorities (Meinzen-Dick and Pradhan, ibid.), and recognizes the multiple sources of law besides the formal law formulated by the State. The moral weight of a particular normative framework, and its capacity to regulate access to land rights on the ground, depends upon contextual factors (Le Roy, Karsenty, Bertrand, 1996), and upon the power relations between actors at the local level, both within the land arena as well as outside (Merlet, ibid.: 2-5).

In this chapter, we will use the concepts of 'practical norms' and 'legal pluralism' to understand why there is a gap between formal norms that should theoretically apply to land conflicts, and on-the-ground 'real

---

[2] Olivier de Sardan uses this concept to explain the gap between 'official' norms on the one hand and everyday practices by actors within the public administration on the other. He adopts this concept, without expressing any moral judgement, to understand how such practices are not arbitrary, but respond to a certain logic.

governance' in land matters. On the basis of three case studies, we will explore the variety of forms of land grabbing by local elites, and we will study the power play between actors in the negotiation over these land conflicts. We will show how land conflicts are dealt with in true 'political arenas' (Olivier de Sardan, 2000); and how power shifts within those arenas continuously alter the odds in land conflicts. Finally, we will consider whether there is a certain window of opportunity for weaker actors involved in such land conflicts: what is their degree of 'agency' (Long, 2001: 241)[3] despite their relative lack of power and wealth?

Land grabbing by political elites in Burundi: three case studies

The three case studies presented in this chapter, are based upon field research that was conducted in November and December 2011.[4] The first case concerns a land conflict between a group of Tutsi families and the formal administration that considers their land as state-owned. The second case study analyses a conflict between a group of Hutu ex-refugees and a Tutsi ex-president. In the third case study, we describe a situation where people are being displaced for what is defined by some as 'public utility', whereas others frame it as a case of land grabbing by current political elites.

In our case studies, we will specifically highlight the role played by land conflict resolution mechanisms. First of all, there is the formal legal mediation, involving the intervention of administrative authorities and of competent juridical instances, being the Burundian courts. At this point, more than 70 per cent of all cases brought to court concern land-related conflicts (Ansoms and Marysse, 2011). However, for many people, access to formal juridical procedures is not guaranteed because of the complexity of the procedures and the costs involved. Therefore, many land conflicts are treated in alternative fora coordinated by civil society organizations (associations and NGOs) or by the Bashingantahe. These mediation initiatives often try to establish a compromise between the competing actors. Civil society organizations do not always take up a neutral role, but can also function as pressure mechanisms in favour of weaker population groups confronted with injustices in the land arena. Finally, there are

---

[3]   In line with Long, we define 'agency' as 'the knowledgeability and capability [of actors] to assess problematic situations and organize "appropriate" responses'.

[4]   We first engaged in a literature review on land-related problems in Burundi to identify which types of conflicts occur. On this basis, we selected particularly interesting case studies that reflect some of the complexities that characterise the land arena. One of the authors engaged in some thirty semi-structured interviews with a variety of actors, being the victims of land grabbing, the intermediaries and mediating actors in those conflicts, and with certain 'land grabbers'. In our analysis, we tried to uncover the rationale of actors in these land struggles beyond their immediate discursive practices.

special mediation mechanisms that have been created by the State to explicitly deal with land matters, for example the 'Commission nationale des terres et autres biens' (CNTB, 2010).

Civilians versus the State: internally displaced Tutsi refugees settled on state-owned land

During the period of conflict (between 1972 and 2000), different successive governments (1966-1976; 1976-1987; 1987-1993; 1996-2000) encouraged displaced refugees, residing in high-risk zones, to regroup themselves along the sides of road axes or in more secure sites that were less accessible to rebel groups. This largely contributed to the emergence of internally displaced groups in Burundi, a phenomenon which appeared for the first time in 1993, when ten thousand of Burundians – mostly Tutsi – abandoned their houses to seek refuge in such 'host places' (*zone d'accueil*) (Buyoya, 2011). Even though these internally displaced groups tried to continue exploiting their land from their new location, their remoteness had several disadvantages. First of all, family members often took advantage of their departure to illegally sell part of the land. In other cases, neighbours took advantage of the displaced absence to enlarge their own land (van Leeuwen and Haartsen, 2005; CNTB, 2008: 2). Finally, the situation of insecurity incited some of the displaced to sell their land for a very modest price. After the end of the conflict, these three mechanisms of land alienation laid the basis of numerous land conflicts.

At the same time, the internally displaced formed new centres in their resettlement sites, referred to as *centres de déplacés*. Those were often located on land, owned by the State or by other individuals. Over the years, these centres – previously isolated – transformed into little poles of commerce and activity. Many of the previously displaced ended up settling themselves there on a more permanent basis, not only because of the precariousness of the situation in their original living environments, but also because they increasingly invested in the housing and infrastructure in their new living environment.

However, after the end of the civil war and the pacification of the country, the local administration in some of these *centres de déplacés* incited the settled population to return to their old living environment. This initiative was part of a wider project to make an inventory of all state-owned land with the aim of recuperating it (CNTB, 2010). This was problematic in several ways. First of all, the newly settled people were often not keen to return to their original habitat, knowing that they were unlikely to be unable to reclaim their old property. Second, many errors were made during the inventory phase, where private land was declared to be state-owned, and was then distributed to new owners. Furthermore, there are instances where the local administration registered some of the indigenous population as internally displaced, and thereby considered the land on which they lived as state-owned.

Such a situation occurred in Muhuta (Muramvya province), where vast tracks of land were owned by a dozen Tutsi families. The commune administrator wrongly decreed this land to be state-owned; and – behind the back of the Tutsi families – he redistributed it to some thirty new owners. Among these new owners were several local Hutu elites, members of the political party in power (the CNDD-FDD – Conseil national pour la défense de la démocratie – Forces pour la défense de la démocratie).[5] When these new owners started to construct on the land they acquired, the legitimate owners realised that their land was being grabbed. This incited them to protest against the commune administrator; but without success. The latter was categorical in his reply: 'This land belongs to the commune, and those who claimed to hold property rights have to prove it by producing the authentic titles.'

The Tutsi families involved had obtained rights over the land through inheritance from an ancestor long ago, who bought the land 'from white men [Belgians] for thirty Burundian francs several decades ago'.[6] But like many other Burundians, they did not possess any formal land title. However, the commune itself also did not possess any legal document that confirmed the legitimacy of its own claim. In fact, as is the case with most non-registered land in Burundi, customary law regulates access and rights over land, and is not based on clearly identifiable land titles (Ntampaka, 2008).[7] Interestingly, whereas the commune demanded the Tutsi families to prove their ownership through land titles, these families themselves did not – in turn – demand the same from the commune. Implicitly, it was thus assumed that in the case of a land conflict between an individual and an administrative entity, it was the individual who had to produce the land title.

Faced with the refusal of the commune administrator to cede the land property, the Tutsi families decided to address the governor of Muramvya province. In fact, the commune administrator had allegedly received certain *pots de vin* ('drinks', a term used in the Burundian context to refer to corruption) from new land occupiers, which made it difficult for him to overturn his decision. Despite the fact that the governor was from the same political party as the commune administrator (CNDD-FDD), the Tutsi families hoped he would conclude the matter in their favour. However, somewhat later, the families found out that some of the new landowners were close acquaintances of the officers at the level of the provincial government. Moreover, several sources confirmed that the commune administrator had the implicit support from the governor in the land conflict; the latter was in fact involved in many other cases of illicit land transfers in his province.[8] Therefore,

---

[5] The CNDD-FDD is dominated by Hutu elites, and is the political party in power (at time of going to press).

[6] Interview, Bujumbura, December 2011.

[7] In most cases, proof provided through testimonies of neighbours.

[8] Interviews with 'Radio publique africaine' and 'Radio-télévision Renaissance', Nov 2011.

it was no surprise that the governor refused to respond to the Muhuta families' demands.

This incited the Tutsi families to take the matter further, and to introduce their claim to the 'ministre de l'Intérieur', again a member of the same political party. The minister asked the governor to clarify the situation. Interestingly, five months later, he ordered the governor to make sure that all construction activities on the disputed sites were stopped. At that time, the government was confronted with an increasing sensitivity of international donors and civil society with regards to the numerous conflicts over land rights, which incited the minister to come up with a solution that would not awaken the national media and civil society organizations. However, the hope of the Muhuta families did not last when four months after the previous order, this ban on construction activities was lifted, accompanied by a note that any complaints should be addressed to the legitimate juridical instances.

What had happened within these four months which made the minister overturn his decision? In fact, at that time, protest against the removal of internally displaced Tutsi refugees from state-owned land had become fiercer. This had inspired UPRONA ('Union pour le progrès national'), a Tutsi opposition party, to denounce the government's way of dealing with land conflicts. The protest had been taken up by the national media and by civil society organizations, which turned the matter into a national issue. In fact, the matter of the internally displaced Tutsi refugees had become the subject of a power struggle between the two major political parties, CNDD-FDD and UPRONA. As a result, the governor changed his decision, not wanting to give in to UPRONA's demands.

During our interviews, the Tutsi families explained that they were not keen on presenting the matter in court for several reasons.[9] First, they highlighted that the procedure would take a great deal of time. Moreover, they claimed to not have the necessary financial means. Finally, they said that magistrates would most likely be corrupt. However, the Muhuta families did decide to expose their problem to a larger public by presenting their case through popular media, the 'Radio publique africaine' (RPA) and the 'Radio-télévision Renaissance' (RTR). Given that in previous cases, 'the mediatization of unjust situations made the government of Burundi overturn its decisions',[10] they hoped that this would help them in their quest for justice. They also contacted civil society organizations that appealed to the international community – and to major donors in particular – to increase pressure on the Burundian government. At the time of our research, the Tutsi families were hopeful that this strategy would turn the odds in their favour.

Overall, this case illustrates how 'practical norms' emerge as a result of the power play between the various actors involved. These norms, that regulate the elite's everyday actions in the land arena, may evolve within the course of a couple of months and drastically change the odds in favour or against particular groups. Less powerful groups, who lack the necessary means and political connections, are less capable to protect their interests and turn these practical norms to their advantage. However, at the same time, the volatility within the dominant normative framework may also provide a window of opportunity for less powerful groups: if they manage to efficiently mobilize certain intermediaries, for example, the media and/or civil society organizations, the odds might turn again sometime in the near future.

Civilians versus old political elites: land contestation between Hutu ex-refugees and a former Tutsi President
As mentioned, the politico-ethnic conflicts of 1972 provoked massive population displacement, both within Burundi, and in neighbouring countries (Reyntjens, 1992: 141-146; Chrétien and Mukuri, 2002). Vast tracks of land were left behind, that were either occupied by neighbours, or reattributed by the administrative authorities (at that point dominated by the political party UPRONA, mostly composed of Tutsi) (Kohlhagen, 2011). In some cases, land was handed over to the civilian population, as well as the political and military elites of Tutsi ethnicity (CNTB, 2010). This case study is an illustration of a land conflict that emerged from such land transactions.

Following the 1972 events, vast tracks of land in Bubanza (we estimate between 100 and 200 hectares) were occupied by Jean-Baptiste Bagaza, a Tutsi who was the president of the Burundian Republic (between 1976 and 1987). After the end of the war, a large number of the Hutu refugees – who had left the country and their land properties behind several decades earlier – returned. In line with the *Arusha Peace Agreement* signed during the negotiations of 2000, they were allowed to recover their land (Buyoya, 2011). Moreover, they had been reassured by successive governments, both the FRODEBU (in power between 2003 and 2005) and the CNDD-FDD government (in power since 2005), during sensitization campaigns in the Tanzanian camps trying to convince them to return to their country.[11] In addition, as the 2005 elections were approaching, the returnees were considered to be an important part of the electorate by some of the political parties. However, on the other hand, Bagaza held official land titles (issued before 1993), which the returnees did not have.[12] In addition, he had held the titles to the land for more than thirty years without them being reclaimed by the original owners, which, according to the law (referred to as *prescription trentenaire*), transferred the

---

[11] Interview with one of the returnees, Bujumbura, 2011.
[12] The authenticity of these documents, transferring the ownership titles to Bagaza, were not called into question by the CNTB. However, one has to keep in mind that Bagaza was himself in power when he acquired these land titles. In fact, all land titles that were issued in that period are called into question. This issue has been raised extensively in Kohlhagen (2011).

property rights over the land once and for all.[13] As a result, the returnees – once having returned to Burundi – could not automatically recover the land they had left behind.

In this case, upon their return to Burundi, the returnees founded a commission with the help of the CNTB. This commission would represent their interests in a mediation, coordinated by the CNTB between themselves and the lawyer of Bagaza. Bagaza argued that state law was on his side: holding the official land titles meant that the legal rights to the land were in his hands. He also referred to the *prescription trente-naire* foreseen in Burundian law that supported his status of legal owner regardless of whether he had occupied the land legitimately or not.[14] The ex-refugees from their side referred to customary law that had transferred the land from father to son, after their ancestors had received their rights from the king.[15] The CNTB, assigned to mediate in this case, had its own political agenda. Being installed by the CNDD-FDD government, the CNTB was sensitive to the demands of the Hutu ex-refugees, being an important part of the electorate of CNDD-FDD. A possible victory of Bagaza, a Tutsi from UPRONA, could have symbolised a victory of the old Tutsi elite over the new Hutu elite. This would not have fitted with the image that CNDD-FDD wanted to promote, at all cost searching for a reinforcement of its power and authority at that time.

In 2011, after months of mediation, CNTB decided in favour of the Hutu ex-refugees and against Bagaza. It called into question the validity of the land titles of Bagaza; and adopted a politically-motivated argument that it was possible to contest legal claims if those had been installed during the period that a dictator had been in power. Bagaza still had the possibility of introducing the case in front of court, in which case a judge would not have been bound by the CNTB decision. However, Bagaza's lawyer understood that state law was not a priority in this case, and believed that 'the judges, who would be occupied with this crucial case, would be carefully selected by the party in power'.[16] The ex-refugees, on the other hand, considered their victory as almost a miracle. One of them confessed that 'from a juridical point of view, our cause was lost in advance, and it is only thanks to a miracle that the odds turned into our favour'.[17]

Indeed, it seems quite spectacular that ordinary citizens, actually ex-refugees in a vulnerable position, managed to reclaim land rights from an ex-president. However, when looking at this case in more depth, this

---

[13] As stipulated by the 'Code civil livre III burundais'. See: Kohlhagen, D., 2010. 'Vers un nouveau code foncier au Burundi ?' In: *L'Afrique des grands lacs. Annuaire 2009-2010*, eds, Reyntjens, F., Vandeginste, S. et Verpoorten, M., L'Harmattan, Paris, pp. 67-98.

[14] The article 29 of Law no 1/008 of 1 Septembre 1986 concerning the land code of Burundi also states that '*celui qui acquiert un immeuble et en jouit paisiblement pendant trente ans en acquiert la propriété par prescription*'.

[15] Interview with an ex-refugee and owner of land at Bubanza, November 2011.

[16] Interview, Bujumbura, November 2011.

[17] Interview, Bubanza, November 2011.

'miracle' was not all that unexpected. Indeed, the case illustrates how a profound shift in the dominant political constellation has a major influence on power struggles at the broader societal scale and in the land arena in particular. In this case, the odds turned against the Tutsi ex-president, given that the ex-refugees had become strategically important for the new political constellation in power (CNDD-FDD). At the same time, this also means that in the minds of people, land conflicts are never over. They are temporarily dealt with at some point in time, and those temporary solutions are shaped by the broader political evolutions taking place. However, the other side waits for its turn, which may come when the power constellation changes once more.

Civilians versus new political elites: land expropriation for
'public utility'
In the beginning of the 2000s, the Chinese government offered to construct a presidential palace in Burundi. The Burundian government proposed a terrain in the northern part of Gasenyi, a location in rural Bujumbura, bordering Bujumbura *mairie*. However, this land was occupied by local population that contested the idea of being expropriated. Nevertheless, the expropriation procedure was launched in line with the land code of 1986, offering very low compensation rates in return for the land (Law no 1/008, 1 September 1986). Some of the expropriated expressed their resentment: 'there is no hope at all that the Government will overturn its decisions, not because the expropriation rules are inflexible, but simply because those who demand their application are extremely powerful'.[18]

Interestingly, it was only after the expropriation that a Chinese expert assessment took place, concluding that the terrain proposed by the Burundian government was not suitable. However, the land had already become state property, and was redistributed among certain political elites a couple of months later. They could resell the land for a prize twenty to thirty times higher than the compensation fees that had been paid to the expropriated people. This occurred despite the fact that the law is clear: if the land is no longer needed for the purpose for which it has been expropriated, it has to return to the original owners (Law no 1/008, 1 September 1986). The administration argued however, that this land had already been inserted into the State's patrimony for good, and that there was no question of returning it to the original owners. In addition, certain expropriated confirmed having been threatened to not pursue their complaints. When simply finding out who the new land owners were, others were terrified enough to remark: 'One does not joke with these people who are capable of killing you at all times'.[19]

Still looking for a suitable terrain to construct the palace, the government proposed to expropriate another piece of land not far from the

---

[18] Interview, Gasenyi, November 2011.
[19] Interview, Gasenyi, November 2011.

original one. Initially, they decided that sixteen hectares had to be expropriated. A little later, this became twenty hectares, and then forty, officials arguing that more land was needed to construct the administrative buildings that would be located in the proximity of the palace. The owners of those forty hectares started to organize themselves. However, a couple of days before the contract was to be signed between these owners and the government, the latter again changed its claim, stating that two hundred hectares were required. It reasoned that the presidential and administrative quarter had to be surrounded by buildings and houses of a 'certain standing'. Some of the original owners assured us that beneath the surface, there was a clear ambition of land grabbing in favour of political elites (field notes, 2011).[20] However, they had no firm proof to support their accusations so they formulated alternative propositions.[21] For example, given that the expropriation of nearly two hundred hectares besides the presidential palace did not concern an expropriation for public utility, the owners asked the authorization to either construct those buildings themselves in line with the plans proposed by the government or to sell their land to those who would be capable of reaching the required standards. They had no expectation that this proposal would be accepted (and indeed, it was refused by the government), but hoped that their apparent spirit for compromise would appeal to the media, to civil society organizations and the political opposition to exert pressure upon the government on their behalf.

The discussions were still ongoing, until 'one good morning, tractors arrived to trace roads to facilitate the transport of materials needed for the construction of the presidential palace, thereby destroying the crops on our fields'.[22] This resulted in immediate contestation from the side of the original owners, but the demonstrators were dismissed with tear gas. The owners knew that they could not take their case to court, given the high ranking positions of the government members involved. Instead, they contacted the media, hoping that a mediatization of the affair would raise the pressure upon the government and increase their chances of not being expropriated. Indeed, according to one of the original owners, the party in power is very powerful but there is no unity. There are 'several decision centres that are not always coordinated'.[23] And thus, the committee of original owners could hope to instrumentalize the internal divisions within the dominant political party through media pressure to 'put the moderate wing of the party into action, and count on their *désolidarisation* with the executors of this expropriation'.[24] The affair was played out in the media. Members of the government were publicly

---

[20] Interview, Bujumbura, December 2011.
[21] These owners, approximately one hundred families, organised themselves to establish a commission that would represent them in their negotiations with the government.
[22] Interview, Bujumbura and Gasenyi, November 2011.
[23] Interview, Bujumbura and Gasenyi, November 2011.
[24] Interview, Bujumbura, December 2011.

asked questions with regards to this land conflict and – in the absence of any legal provision that could legitimize the land acquisition – had to promise to re-examine the affair.

In the end, the original owners called upon the Burundian Ombudsman to mediate in the matter. The function of ombudsman had been foreseen in the Arusha Agreement, according to which the Ombudsman 'receives complaints and investigates cases concerning failures in terms of governance and a violation of citizen's rights by public and juridical agents, and makes recommendations to the competent authorities' (Protocol II, Chapter 1, Article 10,7-1). Furthermore, the Ombudsman may mediate between the administration and ordinary citizens, or between the different ministries of the administration. Finally, he plays the role of observer with regards to the functioning of the public administration. When solicited in this case, the ombudsman formulated a proposal according to which the road tracking work had to be stopped, the population was asked to organise itself to cede forty hectares of land to the government, which as a counterpart had to engage itself to transfer a compensation in line with the law. The original owners were not satisfied with this decision. First of all, the compensation rates that would be paid were calculated on the basis of provisions foreseen in the 1986 land code, whereas the rates foreseen in the new 2011 code were much higher (see Law no 1/13 of 9 August 2011). At the time of going to press, even the modest amounts foreseen have not been paid to the expropriated owners, whereas the law considers this as a precondition for expropriation. In addition, everyone understood that the cession of forty hectares to the government would not impede any further land claims from the side of the government. At the same time, some of the original owners appreciated the Ombudsman's judgements nonetheless. One interviewee stated: 'the Ombudsman could not ridicule the government and did not have enough power to stop the actions of its members in search of this land'.[25] He was of the opinion that the Ombudsman had done everything within his power to assure the rights of the original owners.

In contrast to the previous case studies, the ethnic dimension seemed absent in this case. Indeed, most of the original owners of the land were Hutu, thus sharing the same ethnicity as the principal actors of the party in power. However, in this case, intra-ethnic divisions played an important role. In fact, a majority in rural Bujumbura has always voted for Hutu parties that are rivals to CNDD-FDD. In 2005, this province had voted majoritarily for the political party FRODEBU ('Front démocratique burundais'). In 2010, most people voted in favour of FNL, a political party that later left the electoral arena because of presumed fraud during the elections. This electoral dissent had left a spirit of resentment among the party in power (CNDD-FDD). This was noticeable in the discourse

---

[25] Interview, Bujumbura, December 2011.

of certain authorities after the 2010 elections. In addition, people were killed and numerous people had to flee when FNL rebels were hunted down in the following years.

In conclusion, what is particularly interesting about this case is the fact that the victims of spoliation by powerful elites were capable of defending themselves. They adopted several strategies. First, they decided to not go to court, knowing that juridical institutions would be influenced by the high-ranking positions of the government members involved. Second, they effectively managed to mobilize the media, spreading the message that the law was on their side. Government members were publicly questioned on the matter and could not provide a satisfactory reply to why the land acquisition was necessary for public utility. This strategy probably played an important role when the Ombudsman was involved as a mediator and called some of the government's ambitions into question.

Power relations and agency within the land arena

All our three case studies have shown how a profound gap may exist between formal theoretically applicable norms and 'real governance' with regards to conflicts arising from land grabbing. 'Real governance' in land struggles is framed by a plurality of normative frameworks (legal norms, non-official norms, practical norms, etc.). Indeed, in the case studies, a variety of normative frameworks were taken into account: legal provisions, customary arrangements, arrangements arising from mediation efforts, provisions from the Arusha Peace Agreement, but also norms like 'the law of the strongest prevails', or the principle to support one's electorate at all cost.

This context of 'legal pluralism' allows the actors involved to engage in 'forum shopping', a concept that refers to a situation in which disputants 'use different normative repertoires in different contexts or forums depending on which law or interpretation of law they believe is most likely to support their claims' (Meinzen-Dick and Pradhan, 2002:5). However, the moral weight of a particular normative framework, and its capacity to regulate access to land rights on the ground, depends upon the power relations between the actors involved. Indeed, 'practical norms' emerge out of a power play that is dominated by the interests of the most powerful players. Seemingly 'neutral' mediators, like the courts, the CNTB or the Ombudsman, are bound by this same power play. In the first case, for example, customary arrangements – according to which the Tutsi families involved acquired land rights – were ignored. The authorities, mediating in this case, legitimized the commune's land claim in the absence of any legal title in hands of the Tutsi families. In the second case, however legal land titles in the hands of the ex-president and the *prescription trentenaire* were disregarded in favour of customary land rights in the hands of the Hutu ex-refugees. In the final case, authorities tried to instrumentalize the legal provisions with regards to land expropriation for public utility but failed to do so for the vast area of 200 hectares they tried to expropriate.

However, what our case studies also illustrate is the fact that the application of the dominant 'practical norms' may evolve, dependent upon the way in which power relations are structured and transform as the conflict progresses. Power relations in land conflicts may first of all shift as a result of macro-level societal evolutions in response to a shift in the political power constellation. The ethnic card of actors involved in a land conflict for example plays an important role. Both in the first and the second case, the Tutsi actors involved were relatively disadvantaged in the power play because of the fact that the current party in power (CNDD-FDD) is dominated by Hutu elites. The third case, however, illustrated that the ethnic element is not the only one that plays: intra-ethnic struggles also have their influence upon the way in which land conflicts evolve. The strong influence of shifts in the macro-level power constellation upon evolutions in local-level land conflicts also implies that seemingly definite solutions are never final in the heads of people who feel disadvantaged. When the macro-level power constellation changes once more, the odds in micro-level land conflicts may turn overnight.

Besides macro-level societal evolutions, the power play in land conflicts may also evolve as a result of the numerous strategies developed by subordinate actors at the micro- level in their attempts to turn the odds into their favour. Indeed, in each of the case studies discussed, they proved their 'agency' by exerting pressure upon the government, either in a direct way through open contestation, either in an indirect way through calling upon the media, civil society organizations, opposition parties, and international donors. The mobilization of the media, for example, proved to be core in support of the case of the Tutsi families (first case) and the case of land expropriation for presumed public utility (third case). In the second case, the Hutu ex-refugees instrumentalized the political constellation at the national level to turn the odds against a former president.

Understanding these power relations is of particular importance for international donors that are active in the domain of land governance. Indeed, the capacity of a well-formulated legal normative framework to reinforce the land rights of less powerful groups is limited, given that the way in which land conflicts are dealt with in the Burundian context depends to a large extent upon the power play that takes place within the land arena. Therefore, the pathways to be explored should rather concentrate on the ways in which agency of subordinate groups may be reinforced. Civil society organizations and the media may be impor-tant mobilizers of such agency, and therefore, their reinforcement may be a particularly fruitful strategy in the protection of land rights of less powerful groups.

Bibliography

Ansoms, A. and Marysse, S., 2011. *Natural Resources and Local Livelihoods in the Great Lakes Region of Africa: A Political Economy Perspective.* Palgrave Macmillan, Basingstoke (UK).

Buyoya, P., 2011. *Les négociations interburundaises: la longue marche vers la paix.* L'Harmattan, Paris.

Chrétien, J.-P. and Mukuri, M., 2002. *Burundi. La fracture identitaire. Logique de violence et certitudes ethniques.* Karthala, Paris.

Commission nationale des terres et autres biens (CNTB) – République du Burundi, 2008. 'État des lieux des problèmes fonciers burundais'. Communication à l'*Atelier national de présentation de l'étude sur la problématique foncière et les solutions alternatives face aux défis de la réintégration des sinistrés* (24 et 25 Septembre 2008). Commission nationale des terres et autres biens (CNTB), Bujumbura, République du Burundi.

——, 2010. *Organisation et activité 2006-2010.* Commission nationale des terres et autres biens (CNTB), Bujumbura, République du Burundi, pp. 1-3.

——, 2010. *Rapport sur l'identification des terres domaniales.* Commission nationale des terres et autres biens (CNTB), Bujumbura, République du Burundi.

Gatunange, G., 2005. *La problématique foncière dans la perspective du rapatriement et de la réinsertion des sinistrés.* Observatoire de l'Action gouvernementale (OAG), Bujumbura.

Hatungimana, A. and Ndayishimiye, J., 2005. *Politique de rapatriement, de réinsertion et de réhabilitation des sinistrés ainsi que la problématique de gestion des terres au Burundi.* Observatoire de l'Action gouvernementale (OAG), Bujumbura.

International Crisis Group (ICG), 2003. *Réfugiés et déplacés au Burundi, Bujumbura, 2003. Désamorcer la bombe foncière.* International Crisis Group, Nairobi et Bruxelles.

Kohlhagen, D., 2010. 'Vers un nouveau code foncier au Burundi?' *L'Afrique des grands lacs. Annuaire 2009-2010,* eds, Marysse, S., Reyntjens, F., Vandeginste, S., L'Harmattan, Paris, pp. 67-98.

——, 2011. 'Conflits fonciers sur ordonnance: l'imbroglio juridique et social dans les "villages de paix" de Rumonge'. In: *L'Afrique des grands lacs. Annuaire 2010-2011,* eds, Marysse, S., Reyntjens, F. and Vandeginste, S., L'Harmattan, Paris, pp. 41-60.

Le Roy, E., Karsenty, A. and Bertrand, A., 1996. *Sécurisation foncière en Afrique.* Karthala, Paris.

Long, N., 2001. *Development Sociology: Actor Perspectives.* Routledge, London.

Manirumva, E., 2005. *Étude sur les conflits sociaux liés à la gestion des terres et des propriétés foncières dans les localités de Kinyankonge,*

Nyabugete et Kamenge. Observatoire de l'Action gouvernementale (OAG), Bujumbura.

Meinzen-Dick, R. S. and Pradhan, R., 2002. 'Legal Pluralism and Dynamic Property Rights'. *CAPRI Working Paper*, no. 22. International Food Policy Research Institute, Washington.

Merlet, P., 2010. 'Pluralisme juridique et gestion de la terre et des ressources naturelles'. *Document de travail, réunion de réflexion interne de l'équipe d'AGTER (Améliorer la gouvernance de la terre, de l'eau et des ressources naturelles)*, 2 décembre 2010, Nogent-sur-Marne.

Ntampaka, C., 2008. 'Gouvernance foncière en Afrique centrale'. *Document de travail sur les régimes fonciers*, no. 7, FAO, Bruxelles.

Olivier de Sardan, J.-P., 2000. Anthropologie et développement: essai en socio-anthropologie du changement social. Paris, Karthala.

——, 2008., 'À la recherche des normes pratiques de la gouvernance réelle en Afrique'. *Afrique, pouvoir et politique*, no. 5, pp. 1-23.

République du Burundi, 1986. 'Law no 1/008 of 1 September 1986 concerning the land code of Burundi'. *BOB*, no. 7 à no. 9/86. Bujumbura, République du Burundi.

République du Burundi. 2006. *Codes et Lois du Burundi*. Ministère de la Justice, Bujumbura, République du Burundi.

République du Burundi, 2011. 'Loi no 1/13 du 9 août 2011 portant sur la révision du Code foncier du Burundi'. Bujumbura, République du Burundi.

Réseau citoyens – Citizens Network (RCN) Justice & Démocratie, 2004. *Étude sur les pratiques foncières au Burundi. Essai d'harmonisation.* RCN Justice & Démocratie, Bujumbura.

Reyntjens, F., 1992. 'L'ingénierie de l'unité nationale. Quelques singularités de la constitution burundaise de 1992'. *Politique Africaine*, vol. 12, no. 47, pp. 141-146.

United Nations High Commissioner for Refugees (UNHCR), 2009. *Statistiques sur la situation des réfugiés burundais au 29 juin 2009*. UNHCR, Bujumbura.

van Leeuwen, M. and Haartsen, L., 2005. *Les conflits liés à la terre et les mécanismes locaux de résolution des conflits au Burundi.* DEC-Caritas, Bujumbura.

8

Land Grabbing & Land Tenure Security in Post-Genocide Rwanda

CHRIS HUGGINS

Introduction

Land is of vital importance to the people of Rwanda and the Rwandan State, both in terms of 'access' to this scarce resource in a densely populated country, and in terms of the symbolic and practical ramifications of changes to different kinds of land 'uses' (subsistence or commercial, individual or cooperative, rural or urban, polyculture or monoculture, etc.). In the past, access to land has been a source of socio-political controversy and conflict, particularly during the colonial era and in the decade prior to the 1994 genocide, when land became increasingly concentrated in the hands of political and economic elites. Competition over land is sometimes cited as one of many factors that made the 1994 genocide possible, as will be discussed below. Currently, land tenure is particularly important because of the role of agricultural land, and in particular, in an ambitious programme of national economic growth. The Government of Rwanda is committed to reaching the status of a middle-income country by 2020 (MINECOFIN – Ministry of Finance and Economic Planning, 2000) and wants the rural sector to drive economic growth, through rapid commercialization. Accordingly, the government is engaged in several far-reaching rural transformation strategies including a large-scale agricultural reform which relies upon regional crop specialization and compulsory land use consolidation; and a national land registration exercise. In urban areas, many informal or 'unplanned' settlements are scheduled for demolition in order to accommodate the construction of buildings for the formal sector (housing, commerce, and infrastructure).

Compared to other Sub-Saharan African countries, the Rwandan State has an unusually strong capacity to monitor and regulate the activities of its local representatives as well as private citizens. It has also demonstrated a general willingness to achieve the 'Rule of Law'; and so, the State is unlikely to tolerate outright 'land grabbing' in the sense of illegal acquisition of land through intimidation, and/or corruption. The registration of land holdings across the country and issuance of land leases to landholders (see Ansoms, Cioffo, Huggins and Murison, this volume)

141

may potentially reduce land grabbing. Nevertheless, it is important to realise that the post-genocide Rwandan State has been willing to curtail the land rights of citizens under certain conditions, and that the extent of land grabbing since the 1994 genocide is far from negligible.

This chapter complements the chapters in this volume by Ansoms et al. and Manirakiza and Ansoms by providing more detailed definitions of various kinds of land grabbing in Rwanda, in the form of a systematic typology of land grabbing. Our personal view is that the strict legal definition of land grabbing (i.e. outright criminal theft of land through intimidation, force, or fraud) is too narrow to encapsulate the complexities of changes in landownership and use in countries such as Rwanda. In considering the legitimacy of such changes, it is important to consider not only the domestic legal framework, but also relevant international laws (Leckie and Huggins, 2011). While under international law states are free to choose how land is allocated and how rights will be articulated and administered and they must follow a 'systematic' legal procedure when redistributing rights to land. International law outlaws the 'arbitrary' infringement of property rights. The Universal Declaration of Human Rights (United Nations, 1948) and the African Charter on Human and Peoples' Rights, to which Rwanda is a signatory, bind states to abide by due process guarantees, outlawing arbitrary infringement of property rights. This places responsibilities on the State to provide clear criteria for the redistribution of land rights, and prohibits ad hoc decisions which are not supported by legislation. The Government of Rwanda has generally claimed to have limited the land rights of some citizens only in the interests of the public good; but it has not always explained the logic of those decisions in a transparent way.

The term 'land grabbing' used in this chapter, therefore refers to decisions curtailing the rights to land which have not been part of a systematic process, which lack a clear legal and/or regulatory basis, and/ or which have not been shown to be in the public interest. In order to understand how definitions of land rights are changing, it is important to first consider the general structural issues and historical patterns which affect land tenure security in Rwanda. We then provide a systematic typology of land grabbing in Rwanda, before discussing the various factors that appear to mediate the government's attempts to limit land grabbing.

A brief history of land tenure issues

This chapter does not seek to provide an in-depth historical description of land tenure systems, for which readers are directed to works such as Des Forges (2006) and Burnet and the RISD – Rwanda Initiative for Sustainable Development (2003). Instead, we address some of the major structural and historical patterns that have shaped the way in which land tenure security is framed in contemporary Rwanda.

Pre-colonial and colonial characteristics

In the immediate pre-colonial period, there were a few different land tenure systems in operation in different parts of the country. For example, in the northwest of the country, heads of customary 'landowning' lineages dominated rural life (Newbury, 1988: 141). They enjoyed considerable power over the farmland rights of those local people who were not members of their lineages, while pasture lands came more directly under the control of the King, or *Mwami*. At the risk of over-generalizing, it is possible to say that control over land for the ordinary peasant was generally dependent on forms of tribute to these more powerful lineages: either regular tribute (e.g. a symbolic or more substantial payment of agricultural or pastoral produce) or compulsory unpaid labour known as *ubureetwa* that was contributed by those households who could not claim some connection (through lineage, for example) to the powerful socio-political patrons. The kinds of service performed included fetching water and cultivating the fields of the powerful – normally the hill chief. If ubureetwa was not performed by any individual, the rights to land of his or her family would be forfeit.

From the mid-nineteenth century onwards, when the categories of Tutsi and Hutu became rigid and codified with senses of power and powerlessness, it was only Hutu who had to perform ubureetwa, a situation that was later formalized by the colonial administration's policies of overt ethnic discrimination (Vansina, 2004:135). The Belgian colonial regime imposed conditions of forced agricultural production on the rural population from the late 1920s onwards (Newbury, 1988: 154). Chiefs used the ubureetwa labour of the local Hutu population to meet colonial coffee quotas, as well as to work on their own private farms (ibid.: 142). Therefore, the colonial regime consciously attempted to integrate the political authorities and 'customary' practices into the commercial economy, deepening the inequalities associated with a pre-colonial form of forced labour. By the 1950s, the rural poor, and particularly the Hutu, were complaining loudly about what has been called the 'cohesion' of oppressive practices by local elites and the colonial regime (ibid.). This oppression was closely tied to the fragile nature of land rights, which could be 'withdrawn' by powerful chiefs if their subjects did not comply.

The post-colonial period

The violence of the 1959 'Social Revolution' led to the flight into exile of many chiefs, and the Hutu-led First Republic of Grégoire Kayibanda was established after the formal independence of Rwanda in 1962. The government dismantled feudal structures (for example, *igikingi* land, which in pre-colonial and colonial times was reserved for cattle pasture and owned by the monarchy, became common property) and claimed to have created a more equitable system of landownership. However, over time, members of the new state elite misused their power and influence to gain access to land as well as cheap agricultural labour. New systems of patronage emerged, with access to jobs and education representing the 'currency' through which clients were recruited by administrators and politically-connected elites. Access to land also became linked to patron-client politics, as public land (such as marshland) was distributed by state officials in return for political or other forms of support (Gasana, 2002).

Illegal land grabbing and land concentration through purchase became particularly widespread during the later years of the Habyarimana regime, e.g. the mid-late 1980s onwards (Mullins and Rothe, 2008: 90). As civil servants, businesspeople and some NGO staff became more and more wealthy, they accumulated land they had bought from the poor, becoming absentee landlords. Development projects, which moreover had questionable benefits for local people, also resulted in a loss of private land (Uvin, 1998: 147; Human Rights Watch, 2001). Some examples of abuse of government control over land include the logging of part of Gishwati forest (public land) in the north of the country, for a World Bank-funded cattle-ranching project, the profits of which were allegedly siphoned off by corrupt members of the government and the Bank (Prunier, 1996). Landownership became more and more concentrated. By 1984, according to one source, approximately 15 per cent of the landowners owned half of the land (National Agricultural Survey, 1984, cited in Uvin, 1998). When multiparty politics was introduced in 1991, opposition parties seized upon these patterns, blaming the ruling party for the poverty of the rural masses, in order to build support in rural areas (Gasana, 2002).

The civil war that commenced with the 1990 invasion of the country by the Rwandan Patriotic Front (RPF), led to an increase in ethnic tensions that culminated in the 1994 genocide, in which some 800,000 Tutsi, as well as thousands of Hutu, were murdered. While space does not permit a comprehensive review of the factors behind the genocide, it is relevant to very briefly consider the possible role of land scarcity, and related competition and disputes over land, as a cause of conflict. Scholars have differed in their assessments of the importance of land issues. Percival and Homer-Dixon (1995: 1) argue that, 'environmental and population pressures had at most a limited, aggravating role'. Gasana (2002), in contrast, contends that competition for land and related environmental scarcity and degradation created a favourable environment for intra-Hutu political struggles in the early 1990s. This argument is supported by an in-depth field study which argues that in the early 1990s, competition for land in a particular commune in Gisenyi was so intense that 'the social fabric was at risk of falling asunder' (André and Plateau 1995: 45). Such studies, then, strongly suggest that land scarcity was an important background or indirect cause of conflict.

Land scarcity, exacerbated by inequitable distribution of land, has also been described as one of the 'proximate' or 'direct' causes of genocidal violence. It has been well-documented that extremist politicians urged people to kill Tutsi and moderate Hutu in order to gain access to their land (Human Rights Watch/Des Forges, 1999). Verwimp (2005) finds that the land-poor were more likely to be involved in the genocide than those with average sized landholdings.

In addition, government propaganda claimed that if the RPF were victorious, they would redistribute land in favour of the Tutsi (Percival and Homer-Dixon, 1995). The history of fragile land rights and oppression at the hands of local chiefs and the colonial regime made this propaganda seem more plausible to many people.

In summary, competition for land was both a proximate and a background cause of genocide (though by no means the main cause). This should serve as a reminder of the grave significance of land rights and 'land grabbing', as a socio-political issue as well as an economic one.

The RPF came to power militarily in July 1994, ending the genocide, in the face of international inaction. Some two million Hutu left Rwanda, mainly heading for the Democratic Republic of Congo (DRC) and Tanzania. Meanwhile, hundreds of thousands of Tutsi refugees (the so-called 'old case' returnees) returned to the country, which had been completely devastated during the genocide. The new government policy on land was guided by the Arusha Peace Accords of 1993, which 'recommended' that refugees who had been out of the country for more than ten years and whose land had been occupied by others, 'should not claim their property'.[1] The returnees were to live in specially constructed planned settlements, known in Kinyarwanda as *imidugudu*.[2] While some returning Tutsi refugees settled in the thinly-populated Eastern Province of Umutara, others identified lands which had belonged to their families; most simply chose conveniently-located properties vacated by fleeing Hutu.[3] Probably about six hundred thousand Tutsi refugees had returned by the late 1990s (Van Hoyweghen, 2000, Human Rights Watch, 2001: 65). In a later phase, a total of one million and three hundred thousand Rwandan Hutu refugees (the 'new case' returnees) returned en masse in late 1996 and early 1997. Their land claims often added to the already problematic land struggles that were taking place. The way in which the Rwandan government dealt with these problems will be discussed in more detail further below.

At about the same time, in what is now called Eastern Province, especially Nyagatare and Gatsibo Districts, large ranches were acquired by politically-connected individuals (mostly Tutsi who had returned from exile after the genocide) including senior military officers, politicians, former local administrators and other politically-connected individuals. Extensive areas of the Akagera National Park were excised by the government for the purposes of settling returning 'old case' refugees, and it is reportedly locally that some of this land was 'grabbed'. Other farms and ranches were amassed through the occupation of land belonging to

---

[1] Article 3 of the Peace Agreement between the Government of the Republic of Rwanda and the Rwandan Patriotic Front, 4 August 1993.

[2] The singular noun is *umudugudu*.

[3] For a case study on returning refugees and related land problems, see Leegwater, 2011.

citizens who were displaced, but have since returned to the country. In such cases, those using the land have threatened the original owners, or bribed local officials in order to block administrative efforts to resolve the situation. Land grabbing in Eastern Province will be discussed in more detail further below.

A historical review of dispossession and redistribution of land in Rwanda

Since the Genocide, Rwanda has seen rapid and often sweeping processes of change regarding land tenure; some of them associated with central government programmes, while others are more diffuse and perhaps unintended. The following section is an attempt to distil, from Rwanda's post-1994 experiences of change, some of the more problematic ways in which land has been redistributed by the State, or illegally taken from land users. Not all of the following phenomena are illegal, and many could arguably be justified according to national economic, security, or other priorities. However, they can all be criticized under the criteria developed in the first section of this chapter: they have not been part of a systematic process (and hence are open to accusations of favouritism), and/or lack a clear legal and/or regulatory basis, and/or have not been clearly shown to be in the public interest.

These processes have been categorized according to the category of land involved (privately owned/claimed or public land, controlled by the State), the process involved, and whether or not the dispossession was state-sanctioned.

State-sanctioned uncompensated expropriation of private land (land sharing)
In response to the incredible challenge of dealing with the land claims of more than half a million old case load (Tutsi) refugees and over one million new case load (Hutu) refugees (see above), the Rwandan government used a mechanism of 'land sharing', which is essentially a form of uncompensated expropriation. Land sharing was originally intended to avoid the eviction of secondary occupants who were occupying land belonging to another household: the land was simply divided in two. Those who were compelled to divide their property ordinarily received no compensation for the part lost. Given the general scarcity of land in Rwanda, it is difficult to imagine feasible alternatives that could cope with the massive demand for land as well as the complex legal, political and administrative issues involved. It has generally been implicitly accepted by the international community as a pragmatic response to difficult post-conflict challenges.[4] However, there remains widespread local dissatisfaction over the policy,

---

[4] Land sharing was also adopted in neighbouring Burundi, some years later (Huggins, 2009b).

and/or the way in which it was implemented (see e.g. Leegwater, 2011). For example, even official government agencies have acknowledged that 'it is possible that the experience of land sharing Kibungo and Umutara recently went through has left a bitter taste' (NURC – National Unity and Reconciliation Commission, 2005). The former Kibungo and Umutara provinces experienced the most extensive 'land sharing' programmes, because a large number of 'old case' refugees returned there.

Land sharing is problematic from at least four perspectives:

First, from a strict legal perspective (based on international legal standards; see e.g. Leckie and Huggins, 2011) the policy violates one of the few existing tenets of international law on land and property rights: a requirement that any state action that restricts the property rights of citizens should be done through due process and in accordance with international law.[5] As described above, international law states that expropriation should be done according to transparent criteria universally applied. In Rwanda, some households were made to 'share' their land because former owners came back to claim that specific parcel; but in other cases, returnees who did not know where their ancestral homes were located (such as those born in exile who had lost their parents) were accommodated by the government through land sharing by citizens who had no connection to a specific land claim. In other words, some citizens seem to have been 'arbitrarily' selected to provide land for returnees. There seems to have been no official or publicly-available guidance on how those providing land should be selected. It also appears, based on interviews, that in some places specific sections of society (such as genocide survivors) were exempt from land sharing.[6] Again, there is nothing wrong with such a policy decision, if it had been taken as part of a transparent policy process and had been implemented systematically. It is the arbitrary and *ad hoc* nature of the decision that is problematic under international law.

Second, land sharing was problematic when it provided local authorities and their friends and allies with a means to illegally grab land, or unjustly allocate more land to some people than others. In general, most Hutu were under suspicion of participation in the genocide and were at a great disadvantage in negotiations over land and property. However,

---

[5] Expropriation by the State is permitted under international law, conditional upon five criteria. First, the expropriation must be subject to law and due process. Second, it must be in accordance with general principles of international law; third, it must be in the interests of society and not for the benefit of another private party; fourth, it must be proportionate, reasonable, and subject to a fair balance test between the cost and the aim sought; and lastly, it is subject to provision of just and satisfactory compensation. Relevant sources of international law include United Nations General Assembly Resolution 1803 (1962) and United Nations General Assembly Resolution 3281 (XXIX) (1974), while procedural law related to rights to land (prohibiting arbitrary infringement of property rights) is included in the Universal Declaration of Human Rights (1948) and many regional Treaties.

[6] Interview with member of local land commission, former Murambi Commune, former Umutara Province (now Eastern Province), 25 November 2005. See also Leegwater (2011).

power relations in Rwanda are complex and ethnicity is only one of several dimensions which could affect the process. Vulnerable Tutsi (especially widows and orphans) often found themselves dispossessed by local leaders, who in some cases were Hutu. A government study for example found that land sharing remains a major cause of land disputes in Kirehe District, where in some sectors 'local authorities were allegedly bribed' or gave land to relatives (NLTRP – National Land Tenure Reform Project, 2006: 85). Those who tried to speak out against land grabbing were often intimidated into silence, or fled the country due to fears of punishment. In former Kibungo province (now part of Eastern Province), a study concluded that over half of all land conflicts had their origins in land sharing (Gasarasi and Musahara, 2004). It is impossible to quantify the overall extent of such problems nationwide, but they are by no means unusual.

Third, whereas government officials presented the practice as voluntary, in effect it was forced upon the population by the provincial authorities. Former local administrators stated that the unpopular measure was taken because it was 'an order'.[7] Those who dared to speak out against the policy were harassed. A resident of Nyabwishangwezi, Eastern Province explained: 'When we returned to Umutara in 1996, it was a time of intimidation; there were many arrests and disappearances. The authorities divided the land by force. We accepted in appearance – externally – but internally we were not in agreement. But there was nothing that we could do. There were many people intimidated because of arguing against the sharing of land'.[8] Some of those who refused to cede part of their property to others were punished by imprisonment (Human Rights Watch, 2001). Unsurprisingly, a field study on landownership found that some people who lost their land 'have not accepted this and still believe their land was unfairly given to others' (Republic of Rwanda, 2007: 93).

Fourth, land sharing has continued to be applied on an ad hoc basis in Rwanda. Essentially, the ongoing return of refugees has been used to justify a 'state of exception' to the usual land tenure regulations. As a result, many landholders – particularly those in areas where land sharing has been widespread – do not feel secure in their landownership. For example, a national-level government survey found that citizens living in former Kibungo and Umutara were the most keen to acquire title deeds to land, probably because they feared further land sharing, and assumed that a title deed would protect them from expropriation (NURC, 2005). With the national-level registration of land complete, international land tenure experts have argued that it is now important that the Government of Rwanda ceases 'land sharing' in order to assure that the land leases will be respected. If land sharing continues, it will seriously undermine land tenure security (Bruce, 2007) and complicate the land leasing certification system that has been put in place. At present, based on a draft

---

[7] Interview with former local administrator, Kiziguro sector, Eastern Province, 25 November 2005.

[8] Interview with local resident, Nyagatare town, Eastern Province, 20 December 2005.

version of a new land law, it appears that the government wisely intends to cease the use of the land sharing mechanism.[9]

State-sanctioned expropriation of private land involving unjust compensation

As discussed by Manirakiza and Ansoms (this volume) the government has expropriated land and property from thousands of people, especially those living in urban areas. Such expropriations are justified by the government as an attempt to 'improve' the quality of commercial and residential buildings, to improve infrastructure (such as sewerage and water supply systems), to increase population density (by building multi-story units), and to enforce existing regulations. However, the general trend of urban expropriation arguably represents a particular view of 'modernity' that is biased against local cost-effective building technologies and materials, and is based as much on an image of 'improvement' than a concrete reality. Evidence suggests that only a small percentage of the population can afford to build using government-approved materials, and that the vast majority are trapped in a housing crisis partly caused by government prohibitions on more affordable materials (Sommers, 2012).

Large-scale expropriation of land has been associated with a number of systemic problems. Concerns over the expropriation process are amongst the most common complaints made to Kigali City Council officials (Ndikubwayezu, 2009). One of the most pressing problems is insufficient compensation (RISD, 2012). The undervaluation of land and property represents 'grabbing' of part of the value of these assets from citizens – often the poor – and a subsidization of the activities of the state and commercial investors. By law, landowners should be compensated within a four month period after land valuation, but in practice, payments are often delayed (Payne, 2011).

The 2005 Land Law provides greater tenure security for residents than the earlier law, as it recognizes customary tenure. Nevertheless, expropriation for commercial development accelerated in late 2005 and early 2006 as a draft expropriation law was under development, and speculators wished to expropriate residents using the regulations set out in the 1996 expropriation law rather than the new law (Ilberg, 2008). The Ministry of Lands circulated an official notice in 2005 directing that the compensation values specified in the 1996 law should be tripled to take inflation into account. However, this letter was largely ignored by those calculating compensation packages.[10] The expropriation law was finally promulgated in 2007.

---

[9] Article 68 of the 2013 Land Law retroactively legalises the land sharing that occurred between 'nineteen ninety four (1994) and 30 June 2012'; which may imply that land sharing after that date is not legal. However, it does not categorically ban or declare an end to land sharing.

[10] Interviews with Lands Ministry staff, Kigali, early 2006.

While problems of undervaluation of citizens' assets are arguably the result of 'technical' failings, there seems also to be a lack of political will to protect the assets of the poor, if this is seen to slow down the momentum of economic 'development'. Even in a 'model' resettlement project, citizen's legal rights were violated. This case, in Ubumwe cell in Kigali has been documented by Ilberg (ibid.). Valuations of properties by city staff were much lower than independent valuations (LDGL – 'Ligue des droits de la personne dans la région des Grands Lacs', 2008) and the government Ombudsman ordered that the expropriation await an independent second valuation process. However, demolition of the neighbourhood proceeded despite his order (Gakire, 2008). The new houses for resettlement were located far from the city, which affected livelihoods, and many resettled citizens had problems affording the mortgage payments (Wakhungu, et al, 2010). Moreover, the construction of the resettlement site resulted in the expropriation of former residents, meaning that there were two case-loads of expropriations associated with the project.

State-sanctioned privatization of public land

Increasingly, public land in Rwanda is being leased by corporate entities for the production of food crops, flowers, bio-fuels or other valuable commodities. According to the Rwanda Development Board, US$116,3 million was invested in agriculture in 2011 (of a total of US$598 million for all sectors of the economy combined). Of this US$598 million, approximately US$371 million was foreign direct investment (Anonymous, 2012). While few details are available about these recent investments, older projects have been the subject of research.

One of the earliest cases of foreign investment in the agricultural sector is the Kabuye sugar factory, purchased by investors from Uganda (with roots in South Asia) in 1996. The same investors (the Madhvani Group) also lease 3,100 hectares of marshland in the Nyabarongo valley for sugarcane production. Marshland, which is legally the property of the State, has been one of the main categories of land leased to investors (whether foreign or domestic). The benefits to a small number of local people, some of whom are employed as farm labourers by Madhvani or outgrowers, are probably outweighed by the negative impacts on a larger proportion of the community, which 'feels impoverished' as a result of losing access to marshes (Ansoms, 2009; Veldman and Lankhorst, 2010: 26) and is forced to use hillside plots more intensively to make up for lost production in the marshes. This means that fallow periods have reduced and soil fertility has declined.

Outside the marshes, land acquisition for commercial purposes occurs on a more occasional basis, and usually on smaller land parcels. The Government of Rwanda has prioritized flower and fruit production as high-value sectors where Rwanda has some competitive advantage. It is currently inviting investment in a 200 hectares plot in Eastern Province for the development of a high-tech flower farm.[11] It has also allocated six hundred hectares of land to a maize and soya farm (van der Laan, 2011).

In addition to horticulture, the Government of Rwanda has enthusiastically embraced the potential of biofuel technologies. It is for this reason that one of the largest foreign land acquisitions to date involves the production of jatropha, for the production of bio-diesel. In 2009, the Government of Rwanda granted an Anglo-American consortium a thirty year lease to ten thousand hectares of land near Akagera National Park in Eastern Province, for the production of jatropha (Kagire, 2009) This represents a massive landholding in a country where the average household landholding is about 0.75 hectares (MINAGRI, 2012). According to the *Daily Telegraph* newspaper, the consortium has leased the land 'for a rent of a few thousand dollars a year' (Mendick, 2011).

Non-state-sanctioned grabbing of public land

In order to understand the land question in the contemporary context, it is important to consider not only the question of landownership, but also ways in which forms of control over land use (rather than outright ownership) allows for the value of land – including its productive benefits – to be monopolized by some individuals at the expense of others. For example, access to marshlands (which are all owned by the State) is now possible only through cooperatives (which lease the land – see Ansoms and Murison, 2012) or through state-regulated processes of leasing to large-scale operators such as Madhvani group (see previous section). Evidence from recent research in Rwanda, as well as the problematic history of cooperatives, suggests that while some cooperatives offer real benefits to members, others are extremely poorly managed (Ansoms and Murison, 2012; Huggins, 2012). The term 'ghost cooperatives' has come to be used by Rwandans to refer to institutions which are not based on any collective will on the part of the members, but are rather a legal fiction, and a mere institutional shell, intended to allow a few people to profit while the majority derive only marginal benefits. In such cooperatives, members play little or no role in decision-making, and there is little transparency in the sale of produce and distribution of profits, which are often susceptible to theft. Such cooperatives essentially function as pools of cheap labour, which cooperative leaders can use largely for their private profit. Often, such cooperatives lease marshland or other state-owned property.[12] While land has not actually changed hands (i.e. it remains the legal property of the State), the profits from that land have been privatized, to a greater-or-lesser degree. Such 'grabbing' of profit from public or private lands goes largely unnoticed unless it reaches such proportions that the cooperative simply collapses.

[11] Advertised on the website of the Rwanda Development Board. Online at: http://www.rdb. rw/rdb/agriculture.html [date of last access: 18 July 2012].

[12] Alternatively, cooperatives may use land belonging to the members.

In other cases, public land – such as valleys, hilltops, or land reserved for state infrastructure – is directly taken, without any legal or state backing, by politically-connected individuals. The Gishwati area of Northwest Rwanda (former Gisenyi Province; now Rubavu District) provides an example of land grabbing by local administrators as well as a cabal of state politicians.

The mountainous Gishwati forest, a remnant of ancient woodland in the northwest of Rwanda, was turned into a Forest Reserve in 1930. Following the genocide, large numbers of Tutsi 'old case' refugees from neighbouring Zaïre (now the DRC) entered the forest with large herds of cattle.[13] Their presence was at first accepted by the government, particularly as they formed an obstacle to infiltration of the forest by Hutu guerillas from across the border. The government permitted them to inhabit almost three thousand hectares of forest land (UNDP – United Nations Development Programme, undated). However, in December 1999, this policy was reversed for environmental reasons, and some 10,154 families were evicted from the forest. Those evicted lived for years in very poor conditions in temporary camps organized by local authorities, or in makeshift shelters along the Ruhengeri-Gisenyi road (OCHA – Office for the Coordination of Humanitarian, 2000) before being eventually resettled.[14] Meanwhile, money intended for the resettlement process seems to have been stolen by government officials. In October 2004, the Auditor General's office noted that the Ministry for Land could not account for some 100,500,346 RwF (more than $184,000) intended to assist those evicted from Gishwati (Maguru, 2004).

Following the eviction of the Bagogwe community, more local people were evicted from the forest area in early 2005. They faced massive delays in being resettled, without adequate shelter or access to land.[15] Again, corrupt local authorities grabbed land during the resettlement process, according to local people[16] and the pro-government *New Times* (Bugingo, 2006).

In 2007, flooding – which destroyed houses and killed at least seventeen people – was blamed on environmental destruction on the Gishwati hills, and agricultural activities across a wide swathe of the hills were banned in September 2007 (Tindiwensi, 2007). By February 2008, those affected were still waiting for access to alternative agricultural land, without adequate government assistance or other sources of livelihood (Tindiwensi, 2008a; UNDP, undated). By June 2008, many residents were still waiting to be allocated alternative plots (Tindiwensi, 2008b).

---

[13] Many of the returnees were members of the Bagogwe community with family ties in the area.

[14] Some of the Bagogwe were later housed in *imidugudu* in Gikongoro Province, but were unhappy at local grazing conditions. Many left for the DRC or other parts of the country. Interviews and observations, Gatare Sector, Nyamagabe District, Southern Province, 5 April 2006.

[15] Interview with the Mayor of Kanama District, 19 August 2005.

[16] Interviews, civil society representatives, Gisenyi town, 17 August 2005.

There are two issues here. First is the fact that the State had reversed its previous policy of 'allowing' settlement in Gishwati and hence had a responsibility to provide those evicted with alternative land in a timely fashion; this responsibility was not fulfilled. Second, land was grabbed during the process of resettlement. Corruption was not limited to the local level. A government Agricultural Land Commission allocated land in the area to many people (including several senior government officials) who had no link to the area and were not eligible to receive assistance (Bugingo, 2006). President Kagame has confirmed the corruption, stating: 'The same people who try to appropriate land in the Gishwati forest are the same people who have land in Eastern Province and other places' (Kagame, 2007). Despite this public condemnation, and although some of the land grabbing was overturned, many of those implicated remain in office.

Non-state-sanctioned grabbing of private land
Despite the Government of Rwanda's reputation for a policy of 'zero tolerance for corruption,' there are some examples of administrators and politicians conspiring to grab land, particularly plots belonging to poor citizens who lack the financial or political means to publicly complain or seek recourse in the courts. As noted by organizations such as *Ibuka* (a genocide survivors' organization), many children orphaned by the genocide – who have inherited land from parents and other relatives – have been affected by land grabbing, either by public officials or by relatives. Rose (2005) notes that the majority of orphans' opponents in land disputes were family members, but public officials are often guilty of 'foot-dragging' on orphan's complaints, or are bribed to ignore them. In other cases, state-planned villages (*imudugudu*) were constructed on land belonging to orphans, who have difficulty getting compensation. Orphans who are not genocide survivors also face land grabbing.

The Batwa indigenous minority has also been disproportionately affected by land grabbing. They are historically marginalized socially, economically, and politically, and have thus been largely unable to fight land grabbing. They were expelled from National Parks in the 1980s and early 1990s, without compensation (Huggins, 2009a). Some of the land given to Batwa by the king or his agents during the pre-colonial era was seized during the post-colonial period without any legal basis or compensation. For example, a Batwa community which had been given an entire hill in Mugambazi (Kigali Prefecture) by the Mwami during the colonial period saw some 75 per cent of its land forcibly taken by Bahutu neighbours (Lewis and Knight, 1995). There is also a legacy of 'voluntary' sale of land, at extraordinarily low prices, by Batwa to non-Batwa. Both before and after the genocide, land was often sold for token payments (such as small amounts of food) by Batwa households suffering from food insecurity. These distress 'sales' are typically undocumented and many should be seen as manipulative, and hence legally dubious. However, in a context of general social discrimination against the Batwa, some local administrators still do not take Batwa claims of land grabbing or exploitation seriously.

Along with specific vulnerable groups, other poor farmers suffer land grabbing. Based on fieldwork, a review of legal and regulatory frameworks, and similar experience in several neighbouring countries, it appears to us that grabbing of private farmland is not as systematic or widespread as in other countries in the Central and East African regions, but it is by no means negligible. Mechanisms of grabbing are also different. Often, rather than grab land outright and risk being uncovered, powerful actors force local people to sell for a nominal sum, far below market rates, in order to make the sale seem legitimate. Peri-urban areas close to Kigali are especially badly affected by abuses against the customary land rights of the local peasant population.

An example: forced 'private' expropriation at below market rates
In November 2004, three senior government figures visited Masaka sector, a rural area near Kigali, and identified an area under cultivation by local people, which they wanted to develop.[17] They then enlisted the help of the local administration in forcing the families occupying the land to sell at far below market rates. According to one of the victims of the forcible expropriation,

> They are offering too little money – they offered 100,000 RwF for a plot 20 m x 100-120 m. I have children – what will they do without a plot? There is no negotiation, there is no choice. The councillor of the sector is insisting that we sell.[18]

Other residents affirmed that the local authorities were pressuring them to accept the money. Some residents were intimidated and threatened with imprisonment by the District mayor and other members of the local authorities. At least one resident was also told that he had a 'genocide ideology' because of his opposition to the land purchases.[19]

Despite the unwillingness of the local people to sell, the crops of several of the local residents were destroyed by hired labourers in October 2006.[20] A few days later, the crops of another resident were destroyed, as a large group of angry residents trying to convince the labourers to stop. The owner of the plot had neither verbally agreed to sell, nor signed any contract.

---

[17] Interview with residents of Masaka Sector, Kabuga District, Kigali Ngali, 25 and 29 October 2006.

[18] Interview with residents of Masaka Sector, Kabuga District, Kigali Ngali, 25 October 2006.

[19] Interviews with residents of Masaka Sector, Kabuga District, Kigali Ngali, 25 October and 21 December 2006. In Rwanda, 'genocide ideology' is a crime punishable by severe sanctions. The legal framework around 'genocide ideology' has been vague, resulting in arrests based on minimal or highly questionable evidence.

[20] Interview with residents of Masaka Sector, Kabuga District, Kigali Ngali, 25 October 2006.

One of the most disturbing elements of this case is the inability or unwillingness of state officials to stand up for the right of the local residents. For example, one of the residents called an official from the Office of the Ombudsman. On hearing the names the influential people involved in the land-grab, she reportedly told local people 'what do you think that I can do?'.[21] Someone claiming to be a member of the National Human Rights Commission also colluded with local authorities in trying to persuade local people to accept the money being offered. In the face of continuing intimidation, the local residents eventually sold their land for significantly less than market value.

Official responses to land grabbing

The coverage of land grabbing issues by Rwandan media, reports of the Ombudsman's office and other institutions, and the perspectives of international consultants and observers all tend to suggest that President Kagame has a low level of tolerance for corruption, including outright land grabbing. The government has publicly acknowledged the sensitive nature of landownership and the connections between struggles over land and violent conflict (e.g. MINITERE, 2004; NURC, 2005). Therefore, it makes little sense for the government to allow such a scarce and emotionally charged resource to become a currency in systems of state patronage. However, there appear to be two factors that limit the willingness of the RPF to completely crackdown on land grabbing.

The first factor explaining the somewhat soft approach to punishing most land-grabbers is an economic motive. The Government of Rwanda is completely committed to the radical transformation of the countryside along a paradigm of 'modernization' and 'consolidation' of the agricultural sector. The Land Policy argues that customary smallholder agriculture is 'mediocre' and 'has no future' (MINITERE, 2004: 43) and the government generally has little faith in local knowledge or the productive capacities of smallholders (see Ansoms, 2010). The State believes in economies of scale – for example, it removed a proposed fifty hectare landownership ceiling from the 2005 Land Law – and wants to actively encourage the commercialization of agriculture, the transfer of land to the most profitable uses, and direct investment by domestic and foreign investors. It therefore seems unwilling to punish wealthy actors for land grabbing, on the assumption that it is these actors, not smallholders, who will lead 'economic development'.

The second factor is political. Evidence suggests that while low-level government officials routinely risk losing their jobs for land grabbing behaviour, higher-level personnel (such as those named in the Presidential Commission for Eastern Province) often enjoy impunity, presumably

---

[21] Interview with residents of Masaka Sector, Kabuga District, Kigali Ngali, 21 December 2006.

because of their political influence. In particular, it is noticeable that many of those accused of grabbing large plots of land are current or former members of the Rwandan military (RDF – Rwanda Defence Forces). Some of these same high-ranking army officers are now amongst the 'inner circle' of RPF (Rwandan Patriotic Front) decision-makers. It appears that in order to maintain support amongst the high-level cadre of the RPF, the Rwandan government has chosen to either turn a blind eye to some past episodes of land grabbing, or (in cases which have become too high-profile to ignore) to redistribute some of the grabbed land without punishing those accused of grabbing (see the section below on Eastern Province). This policy has given rise to a perspective amongst many Rwandan, and international policy and political science experts, that the RPF leadership sometimes allows party loyalists to indulge in a degree of corruption as long as they remain useful to the party. However, if such individuals become seen as disloyal to the party, or if their appetite for graft is seen as unacceptably blatant, then the 'file' on their corrupt activities is leaked, forcing the individual to resign, face legal action, or flee the country.[22]

The co-optation of civil society groups by the government (see Gready, 2010), as well as the various legal and extra-legal means used to undermine and destabilize civil society groups in Rwanda (Longman, 2011; Reyntjens, 2011), has meant that there are few organizations able and willing to comprehensively and systematically monitor land grabbing, and fewer still who are willing to speak out about it publicly. Instead, citizens are encouraged to channel complaints through state-controlled institutions and processes, such as the Ombudsman's office. Where specific 'clusters' of grabbing are detected, these are seen as an internal matter, to be handled by the government, without external interference (see, for example. Ngarambe, 2012), and generally, these cases are dealt with behind closed doors.

There are, however, occasional exceptions. In response to land grabbing in Eastern Province by military leaders, administrators and other powerful figures in the months and years following the end of the genocide, President Kagame established a land commission in mid-2007 to redistribute land in the province. The then State Minister in Charge of Lands and Environment, Patricia Hajabakiga, stated that some top government officials' plots were likely to be redistributed and that about two hundred more officials owned over fifty hectares each, a suspiciously large landholding in the Rwandan context (Musoni, 2008). President Kagame has stated that, 'certain leaders are indeed guilty... There are also some Ministers implicated' (Kagame, 2007), and has acknowledged that land grabbing has negatively impacted local people: 'sometimes families flee the country because someone has chased them from their land; some have gone to Tanzania and others to Uganda' (Musoni, 2007).

---

[22] Phone interview with international academic, 22 February 2012, as well as numerous interviews in Kigali, 2005-7.

However, the overall results of this commission's work were disappointing for several reasons. First, many members of the commission had been involved in land grabbing themselves, which presented a clear conflict of interest. Second, unlike many state land commissions which investigate land grabbing, such as the Ndungu and Njonjo Commissions in Kenya, the results of the Presidential Commission were not made public. Second, there was no difference in the treatment of those who acquired large landholdings legally (for example, through purchase) and those who acquired land irregularly. This means that legal owners had their land expropriated and redistributed without compensation, while 'land-grabbers' were not given appropriate punishments (Ntagungira, 2008). Third, the commission's way of dealing with cases of land grabbing was ambiguous given that owners of large parcels (including those accused of having 'grabbed' the land) were permitted to retain twenty-five hectares, while their relatives who live on the land were allowed to retain ten hectares each. In practice, this amounted to legalizing land grabbing. For example, General Ibingira, the head of the commission, originally owned 320 hectares. The commission allowed him and his family members to retain ninety-five hectares (Kimenyi, 2008).

Conclusion

Rwanda is generally perceived by the international community as an island of integrity in an otherwise very corrupt region. While the government tends to have a lower tolerance for land grabbing than its neighbours, it seems nevertheless to be a not uncommon occurrence in contemporary Rwanda. As this small, densely populated country undergoes rapid changes in both the urban and rural context (brought on by legislative changes, foreign assistance and domestically-created economic growth) the risks of land grabbing are likely to increase as market prices of land go up. While the government generally follows the liberal economic doctrine that stresses the importance of secure private property rights, it also tends to prioritize economic growth and the demands of investors over the demands of the poor. In order to understand the various ways in which Rwandan citizens are being divested of land or part of the 'value' of their land and properties, it is important to recognize various forms of land grabbing. To this end, the chapter has attempted to create a typology of land grabbing in Rwanda, which includes, for example, deliberate undervaluation of land during expropriation processes, as well as the more well-known forms of land grabbing.

The chapter has also argued that the highest levels of government generally have a vested interest in cracking down on land grabbing in order to avoid public unrest. Indeed land grabbing is less common than elsewhere. However, perhaps due to a desire to avoid a recognition of the role of state officials in land grabbing (which might risk bringing the

RPF into disrepute), state responses have generally been both opaque and somewhat lenient towards land-grabbers, particularly those who hold influential positions within the RPF or the army.

In the context of a stated government intention to move hundreds of thousands of rural people off the land and out of agriculture over the next eight years (MINECOFIN, 2000), as well as widespread urban expropriation, efforts to study land grabbing in Rwanda should examine the phenomena from a broad, critical perspective which looks not only at laws and policies; but also at how they are implemented in a context of rapid change and significant inequalities in wealth and political influence. Rather than utilize a narrow 'rule of law' approach, it is important to enquire more comprehensively into the political economy of land tenure and land grabbing in Rwanda, especially through detailed fieldwork.

Acknowledgements

The author would like to thank the editors of this volume for their insightful comments. The advice of several anonymous reviewers was also very useful.

Bibliography

André, C. and Plateau, J.-P., 1995. *Land Relations under Unbearable Stress: Rwanda Caught in the Malthusian Trap.* Centre de recherche en économie du développement, Namur (Belgique).

Anonymous, 2012. 'Agriculture tops 2011 investments as overall investments hit US$598million'. *The New Times*, Kigali. Online at: http://business.rwanda.rw/spip.php?article1153 [date of last access: 18 July 2012].

Ansoms, A., 2009. 'Privatisation's bitter Fruit: The Case of Kabuye Sugar Works in Rwanda'. *L'Afrique des Grands Lacs: Annuaire 2008-2009*, eds, Marysse, S., Reyntjens, F. and Vandeginste, S., L'Harmattan, Paris, pp. 55-71

——, 2010. 'Views from Below on the Pro-poor Growth Challenge: The Case of Rural Rwanda'. *African Studies Review*, vol. 53, no. 2, pp. 97-123.

Ansoms, A. and Murison, J., 2012. 'De "Saoudi" au "Darfour": l'histoire d'un marais au Rwanda'. *L'Afrique des Grands Lacs: Annuaire 2011-2012*, eds, Reyntjens, F., Marysse, S. and Vandeginste, S., L'Harmattan, Paris.

Bruce, J., 2007. 'Drawing a Line under the Crisis: Reconciling Returnee Land Access and Security in Post-conflict Rwanda'. *Humanitarian Policy Group Working Paper.* Overseas Development Institute.

Bugingo, S., 2006. 'Agriculture Land Commission: The solution or the Problem?' *The New Times* (5 September), Kigali.

Burnet, J. and the Rwanda Initiative for Sustainable Development (RISD),

2003. *Culture, Practice and Law: Women's Access to Land in Rwanda.* RISD, Kigali.

Des Forges, A., 2006. 'Land in Rwanda: Winnowing out the Chaff'. *L'Afrique des Grands Lacs. Annuaire 2005-2006,* eds, Reyntjens, F. and Marysse, S., Centre d'étude de la région des Grands Lacs d'Afrique/ L'Harmattan, Anvers (Belgique)/Paris, pp. 353-371.

Gakire, A., 2008. *La population de Rugenge passe la nuit à la belle étoile après démolition de leurs maisons.* Ligue des droits de la personne dans la région des Grands Lacs (LDGL) (23 July 2008), Kigali.

Gasana, J. K., 2002. 'Natural Resource Scarcity and Violence in Rwanda'. *Conserving the Peace: Resources, Livelihoods and Security,* eds, Matthew, R., Halle, M. and Switzer, J., International Institute for Sustainable Development, Winnipeg, Canada.

Gasarasi, C. and Musahara, H., 2004. 'The Land Question in Kibungo Province: A Research Report'. *Cahiers du centre de gestion des conflits,* série no. 12, NUR, Butare.

Gready, P. 2010. 'You're either with Us or against Us: Civil Society and Policy Making in Post-Genocide Rwanda'. *African Affairs,* vol. 109, no. 437, pp. 637-657.

Huggins, C., 2009a. *Historical and Contemporary Land Laws and their Impact on Indigenous Peoples' Land Rights in Rwanda.* Forest People's Programme, London

——, 2009b. 'Land in Return, Reintegration and Recovery Processes: Some Lessons from the Great Lakes Region of Africa'. *Uncharted Territory: Land, Conflict and Humanitarian Action,* ed. Pantuliano, S., Practical Action Publishing, Rugby (UK), pp. 67-93.

——, 2012. 'Consolidating Land, Consolidating Power: What Future for Smallholder Farming in Rwanda's "Green Revolution"?' Paper presented at the *International Academic Conference on Global Land Grabbing II,* Cornell University, Ithaca (NY), 17-19 October 2012.

Human Rights Watch/Des Forges, 1999. *Leave None to Tell the Story: Genocide in Rwanda.* Human Rights Watch and FIDH.

Human Rights Watch, 2001. *Uprooting the Rural Poor in Rwanda.* HRW, Washington, DC.

Ilberg, A., 2008. 'Beyond Paper Policies: Planning Practice in Kigali'. Paper presented at *N-AERUS conference,* Edinburgh, 12 December 2008.

Kagame, P., 2007. *Comments of President Paul Kagame.* Presidential Press Conference, Village Urugwiro, Kigali, Broadcast on Radio Rwanda, 20 April 2007. Unofficial Human Rights Watch translation from the original Kinyarwanda.

Kagire, E. 2009. 'Cabinet approves US35m Bio-diesel project'. *The New Times* (30 October), Kigali. Online at: http://www.newtimes.co.rw/ news/index.php?i=14064&a=21874

——, 2011. *PM Extends Deadline for Land Lease Fees. The New Times* (30 December), Kigali. Online at: http://allafrica.com/stories/ 201112300984.html

Kimenyi, F., 2008. 'Share Resources, Kagame Tells Rwandans'. *The New Times* (24 January), Kigali.

Ligue des droits de la personne dans la région des Grands Lacs (LDGL), 2007. Expropriation – Le dépit des propriétaires de Batsinda. Online at: http://www.ldgl.org/spip.php?article1721 [date of last access: 3 July 2009].

Leckie, S. and Huggins, C., 2011. *Conflict and Housing, Land and Property Rights: A Handbook on Issues, Frameworks and Solutions*. Cambridge University Press, Cambridge.

Leegwater, M., 2011. 'Sharing Scarcity: Issues of Land Tenure in Southeast Rwanda'. *Natural Resources and Local Livelihoods in the Great Lakes Region: A Political Economy Perspective*, eds, Ansoms, A. and Marysse, S., Palgrave Macmillan, Basingstoke (UK).

Lewis, J. and Knight, J., 1995. *The Twa of Rwanda: Assessment of the Situation of the Twa and Promotion of Twa Rights in Post-War Rwanda*. World Rainforest Movement and International Work Group for Indigenous Affairs.

Longman, T., 2011. 'Limitations to Political Reform: The Undemocratic Nature of Transition in Rwanda'. *Remaking Rwanda: State Building and Human Rights after Mass Violence*, eds, Straus, S. and Waldorf, L., Wisconsin University Press, Wisconsin.

Maguru, L., 2004. 'Les Aigrefins se sont réjouis à faire les détournements'. *Ubumwe* (Kigali), no. 129, [Human Rights Watch translation from the original Kinyarwanda], pp. 3-9.

Mendick, R., 2011. 'Tony Blair, Trips to Africa and an Intriguing Friendship'. *The Telegraph*, 12 Nov 2011. Online at: http://www.telegraph.co.uk/news/politics/tony-blair/8885987/Tony-Blair-trips-to-Africa-and-an-intriguing-friendship.html

Ministry of Agriculture and Animal Resources (MINAGRI), 2012. *Farm Land Use Consolidation in Rwanda: Assessment from the Perspectives of Agriculture Sector*. Kigali, Republic of Rwanda.

Ministry of Finance and Economic Planning (MINECOFIN), 2000. *Rwanda Vision 2020*. Kigali, Republic of Rwanda.

Ministry of Lands, Environment, Forestry, Water and Mines (MINITERE), 2004. *National Land Policy*. Kigali, Republic of Rwanda.

Mullins, C. W. and Rothe, D. L. (2008). *Blood, Power, and Bedlam: Violations of International Criminal Law in Post-Colonial Africa*. Peter Lang, New York

Musoni, E. 2007. 'Military, Police Team Probe Land Ownership'. *The New Times* (28 June), Kigali.

——, 2008. '54,000 hectares of Land to Be Re-distributed in Eastern Province'. *The New Times* (27 January), Kigali.

National Land Tenure Reform Project (NLTRP), 2006. 'Phase 1 of the Land Reform Process for Rwanda: Developing the Strategic Road Map'. *Land Sector Stakeholder Group Mid-Term Briefing Note*. Kigali, Republic of Rwanda.

National Unity and Reconciliation Commission (NURC), 2005. *Land Property and Reconciliation*. NURC/IRC, Kigali, Republic of Rwanda.

Ndikubwayezu, B., 2009. 'Land Issues Feature Prominently Among Kigali Residents' Queries'. *The New Times* (8 May), Kigali.

Newbury, C., 1988. *The Cohesion of Oppression*. Columbia University Press, New York.

Ngarambe, A., 2012. 'Local Leaders in Rubavu Face Probe over Land Grabbing'. *The New Times* (11 January), Kigali.

Ntagungira, G., 2008. 'Not all Re-distributed Land was Grabbed'. *The New Times* (26 March), Kigali.

Office for the Coordination of Humanitarian Affairs (OCHA), 2000. *Rwanda Humanitarian Situation Report March/April 2000*. OCHA, Kigali.

Payne, G., 2011. 'Land Issues in Rwanda's Post Conflict Law Reform'. In: *Local case studies in African land law*, ed. Home, R., Pretoria University Law Press, Pretoria, pp. 1-19. Online at: http://www.pulp.up.ac.za/pdf/2011_16/2011_16.pdf

Percival, V. and Homer-Dixon, T., 1995. *Environmental Scarcity and Violent Conflict: The case of Rwanda*. Trudeau Centre for Peace and Conflict Studies, University of Toronto, Toronto, Canada.

Prunier, G., 1996. *The Rwanda Crisis: History of a Genocide, 1959-1994*. Fountain Publishers, Kampala.

Republic of Rwanda, 2001. *Ministry of Lands, Human Settlement and Environmental Protection*. Brookings Initiative in Rwanda: Land and Human Settlements, Kigali.

——, 2007. *Phase 1 of the Land Reform Process for Rwanda: Results of Preparatory Field Consultations in Four Trial Districts. March-October 2006*. DFID/HTSPE/MINITERE, Kigali.

Reyntjens, F., 2011. 'Constructing the Truth, Dealing with Dissent, Domesticating the World: Governance in Post-genocide Rwanda'. *African Affairs*, vol. 110, no. 438, pp. 1-34.

Rwanda Initiative for Sustainable Development (RISD), 2012. *20 Year Land Lease in Urban Areas too Short-Kairaba*. RISD, Kigali. Online at: http://risdrwanda.org/spip.php?article141

Rose, L., 2005. 'Orphans' Land Rights in Post-War Rwanda: The Problem of Guardianship'. *Development and Change*, vol. 36, no. 5, pp. 919-936.

Sommers, 2012. *Stuck: Rwandan Youth and the Struggle for Adulthood*. Universtity of Georgia Press, Athens (GA).

Tindiwensi, M., 2007. 'Agricultural Activities Banned in Gishwati'. *The New Times* (6 October), Kigali.

——, 2008a. 'Floods: Bigogwe Residents Remember Irish Potatoes'. *The New Times* (6 February), Kigali.

——, 2008b. 'Minister Sets Deadline for Land Allocation in Gishwati'. *The New Times* (2 June), Kigali.

United Nations (UN), 1948. *Universal Declaration of Human Rights*. Online at: http://www.un.org/en/documents/udhr/

United Nations Development Programmes (UNDP), (undated). *Rwanda: Reducing Vulnerability to Climate Change by Establishing Early Warning and Disaster Preparedness Systems and Support for Integrated Watershed Management in Flood Prone Areas.* Project Document. Online at: http://www.undp.org.rw/ProDroc_69648.pdf [date of last access: 15 October 2012].

United Nations High Commissionner for Refugees (UNHCR), 1997. *Report on the Situation of Human Rights in Rwanda.* UNHCR, Geneva.

US Department of State, (2009). *Rwanda: Human Rights Report 2009.* Washington DC.

Uvin, P., (1998). *Aiding Violence: The development enterprise in Rwanda.* Kumarian Press, West Hartford.

van der Laan, J., (2011). *'Going Local': the Case of Minimex.* Agri-Pro-Focus, Arnhem (Nederland).

Van Hoyweghen, S., 2000. 'The Rwanda Villagisation Programme: Resettlement for Reconstruction?' *Conflict and Ethnicity in Central Africa,* ed. Goyvaerts, D., Institute for the Study of the Languages and Cultures of Asia and Africa (ILCAA), Tokyo.

Vansina, J., 2004. *Antecedents to Modern Rwanda: The Nyiginya Kingdom.* University of Wisconsin Press, Madison (WI).

Veldman, M. and Lankhorst, M. (2010). *Socio-Economic Impact of Commercial Exploitation of Rwandese Marshes – A Case Study of Sugar Cane Production in Rural Kigali.* International Land Coalition, Rome.

Verwimp, F. 2005. 'An Economic Profile of Peasant Perpetrators of Genocide: Micro-level Evidence from Rwanda'. *Journal of Development Economics*, vol. 77, no. 2, pp. 297-323.

Wakhungu, J.W., Huggins, C., Nyukuri, E., Lumumba, J. 2010. *Approaches to Informal Urban. Settlements in Africa: Experiences from Kigali and Nairobi.* ACTS Press, Nairobi.

9

The Reorganization of Rural Space in Rwanda

Habitat Concentration, Land Consolidation & Collective Marshland Cultivation

AN ANSOMS, GIUSEPPE
CIOFFO, CHRIS HUGGINS &
JUDE MURISON

> Any attempt to completely plan a village, a city, or, for that matter, a language is certain to run afoul of the same social reality. A village, city, or language is the jointly created, partly unintended product of many, many hands. To the degree that authorities insist on replacing this ineffably complex web of activity with formal rules and regulations, they are certain to disrupt the web in ways they cannot possibly foresee. (Scott, 1998: 256)

Introduction

'How do Rwandans envisage their future? What kind of society do they want to become? What are the transformations needed to emerge from a deeply unsatisfactory social and economic situation?' These are the promising opening questions of the Rwandan Vision 2020 document, which was finalized in July 2000 (GOR – Government of Rwanda, 2000). In the early years of the new millennium, ambitions for economic growth within Rwandan government circles primarily concentrated on the service sector. The first Rwandan PRSP (*Poverty Reduction Strategy Paper*) actually contended that there was a window of opportunity 'to leap-frog the stage of industrialisation and transform [Rwanda's] subsistence economy into a service-sector driven, high value-added information and knowledge-based economy that can compete on the global market' (GOR, 2002: 69). With time, however, policymakers have become increasingly aware of the small likelihood of a knowledge-based service sector absorbing a massive unskilled labour force previously employed in agriculture. Hence, the Rwandan government has turned to agriculture as the main engine of economic growth (see for example EDPRS – Economic Development & Poverty Reduction Strategy 2008-2012 and EDPRS 2012-2016).

In fact, Rwandan policymakers' attention to the agricultural sector is justified: agriculture represents the main economic activity in the country, and it is a source of livelihood for about eighty per cent of the populations (GOR, 2012). However, the way in which benefits and wealth created by agricultural-led growth impact upon the population, depends on how the primary sector is 'upgraded'. The Strategic Plan for the Transformation of Agriculture (SPAT) outlines an operational framework for agricultural sector development. The document focuses on agricultural modernization, intensification, professionalization and enterprise development (GOR, 2004a). The government introduced policies for promoting monocropping and regional crop specialization, land registration and agricultural plot consolidation, combined with a market-oriented approach to be adopted in all the sector's productive activities (MINAGRI – Ministry of Agriculture and Animal Resources, 2011). Such policies are inspired by a concern for improving primary sector efficiency and for realizing economies of scale in the production of agricultural commodities, with the ultimate goal of contributing to economic growth and poverty reduction.

However, the government's vision for a professional, market-driven and efficient agricultural sector appears incompatible with traditional Rwandan habitat and cultivation patterns as well as landownership arrangements (scattered homesteads with scattered fields across different hills) and risk-averse agricultural practices, common among Rwandan peasants. Therefore, Rwandan authorities believe that a profound reorganization of rural space is required. Through the reorganization of human habitat, land tenure, and cultivation systems, the government aims at reconfiguring traditional agricultural systems in line with criteria focusing on efficiency and profit maximization. In this paper, we analyse three of the policies guiding this process: the villagization policy, the land registration and consolidation policy, and the collective marshland cultivation policy. In our conclusion, we argue that these processes of reorganization of rural life – while making economic sense to rural households that are willing and able to insert themselves into the modernization logic – risk endangering the livelihood strategies and reproduction basis of risk-averse smallholder producers. Further research will have to resolve the question of how many will lose their productive assets, and what kind of future they will face in a context of poor non-agricultural job opportunities.

The reorganization of rural space

Habitat concentration

Traditionally, Rwandans do not group together in clearly identifiable villages, but live scattered on the country's many hills. Young men must traditionally ask their fathers for part of the family's land in order to build their own dwellings, a crucial condition for marriage and the transition to adulthood (De Lame, 2005; Sommers, 2012). Subsequently, male heads may – according to their needs and financial resources – expand and improve their homes as they see fit. However, this pattern of scattered living does not tie in with the Government's vision of the spatial organization of a modern State. The government, in fact, aims to rehouse the rural population in grouped houses within clearly delimited settlements – or *imidugudu* (what would be generally called 'a village'[1]) – by the year 2020 (GOR, 2000). Different reasons motivate the villagization policy. First, grouped settlements should facilitate service delivery such as the provision of water and electricity, schools, hospitals. Moreover, imidugudu can be better connected to the broader infrastructural network and might therefore improve households' access to markets and services at the provincial level. In addition, when housing plots are clearly separated from agricultural plots, agricultural land can more easily be consolidated into large plots on which crops can then be cultivated in a synchronized way, with neighbours growing similar crops according to similar cultivation schedules (MINAGRI, 2011).

Villagization programmes (whether compulsory or not) are not new to African countries. Particularly in the aftermath of independence, socialist countries attempted to organize the living patterns and productive systems of rural populations into settlement programmes, agricultural communities, and newly created villages. Two of the most notorious examples are the Ethiopian villagization programme and the Tanzanian *ujamaa* villagization programme, both carried out between the 1960s and the end of the 1980s. Both Ethiopian and Tanzanian planners aimed at breaking with the traditional living and cultivation patterns to strive towards more efficient service delivery, better local administration, and increased agricultural production (de Wet, 1991; Scott, 1998; Gascon, 2007). However, according to Scott, the tacit aim of such programmes is rather the reorganization of 'human communities in order to make them better objects of political control and to facilitate the new forms of communal farming favoured by state policy' (Scott, ibid.: 224).

Planners, therefore, must defy the character of traditional 'social life' which appears 'illegible and resistant to the narrow purposes of the State' (ibid.). These historical examples have utterly failed in their ambition of reorganizing social life and improving overall agricultural production efficiency. Scott (ibid.) adduces this failure to the 'aesthetics' of 'high modernity' that brings planners to treat human settlements, and humans along with them, as standardized units which can be scientifically arranged to 'improve' production, livelihoods and profitability. As colonial administrators before them, planners operated within a standardized model of rural development 'assuming that all peasants would desire roughly the same crop mix, techniques and yields' (ibid.: 228). Scott's critique of the Tanzanian villagization experience is important to understand the Rwandan villagization policy for two main reasons. First, it points to the antagonism between a ruling elites' attempt to bring about social transformations towards a certain image of modernity on

---

[1] In addition to its literal translation as 'village', the term *umudugudu* has since 2006 also been used to refer to a local administration unit, which is now the smallest administrative unit in Rwanda.

the one hand, and the reality of social life on the other, with its web of connections, survival strategies and informal arrangements that exist within rural settings. Second, it gives us an insight into the multiple functions of forced villagization: such programmes do not only follow the modernist imperatives of efficiency and profit maximization; they also call into question the autonomy and initiative of the individual *vis-à-vis* political control by the state apparatus and the administrative machine.

In Rwanda, 'villagization' was introduced as a strategy for resettling refugee households in the aftermath of the violent conflict of 1990-1994. In later years, however, it was used to forcefully re-house non-refugee households, especially in the eastern part of the country. Families were made to burn their houses and move out, often to dwellings or shelters of inferior quality. Different authors analysed the perverse effect of this policy upon the livelihoods and social relations at the local level (see Leegwater 2011; Newbury, 2011). Such critiques basically focused on the lack of the promised service delivery in the new village settings, the loss of agricultural land by resettled people, the increased distance between new houses and farming land, an increased feeling of social insecurity due to increased distance to the fields and the obligation to share life and resources in a new social setting, a dynamic that often triggered the collapse of pre-existing social safety nets (Van Hoyweghen, 1999; Human Rights Watch, 2001; Newbury, 2011; Leegwater, 2011).

The current version of the villagization approach is less strict, however: only newly established households are required to settle at specified sites within grouped communities. Nonetheless, this policy still fails to take account of the needs and means of the populations. Land prices and construction costs at the officially designated umudugudu sites are in fact often prohibitively expensive for rural youth. As noted by Sommers and Uvin (2011: 3): 'regulating the standard size of an umudugudu house helps make the quest toward completing a house virtually impossible for nearly all poor male youth in rural Rwanda.' An additional problem is that the building requirements of a house in the umudugudu are very strict: local authorities determine the minimal size of the house, one is obliged to build a separate kitchen, a stable (in case the household possesses cattle), and the whole house has to be covered with tiles (banana leave roofing is strongly prohibited). Sommers and Uvin (on the basis of research conducted in 2006) recount that male and female youth try to save as much as possible to buy roof tiles, adding that 'what was striking about this situation was how many male youth in rural Rwanda stated that they know they might never complete a roof for their house in their lifetime' (Sommers and Uvin, 2011: 4). Since then, the price of tiles has dramatically increased because of the government's ban on traditional tile- and brick-making (Ansoms and Murison, 2013).

Indeed, the impact of the current habitat concentration policy is particularly strong on youth. Ansoms and Murison (ibid.) found in their research that many young men are obliged to stay with their parents and cannot live independently as adults as they cannot gain productive employment, generate income and afford a house. This represents an important cultural change, but it also follows economic constraints that lead the poorest young adults to not be able to afford rising rents.[2] Others get married in a 'clandestine' way: a young couple, for example, might occupy the new husband's parents' kitchen (generally a separate building, as is required by the current housing policy), even without asking the parents' permission. When a girl becomes pregnant outside of a marriage (an increasingly frequent phenomenon), it is not unusual for the father to move away from his native setting, ashamed of not being able to provide for his family (Sommers, 2012; Ansoms and Murison, 2013).

Land registration and consolidation
As mentioned before, the reorganization of rural habitat also aims at restructuring the way in which agricultural land is cultivated and managed. This aim is further pursued through a profound agricultural sector reform, which is designed to create 'a sustainable agricultural sector that can protect Rwanda from food and nutrition insecurity, by increasing productivity per hectare, and generating additional income through export crop production and well-developed national markets and value-chains [...] This will see the sector transformed into one where farming is seen as a business, rather than subsistence, activity. This will create a sector that uses its comparative advantage, for example in labour-intensive, high-value crops, to compete in open regional and international markets' (MINAGRI, 2010: 8). Key to this vision is the realization of economy-of-scale effects: regional crop specialization, monoculture, land use consolidation and the organization of rural producers into large cooperative structures, (amongst other means) are promoted by the Rwandan government in order to move towards an industrial-commercial model of agriculture.

Land rights are a crucial element in this process. Customary land tenure arrangements are seen by policy makers as inherently insecure, and therefore an obstacle to trigger investments in the agricultural sectors. The solution to this problem lays, in their opinion, in the establishment of legally enforced property rights in a context of a transparent, generally market-driven, land tenure system (MINITERE, 2004). Thereby, the Rwandan government largely aligns to the technocratic approach to land governance – promoted by international donors such as the World Bank – in favour of individualized and private land rights protected by centrally registered legal titles (see e.g. De Soto, 2000; World Bank, 2007; Deininger and Feder, 2009) as a means for increased investments in soil fertility conservation and mechaniszed agriculture (GoR, 2004b). However, Rwanda is somewhat unusual in granting landholders only lease rights,

---

[2] According to Ansoms and Murison (2013), the rent for a two-room house can easily amount to seven thousand Rwandan francs (RwF) per month.

rather than full ownership rights. Rural landowners have 99-year leases, but urban dwellers have much shorter leases, sometimes of just twenty-five years. This technocratic and market-orientated approach to land rights can be contrasted with models which emphasize equity rather than just economic growth, and which include mechanisms to manage the political and social aspects of land tenure patterns, for example through the redistribution of land by the State to landless or land-poor households (Ridell, 2000).

The Government of Rwanda's approach emerged following a long process of consultation. In 1998, the ministerial cabinet put in place an inter-ministerial commission for the development of a land law, headed by the Ministry of Agriculture. It is during this period (1997-1998) that most of the contents of the Land Law were drafted, and the first draft was ready in early January 1999. However, it was 'shelved' until a policy could be formulated to frame the bill.

Preliminary consultative meetings of local administrators, members of local organizations and farmers' representatives were organized through-out the country; they recommended that 'full ownership' of land be given to all landowners. This recommendation was, in the end, ignored in favour of a land lease model. In September 1999, a workshop was held on 'Land Use and Villagization in Rwanda', convened by a Rwandan NGO. This workshop, initiated in a context of distrust between civil society and government, reportedly created greater space for dialogue.

In 2000, the ministry in charge of land began the development of a national land policy, and in November the first national consultation was convened to discuss the first draft of the policy. The conference recom-mended consultations be held at the grassroots level. This process was done through participation of some NGOs working closely with local people in rural areas. The Ministry of Land organised other consultative meetings in all provinces. These meetings tended to involve adminis-trators at the district level, rather than members of the general public (Bledsoe, 2004).

The draft land policy was almost complete by 2001, and was dis-seminated for comments to local and international organizations including the Rural Development Institute, Oxfam GB and others. These comments were incorporated to varying degrees. In particular, concerns over the rights of access to marshlands by the indigenous Batwa community, which were consistently raised by LandNet Rwanda (a group of local and international NGOs) were ignored. In the words of one analyst:

> [...] because the changes envisaged by the land policy are so far-reaching, the government has declared its intention to consult with the population as widely as possible and to modify the policy on the basis of their views. However, the government is very clear on the direction it wishes to take. (Jones, 2003)

From 2001 until the final draft of the land policy and land law, which were sent to the ministerial cabinet for adoption in February 2004, key issues were being debated within government, largely behind closed doors. The fact that a high-priority law spent three years under discussion shows the sensitivity of the issues. The law was promulgated in 2005. It took several years for the required pieces of secondary legislation to be developed to allow implementation to start in 2008. The secondary legislation and procedures for registration of land were developed by an international consulting organization, in close cooperation with the Ministry of Lands and the National Land Centre. The land registration process was preceded by a period of local awareness-raising. However, this process mentioned land 'ownership' rather than leaseholder rights, which meant that many citizens were surprised to receive only leasehold rights, rather than full ownership rights (interviews with local householders, Kigali, June 2010). The 2005 land law (known as the Organic Land Law or OLL) and the 2013 Land Law profoundly reshaped land tenure arrangements in Rwanda. Land registration became compulsory and land transactions are to be regulated through formal legal procedures (GOR, 2005, art. 26). In addition to assigning official leaseholder rights, the land law attempts to tackle the problem of land fragmentation by prohibiting the division of bequeathed land parcels which fall below one hectare (GoR, 2005, art. 20 and GoR, 2013, art. 30). However, this is problematic given that in Rwanda, three quarters of all households have landholdings below one hectare (0.71 hectares per household on average 2000 figures, Jayne *et al.*, 2003), in most cases spread over multiple plots.[3]

Based on the 2005 law and various pieces of supporting legislation, land tenure registration took place across the country, concluding in 2012. The National Land Tenure Reform Programme (NLTRP) was designed by international consultants, in conjunction with Rwandan government staff, and received considerable funding from the UK's Department for International Development (DFID) and other major donors. In contrast to neighbouring countries such as for example Uganda, the implementation of land registration in Rwanda has been extremely rapid. Indeed, the highest levels of the Rwandan government saw land reform as a high-priority issue, and directed the Ministry of Land to act quickly. Moreover, the government's formidable administrative capabilities were efficiently deployed during the registration process. Land committees, incorporating local authorities and citizens, were established at the cell level to coordinate the process.[4] Local dispute adjudication committees were formed to resolve disputes related to registration, reducing the costs and time loss of dispute resolution in front of formal courts. Local teams of specially trained para-surveyors oversaw the delineation of plot boundaries using

---

[3] On the basis of a 2001 representative dataset, Ansoms et al. calculated that an average farm disposes of 0,82 hectares, on average divided over 3,15 plots (Ansoms et al., 2008).

[4] The cellule is the second-smallest administrative unit in Rwanda, larger than the umudugudu.

high-resolution aerial photography in combination with site-visits. These innovative approaches increased the speed and transparency of the process. However, as discussed in further detail below, there is a possibility that local dispute resolution committees may have been unable to prevent some disputes being suppressed by powerful members of the community, especially administrators.

Once the plots have been delineated, landholders can obtain a lease. In the countryside, leases last up to ninety-nine years[5] (and they can be renewed), while shorter-term leases – generally for twenty years – are provided in urban centres (RISD, 2012). Each parcel of land has a primary leaseholder, while other family members (usually the leaseholder's spouse or children) may be registered as having an interest in the parcel. Co-ownership is also possible, for example by husband and wife. By law, those with an interest in a parcel must give consent before any transaction can take place, such as the sale of a parcel. The land tenure reform exercise has widely been described as a success (Ali, Deiniger and Goldstein, 2011), particularly from the perspective of women's land rights (Daley, Dore-Weeks and Umuhoza, 2010).

It is likely that the intimate involvement of DFID and international consultants in the land registration process, as well as the high priority accorded to this process by the RPF leadership, helped to reduce land grabbing by powerful actors immediately prior to the land registration process. However, it remains to be seen whether the registration process has led to universally improved tenure security at the micro-level. The National Land Tenure Reform Programme (NLTRP) reported very low rates of disputes during the registration process – less than one percent of all landholding claims were disputed – and those involved have stated that 'most land disputes that have come before the new sector authorities have been easily resolved' (Sagashya and English, 2010). However, there is evidence from outside of the NLTRP that disputes still exist: the number of land-related cases referred to the National Ombudsman's office more than doubled from 2009-10 (two hundred and twelve cases) to 2011-12 (five hundred and twenty-five cases). The Ombudsman's staff attributed this increase to intensified competition for land due to the registration process, and 'negligence' and 'corruption" by local authorities (Ndoli, 2012). This was confirmed in Ansoms and Murison's research (2011), where respondents in several settings referred to cases of existing land conflicts during the land registration process that were not considered as 'conflictual' by the registration authorities. It therefore remains unclear to what extent the disputes encountered during the registration process nationwide were indeed officially registered and 'resolved', or whether they were rather temporarily quashed by authorities, in which case they may re-emerge in the future.

---

[5] Marshlands, however, are subject to different regulations for with regards to leaseholding.

Despite the generally sound design of the registration mechanisms, some citizens have raised a number of broader concerns. Part of these concerns relate to the way in which the land registration programme was communicated to the larger public. People expected that registration would give them ownership rights, and many were unpleasantly surprised to find out that they are leaseholders rather than landowners. Rural leaseholders must also pay a small fee before being given the definitive leasehold document (generally 1000 RwF per plot, or about $1.5). In research conducted by Ansoms and Murison (2011), economically better-off interviewees had often paid part of the due fees, mostly for their larger land plots, or for plots on which they feared a counterclaim. However, land titles did not seem a priority for poorer landholders. In fact, only few of the poorer landholders had paid the fees to obtain formal land titles at the time of the research. When purchase of official land titles took place, it was often in response to local authorities' pressures (Ansoms and Murison, 2011). This aligns with the observation of the Director of the National Land Centre that the rate of collection of the documents is 'very low' (Kanyesigye, 2012).

In addition, legal requirements can pose two further constraints on the land registration process (ibid.). First, people will have to register a land transfer, which for larger land plots would be accompanied by an additional cost. This might prove to be an obstacle to continued formal land registration and an incentive for informal sales out of the legal context. Needless to say, a large number of illegal transactions would undermine the whole land registration process. Second, a major impeding factor for land registration is landholders' reticence to reveal the true size of their extensions: reticence towards researchers; towards fellow community members;[6] and most certainly towards the authorities. In Ansoms and Murison's research, better-off (and some poorer) interviewees in various settings expressed their worries that the newly registered titles could be used as a basis for taxation. Moreover, poorer population groups were worried that a clear track-record of who-owns-what would be a facilitating tool for the Rwandan government's land consolidation ambitions (Ansoms and Murison, 2011). Land consolidation is a process through which plots in a given area are brought together to grow food crops in a synchronized fashion. Many of the interviewees considered such a process to be problematic. Different socio-economic categories have divergent interests, which makes agreements on joint cultivation projects nearly impossible (see also Ansoms, 2010).

Reorganizing the marshland
The swamplands represent an important locus of spatial reorganization in rural areas. As is the case for hillside land, swamplands are also subject

---

[6] Rural inhabitants of a particular setting often have a rather accurate idea of the extent of each other's property. However, a person can always own an additional plot from an inheritance or a purchase in another setting. People generally prefer to hide this from their neighbours.

to land consolidation. However, in comparison to the hills, a different approach is adopted. In line with the 2005 land law, no private property rights on marshland plots can be allocated to individuals (GOR, 2005). The Rwandan government has made marshlands available as a concession to private investors. In other cases, the national government has mandated local authorities to consolidate the traditional patchwork of marshland exploitations into larger plots of land to be cultivated in a collective fashion. In a first phase, marshland plots were given into concession to farmer's associations (this started in 2005-2007). These associations have recently (2009-2011) been obliged to group themselves into officially recognized cooperatives. Such reorganization of marshland areas has also entailed a change in cultivation practices, as farmers are no longer allowed to combine different crops but have to specialise in market-oriented 'high-value' crops such as rice or maize, defined by the government.

In this section, we focus on a case study of one particular setting in Rwanda's Southern Province to describe the impact of the national policy on the livelihoods of the rural population engaged in marshland production. The research data was gathered in 2006, 2007 and 2011 by Ansoms and Murison (2011) through in-depth focus group interviews with a variety of socio-economic groups in a particular umudugudu.

The story of a marshland: from Saudi Arabia to Darfur

In 'old times',[7] the marshland was heavily overgrown with invasive papyrus, and used for hunting and grazing cattle.[8] Between 1974 and 1976, the population began to cut down the papyrus – dangerous work, as peasants would risk being attacked by the lions living in the area. The available space in the marshland was so large that nearly anyone who desired to cultivate could occupy a plot. One of our informants (Focus group 2011) highlighted how 'people of all ethnic groups were there', and had a very good harvest. Peasants were involved in a *métayage* (sharecropping) system with the authorities who collected taxes at harvest time. The marshland was actually referred to as 'Saudi Arabia', pointing to the richness that the local population extracted from the marshland and the importance of this space for local livelihoods.

In the past, access to land in the marshland depended on the ability to clear a plot. The hardwork involved in plot clearance, compounded by frequent floods, represented the main 'entry cost'. Although at the national level, the Habyarimana government in the 1980s frequently urged peasants to group themselves into cooperatives,[9] this was not the

---

[7] Our interviewees did not mention whether this referred to pre- or post-independence history.

[8] For a more historical perspective on agricultural changes in this time period, see Leurquin, P., 1963. 'Agricultural change in Ruanda-Urundi: 1945-1960'. *Food Research Institute Studies*, vol. 4, no. 1, pp. 39-89.

[9] See e.g. Jeffremovas, V., 2002. *Brickyards to Graveyards: From Production to Genocide in Rwanda*. State University of New York Press, New York.

case in this marshland, as none of our interviewees referred to collective forms of cultivation before 1994. During the civil war (1990-1993) and genocide in 1994, people abandoned the marshland.[10] In 1997, the marshland witnessed an attempted production revival through a World Food Programme (WFP) project. As the marshland was said to be used as a refuge by Hutu extremists, the WFP project security was ensured by a military unit of the Rwandan army. This unit was led by Eugene,[11] who took advantage of his position in the military to gain control over the marshland management when the project ended. Eugene left around 1999, following adverse weather conditions and the flooding of a large part of the marshland (Focus group 2006).

The flood meant that the population had to once more clear up the marshland. Many did so, and restarted cultivating food crops (beans, sorghum, cassava, sweet potatoes), mainly for their own consumption and for the market, when production was sufficient to do so. In the early 2000s, however, the commune intervened and decided to start a campaign to 'help the population find a project that could bring them money' (Focus group 2007), through more market-oriented production. In 2002 the commune handed the control over a large part of the marshland to a local entrepreneur,[12] Alphonse, who had gathered external funding to increase agricultural production.[13] One year later, Eugene returned to the Marshland and claimed that Alphonse had appropriated his area (referring to the area previously included in the WFP project). Eugene was able to make his case to the commune (now district) authorities and to reinstate his control over the old WFP parcels. Some interviewees suggested that it was Eugene's link to the military that enabled him to reclaim the land.[14] Local peasants divided their allegiances between the two claimants, which resulted in increased tensions. However, the antagonism did not turn into overt violence.

For their part, Alphonse and Eugene organized marshland production differently. Alphonse allowed people to cultivate the same plots that they had dug prior to his arrival, and serviced the people with seeds, manure and fertilizer. To this he added two major conditions: the population had to grow only maize; and they had to sell the harvest to him at a predetermined price.[15] Some peasants considered such price to be decent,

---

[10] For more information on the impact of the war on agriculture production, see Sperling, L., 2001. 'The Effect of the Civil War on Rwanda's Bean Seed System and Unusual Bean Diversity'. *Biodiversity and Conservation*, vol. 10, no. 6, pp. 989-1009.

[11] We use pseudonyms for all names in this chapter.

[12] The formal way through which the management of the marshland had been granted to Alphonse was not clear during our research.

[13] Some interviewees refer to an NGO; others mention that Alphonse got inputs from the Rwandan government's Rural Sector Support Project. Probably both were involved at some point.

[14] Some mention that his marshland project served to provide an income-generating activity to demobilized soldiers.

[15] For a comparative study see Nabahungu, N. L. and Visser, S. M., 2011. 'Contribution of

and noted that Alphonse had provided them with a market for maize, which was difficult to find. Others thought Alphonse was 'taking' [their] production not fulfilling his promise to pay a right price. Peasants who attempted to surreptitiously take their maize harvest from the marshland were roughly dealt with by the local security forces operating on behalf of Alphonse. When farmers refused to hand over their harvest because of price disagreements, farmers claimed that Alphonse used 'force' to 'grab our production' (Focus group 2007).

When the government of Rwanda began promoting associations as a means to collectively increase and organize production in the marshlands, Alphonse organized the peasants into groups. However, participants of several focus groups (2007 research) referred to these as 'phantom associations' that only served as a showcase to the authorities. Our research in 2007 reveals that Alphonse asked peasants for financial contributions when setting up the association ('at some point he asked us 1000 RwF as a rent for a five year period', but shortly thereafter 'he asked again 1000 RwF and later again 1700 RwF'). Peasants reported irregularities in the allocation of user-rights, through associations, in the marshland. One peasant recalled how Alphonse had his *préférés*, generally people from outside the umudugudu, who had many plots and large harvests. Alphonse also set a fixed cultivation programme and calendar to which peasants had to conform. At the end of this reorganization, about one third of peasants had lost access to the marshland. Our interviewees identified multiple causes: the imposition of crop choice and cycle, exclusion during the creation of peasant associations, during further marshland reorganization.

On the other side of the marshland, Eugene had a collective management approach to agricultural production right from the moment he returned (2003-2004) and encouraged the population to cultivate collectively in groups. Under his control, he created a cooperative ('cooperative A' onwards) that grouped about sixty associations (approximate figure; focus group 2007) encompassing all villages located around the marshland. The cooperative organized the work of the associations, each of them cultivating a specific crop. In line with government policy, production was carried also on under monocropping arrangements. The association fees were in 2006 rather low, therefore accessible to poorer farmers. However, the system was soon changed to a one-off fee of 100,000 RwF to be paid by each association,[16] in addition to an annual

---

(contd) Wetland Agriculture to Farmers' Livelihoods in Rwanda'. *Ecological Economics*, vol. 71, no. C, pp. 4-12; and Nabahungu, N. L. and Visser, S. M., 2011. 'Farmers' Knowledge and Perceptions of Agricultural Wetland Management in Rwanda'. *Land Degradation and Development* (July).

[16] This amount was due, regardless of the land allocated and regardless of the number of members. The exact destination of this money was unclear to most focus group participants. Some mentioned that part of the money would remain at the individual association's disposal; others mentioned that it served to pay the needs of the cooperative (referring to operating costs); still others claimed that it went into the pockets of the associational

fee (referred to by our respondents as 'tax rate') of 1200 RwF per member.

Despite their respective differences, these two systems of access to the marshland organized through the granting of management rights to particular associations or stakeholders, presented important common aspects. First, in both systems, peasants had to leave their associations when unable to work. While in such cases better-off peasants could hire labour to work on their plots, this represented a crucial constraint for poorer categories. Second, the better-informed had an advantage in joining an association at earlier times (when marshland was still relatively abundant). Moreover, the financial fees involved impeded poorer farmers from joining or remaining members of a marshland association. Such fees were collected several times, often without the communication of a clear reason. In addition, well-connected farmers instrumentalised the system for personalized control over marshland areas.

In 2006, Alphonse left the marshland under unclear circumstances.[17] Immediately after his departure, the peasants freely occupied their marshland plots and cultivated what they wanted. However, in 2007 this again changed after the district gave control over the marshland to a cooperative (further referred to as 'cooperative B' – see below). Under cooperative B's management, the marshland was redivided into plots of equal size. Initially, the membership fee was set at 3000 RwF but shortly afterwards it was raised to 5000 RwF (some members said that they had even paid 6500 RwF). High entry fees meant that the marshland became only accessible to a certain category of peasants. As a result, poorer peasants who had been able to produce under Alphonse's system, found themselves excluded. At the same time, rumours spread that additional plots were available to those wealthy farmers who could afford to register under family members' name, and that some association *encadreurs* did not have to pay the fees (Focus group 2007).

When we returned to the marshland in 2011, the controversies around cooperative B's functioning had calmed, despite membership fees being raised to 20,000 RwF, more than a monthly salary for daily labour activity (600-700 RwF per day). Poorer research participants seemed to have reluctantly acquiesced in the situation. Under cooperative B, farmers individually cultivated the crops identified by the cooperative (maize and rice). The cooperative provided maize seeds as farmers were not allowed to use seeds from previous harvests.[18] At the time of our research the cooperative was buying maize production from its members at 400 RwF

[contd] presidents and the cooperative coordinators while the local peasants had no clue what purpose it served. The financial requirement was described by a participant as 'a delicate problem' as many people did not find the necessary means.

[17] There are different versions of why Alphonse departed, including that he was pushed by the district authorities; he had a disagreement with a local NGO; and his contract with the district had ended. In 2011, our respondents gave an entirely new version of events: they claimed it was Eugene who had been behind the 'chasing of Alphonse', denouncing him to the district authorities for not having treated the local population correctly.

[18] The marshland, in fact, was involved in a RADA project for seed multiplication.

per kilo, of which 100 RwF was taken by the cooperative for management costs. Nearly all our interviewees who were member of this cooperative, seemed satisfied by this price, 'more than we could get elsewhere'. While maize was guarded by cooperative security forces in order to avoid it being 'stolen' by producers, peasants were allowed to take rice home against a contribution of 1000 RwF to the cooperative.

The rather positive appreciation of cooperative B's management stands in sharp contrast with local people's assessment of the organizational arrangements of cooperative A, managed by Eugene. Apparently, between 2007 and 2009 there were no clear rules on peasants' financial contribution to the cooperative. One interviewee recalled how at some point, in 2008, they forcibly had to contribute 5000 RwF for Eugene's marriage, 'of which we are not even sure if it took place'. 'Those who did not contribute could be chased from the marshland' (Focus group 2011). However, in 2009 the cooperative was 'restructured'.[19] At that point, all members had to pay 2000 RwF as a tax per plot, 10,000 RwF per block as *part social* (financial share of the cooperative), and another 10,000 RwF per block to keep access rights after the harvest. As a result, on the one hand, dozens of households could not pay the fee and lost access to their marshland plots. On the other hand, many of those who paid part of the fee (hoping to pay the other part after the harvest), received a different plot than the one they previously occupied, often located in the marshland area called 'Darfur',[20] an area subject to frequent floods.

While poorer peasants lost access to the marshland, better-off categories – often not even from the local setting – largely exploited the opportunity provided by this reorganization. Some obtained plots 'subscribing fictitious people that did not really exist', while an individual from the army was known to have at least one hundred seventy plots. Locals ironically identified the military group associated to Eugene as 'partners of the cooperative', and as such its members appropriated a large zone consisting of one hundred forty plots (Focus group 2007). These better-off categories often employed local labourers to harvest their production and although such labour force was paid more than average agricultural wage (600-700 RwF[21] per day), it often consisted of peasants who previously occupied marshland plots but were not able to buy their way into the marshland after its reorganization.

Access to land was not the only issue in the newly reorganized marshland. In cooperative A, for example, peasants who had managed to secure access to land also experienced problems. The cooperative

---

[19] Our informants referred to 'the military' as the one who reorganised access to the marshland: 'they came and put us in a bad part of the marshland, in Darfur.'

[20] Many of them decided to no longer invest in the marshland shortly thereafter, given that they could barely cultivate these plots, facing the continuous risk of a flooding destroying the harvest.

[21] As a basis of comparison: a kg of beans cost 450 RwF per kg in the beginning of the season, and 250-300 RwF around harvest time (Focus group 2011).

promised a price of 250 RwF/Kg of harvested maize. However, at harvest time, the price was set at 80 RwF/Kg, about half of what peasants would have got selling their produce to individual traders. Even at such a low price, the cooperative did not find a market for the produce, so it milled the maize into flour and allowed peasants to collect an amount of flour. In the 'Darfur' part of the marshland, people cultivated beans that they were allowed to take home if the multiple floodings did not ruin the harvest before it was ready. Nonetheless, they had to pay the same membership fees or risked to be evicted from the marshland.

In 2010, rumours suggested that cooperative A had gone bankrupt, and Eugene withdrew as a president. After that, a new committee took over the organization, changed the cooperative name and elected a new president. However, as the following conversation shows, peasants who had experienced poor associational management, as in the example of co-op A, had become highly disillusioned about new marshland reorganizations.

A: Even though the military people are no longer members of the committee, we do not hope to get plots in the marshland.

B: Oh, but if you would approach them [the new committee] with money, you would have a plot because there will be reorganizations of the marshlands all the time.

C: Yes, they are really thirsty for money. If you have 35,000 RwF, you will get a parcel.

We: Given that the marshland is fully occupied, where would they find those plots?

All: Oh, but they would definitely arrange themselves so that they would find such space [ironical tone].

(Focus group discussion, 2011)

Reorganizing the marshland, re-structuring social life
Since the first reorganization in 1999, the system of production deployed by local peasants in the marshland – based on clearance capacity and food production – gradually became replaced by market relations and top-down cooperative arrangements, introduced by changes in the productive organization of such areas. Such shift from traditional to 'modern' practices had important consequences on the livelihoods of local communities.

First, whereas the initial entry barriers to cultivate the marshland were physical capacity to cultivate and land availability, the associational/cooperative system introduced two new elements in the negotiation over marshland user rights: financial capacity and personal connections. Farmers had (and still have) to make significant financial contributions to enter marshland associations (in the first instance) and cooperatives (as from 2009 onwards). In the case under analysis, while financial contributions were initially still relatively affordable, they soon reached virtually prohibitive prices for smallholder farmers. Thus, the reorganization of the marshland has resulted in a reorganization of access to marshland plots to the disadvantage of poorer social classes. On the other hand, well-connected and better-off farmers managed to gain access to more plots than they were entitled to, and often in the better parts of the marshland.

Second, small farmers who managed to pay the membership fees and to access a plot in the marshland were not allowed to take part in any decision-making process within cooperatives. On the contrary, while the rhetoric of cooperative management is paired with the imperative of 'participation', such assumption seems not to be borne out by the facts. Actually, while cooperative B management met some of the peasants' needs, the management of cooperative A was a complete failure (see Ansoms and Murison, 2012). Farmers were bluntly denied access rights despite having paid access fees. They were flagrantly exploited when – despite a good agricultural season – they earned less than they had initially invested. Even when cooperative A management failures led to an organizational restructuring (with the instalment of a new committee), many people had lost all hope that they would be handled fairly by the new committee.

Third, the top-down, compulsory choice of the crop and its cycle, dramatically changed peasants' cultivation practices. Both cooperatives imposed crop types and the use of particular seeds upon farmers, without providing (at least to our knowledge) any crop insurance. After our research in 2011, we came to know that in that same year a flood ruined the entire maize harvest. Practically, this not only meant that people lost all their harvest, but they were unable to recuperate their expenditures on seeds and fertilizer. Furthermore, the cooperative imposes the cultivation of commercially-oriented crop types with long cultivation cycles. As a result, poorer farmers cannot use their marshland production as an 'emergency' food source as they used to do before the reorganization took place. In addition, collective cultivation implies fixed cultivation schemes. This represents an important constraint for poorer farmers, whose livelihood strategies are highly differentiated in their continued search for petty jobs and revenues. They may lack the time to invest in marshland production when being confronted with immediate needs.

Fourth, the harvest has to be handed over to the cooperative who decides what happens to it, and looks for a suitable market. This situation is compounded by the virtually non-existent bargaining power of small peasants on produce prices *vis-à-vis* cooperative management. While selling to the cooperative may provide a good price (see the case of cooperative B), inefficient management and volatile prices on local and regional markets mean that the price paid by cooperatives (see cooperative A) to farmers may be well below market prices. On top of this, the poorer groups of peasants working on the marshland are often confronted with immediate cash constraints and cannot afford to wait for the cooperative to find a suitable market for their produce. As a result, they may be obliged to take loans during the cultivation season, which they have to pay back with interest at harvest time, which further increases their financial burden operating as cooperative members.

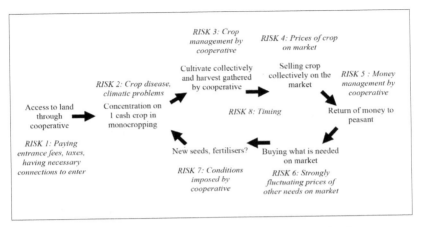

Fig 1 The system of production in cooperatives and associated risk
(Source: Ansoms, A. and Murison, J, 2012)

Fifth, marshlands are no longer fulfilling their traditional role of 'food safety nets'. The monocropping policy has limited the variations of food types that smallholder farmers have access to. As a result, they are increasingly dependent upon the market to get access to other food crops. However, prices on those markets are highly volatile; and the overall trend of food price rises of the last years has generally not been matched by an equally substantial increase in peasants' daily income. As a result, people have become less food secure. They are now dependent upon an unstable market to buy food that they used to cultivate themselves in the past.

Sixth, farmers must exclusively rely on the cooperative for access to inputs such as seeds and fertilizers and, in most cases, they are not allowed to regenerate seeds from their harvests. Instead, they are obliged to buy new seeds.[22] The new system of cooperative access to productive inputs in the marshland is problematic in two ways. First, cooperative managers hold a monopoly on the local provision of agricultural inputs, which might open opportunities for abusing such a dominant position. Second, peasants have to deny their locally-built knowledge about cultivation cycles and local eco-systems, and have to submit themselves to the experiments the cooperative decides to engage in. However, when these experiments go wrong (and this occurs regularly) farmers bear the burden of harvest failure.

---

[22] On this topic more generally, see Pritchard, M. F., 2013. 'Land, Power and Peace: Tenure Formalization, Agricultural Reform and Livelihood Insecurity in Rural Rwanda'. *Land Use Policy*, vol. 30, no. 1, pp. 186-196.

Overall, the cooperative conditions on access to and cultivation of the marshlands have often resulted in the poorer categories of peasants being obliged to give up marshland cultivation. Even in the case of cooperative B – a relative success story of sound and transparent management – increased output where available only to those who could afford to pay their way into the marshland. In the case of cooperative A, poorer peasants were flagrantly and bluntly exploited. Therefore, we may conclude that the reorganization of the marshland contributed to the replication and even reinforcement of structural forms of poverty and inequality within but also beyond the marshland arena. Interviewees referred to pre-existing socio-economic categories to differentiate between those who had profited (the already better-off) and those who had lost out (the already poor) in marshland use and redistribution.

Conclusion

Rwanda is a small country with an increasing population overwhelmingly involved in small-scale agricultural activities. The government's ambitions to deal with this situation involve a profound reorganization of agricultural space, which also impacts access to land, agricultural inputs and the organization of labour. This chapter has shown that such reorganization cannot leave social relations unaffected: changing dynamics of access to and control of natural resources and agricultural production call into question the effects of changes on social differentiation within rural populations. As we have seen, the reorganization of rural life and changes in patterns of land use and access open up important social questions not only about youth's transition to adulthood (Sommers, 2012), but also regarding broader social relations of production in the countryside. While better-off rural actors, in fact, might manage to pay their way into the system (being able to purchase a plot in the umudugudu and buy roof tiles, to register land, or to pay membership fees for the cooperative), poorer social categories are left in a limbo where older forms of life and production are no longer available in the growing space of 'modernity'.

The result is likely to be a redistribution of power and wealth in favour of richer farmers in the agricultural sector. This means that despite the rhetorical emphasis on smallholder farming in the agricultural reform, and the delivery of subsidized inputs (notably seeds and fertilizer) to smallholder farmers as cooperative members, the impacts of the reorganization policies are likely to be highly differentiated amongst smallholders. While some may prosper, others will accumulate debts which may lead to the sales of their productive assets (notably agricultural land). In the lack of credible non-agricultural employment opportunities, a likely scenario is the expansion of a class of landless unskilled labourers. Such development may impede upward social mobility, especially for the youth who, even when they have access to higher education, lack opportunity in non-agricultural sectors (see also Sommers, 2012).

Broad-based growth founded on small-scale agricultural activity appears as an appealing alternative to industrial agriculture for Rwanda, but also more generally, for Sub-Saharan Africa. This could be achieved through a thorough evaluation of the productive potential of various socioeconomic peasant categories and search for mechanisms to activate it. In line with this thinking, the relevant scholarly literature points to viable policy alternatives to the large-scale biased model and highlights the way in which such alternatives have been 'sabotaged' in the recent past. Akram-Lodhi (2008: 471), for example, denounces that smallholder agriculture is now declared unviable, after 'smallholders [have been systematically undermined] by disinvesting and exposing them to "free" market forces on an uneven playing field'. Cribb (2010) observes how a shift from public to private-sector investment in agricultural innovation has stimulated the development of a technology that is tailor-made for a high-energy (large-scale) model of farming. He further notes how 'science has largely neglected the equally promising but far less understood low-input systems [that characterise smallholder agriculture]' (Cribb, 2010: 133). Moyo (2008: 23) argues in the same vein that 'the concentration of public resource allocations for agricultural technological progress as well as for market protection has been directed at [large-scale agrarian capitalist farming], particularly the export farmers'. He concludes that 'this is at the expense of broad-based transformations of farming techniques and institutions'. Therefore, the choice for an agricultural model based on smallholder farming is not just a matter of short-term fixes, but it also requires a profound investment in the restructuring of production relations and public institutions. Besides 'romantic' ideas of peasant family farming, we argue for thorough and consistent investments in the development of a smallholder farming base, the productive potential of which will continue to deliver poor yields if not appropriately supported by funding and research.

A first pro-smallholder policy initiative might shift the focus of research and policies to techniques that lower the capital-to-labour ratio (for example by introducing new land/financial capital-saving techniques that allow smallholders to increase their productivity). Indeed, broad-based agricultural growth should be focused on an acknowledgement of the low opportunity cost of labour and the high opportunity cost of capital that small-scale peasants face.

Another possible way forward is to identify and remove the institutional constraints that prevent smallholders from accessing capital at a relatively low cost. Providing access, at the (most) local level, to credit and risk-insurance mechanisms could enhance peasants' capacity for coping with risk and uncertainty related to new types of agriculture. The ambition of the Rwandan policymakers to strongly involve the private sector in local credit mechanisms may restrict accessibility to these resources for many small-scale peasants with an unfavourable risk profile (i.e. those unable to provide collateral as a guarantee).

A third key strategy is to facilitate smallholders' access to markets, increase the number of marketing options available to them, and to improve their bargaining position. In this respect, Rwandan cooperatives often function poorly and not infrequently they adopt coercive methods to oblige farmers to sell their crops collectively. Instead, smallholders should have ownership over the collective mechanisms whereby they may profit from exchange opportunities in the market. This may be achieved through putting in place effective mechanisms of farmer-initiated cooperative participation and collective bargaining instead of 'formal' cooperative arrangements centred on the initiative of a few 'big men' and the coercive 'mobilization' of farmers by the State.

Fourth, it is important to incentivize local small-scale entrepreneurs to invest accumulated surpluses from agricultural production in non-farming, job-generating economic activities. Although the often informal character of small rural enterprises remains to be addressed, such initiatives would offer opportunity for (decent) wages for the rural youth, favouring the redistribution of wealth towards the poorer social categories. The current government's effort to incentivize non-farming enterprises is laudable, but its strategy of 'formalization of the informal' has burdensome consequences for the poorest categories (Ansoms and Murison, 2013).

Finally, and probably most importantly, policy makers and researchers should reassess the importance of local knowledge and know-how. For generations, Rwandan farmers have survived in extremely challenging conditions. They have adapted themselves to increasing population pressure, to crop diseases, to climate changes, to multiple risks and challenges. They should therefore be considered as true partners in the elaboration of rural development policies, and not as simple recipients that have to be 'taught' how to insert themselves in the modern age. Otherwise, one risks that policy measures and regulations promote the 'esthetic' of modernity (Scott, 1998), while being instrumentalised by local and national elites – paying lip-service to the 'appearance' of development – to reinforce their own power and wealth.

Acknowledgements

This chapter is partially a compilation of several previously published papers. We thank the journals for their permission to republish parts of the original papers.

Ansoms, A. and Rostagno, D., 2012. 'Rwanda's *Vision 2020* halfway through: What the eye does not see'. *Review of African Political Economy*, vol. 39, no. 133, pp. 427-450.

Ansoms, A. and Murison, J., 2012. 'De "Saoudi" au "Darfour": L'histoire d'un marais au Rwanda'. In: *L'Afrique des Grands Lacs: Annuaire 2011-2012*, eds. Reyntjens, F., Vandeginste, S. and Verpoorten, M., L'Harmattan, Paris, pp. 349-369.

Bibliography

Ali, D. A., Deininger, K. and Goldstein, M., 2011. 'Environmental and Gender Impacts of Land Tenure Regularization in Africa: Pilot evidence from Rwanda'. *World Bank Policy Research Paper* 5765. World Bank, Washington DC.

Akram-Lodhi, A. H., 2008. '(Re)imaging Agrarian Relations? The World Development Report 2008: Agriculture for Development. *Development and Change*, vol. 39, no. 6, pp. 1145-1161.

Ansoms, A., Verdootd, A. and Van Ranst, E. 2008. 'The Inverse Relationship between Farm Size and Productivity in Rural Rwanda'. *Discussion Paper 2008.9*. Institute of Development Policy and Management, Antwerp, Belgium.

Ansoms, A., 2010. 'Views from Below on the Pro-poor Growth Challenge : The Case of Rural Rwanda'. *African Studies Review*, vol. 53, no. 2, pp. 97-123.

Ansoms, A. and Murison, J., 2012. 'De "Saoudi" au "Darfour": L'histoire d'un marais au Rwanda'. *L'Afrique des Grands Lacs: Annuaire 2011-2012*, eds, Reyntjens, F., Vandeginste, S. and Verpoorten, M., L'Harmattan, Paris, pp. 349-369.

———, 2013. 'Formalising the informal in Rwanda: From artisanal to modern brick and tile ovens'. *Informal Economy, Vulnerabilities and Popular Security Enhancing Practices*, eds, Lemaître, A., Hillenkamp, I. and Lapeyre, F., Oxford University Press, Oxford.

Bledsoe, D., 2004. *Republic of Rwanda Land Policy and Law, Trip Report: Findings and Recommendations*. RDI/USAID/MINITERE.

Cribb, J., 2010. *The Global Food Crisis and What We Can Do about It*. University of California Press, Berkeley and Los Angeles.

Daley, E., Dore-Weeks, R. and Umuhoza, C., 2010. 'Ahead of the Game: Land Tenure Reform in Rwanda and the Process of Securing Women's Land Rights'. *Journal of Eastern African Studies*, vol. 4, no. 1, pp. 131-152.

Deininger, K. and Feder, G., 2009. 'Land Registration, Governance, and Development: Evidence and Implications for Policy'. *World Bank Research Observer*, vol. 24, no. 2, pp. 233-266.

De Lame, D., 2005. *A Hill among a Thousand: Transformations and Ruptures in Rural Rwanda*. University of Wisconsin Press, Madison (WI).

De Soto, H., 2000. *The Mistery of Capital: Why Capitalism Triumphs in the West and Fails Everywhere Else*. Basic Books, New York.

de Wet, C. (1991). 'Some Socio-economic Consequences of Villagization Schemes in Africa, and the Future of "betterment villages" in the "new South Africa"'. *Development Southern Africa*, vol. 8, no. 1, pp. 3-17.

Gascon, A. 2007. 'Les modifications coercitives du peuplement en Éthiopie: Staline et Pol Pot en Afrique ?' *L'information géographique*, vol. 1, no. 71, pp. 27-46.

Government of Rwanda (GOR), 2000. *Rwanda Vision 2020*. Ministry of Finance and Economic Planning (MINECOFIN), Kigali.

——, 2002. *Poverty Reduction Strategy Paper*. National Poverty Reduction Programme, Ministry of Finance and Economic Planning (MINECOFIN), Kigali.

——, 2004a. *Strategic Plan for Agricultural Transformation in Rwanda*. Ministry of Agriculture and Animal Resources (MINAGRI), Kigali.

——, 2004b. *National Land Policy*. [Draft, January].Ministry of Lands, Environment, Forestry, Water and Natural Resources, Kigali.

——, 2005. *Organic Law no. 08/2005 of 14/7/2005 Determining the Use and Management of Land in Rwanda*. Kigali.

——, 2012. *The Evolution of Poverty in Rwanda from 2000 to 2011: Results from the Household Surveys (EICV)*. National Institute of Statistics (NIS), Kigali.

——, 2013. *Law no. 43/2013 of 16/06/2013 Governing Land in Rwanda*. Kigali.

Human Rights Watch, 2001. *Uprooting the Rural Roor in Rwanda*. Human Rights Watch, New York.

Jayne, T. S., Yamano, T., Weber, M. *et al.*, .2003. 'Smallholder Income and Land Distribution in Africa: Implications for Poverty Reduction Strategies'. *Food Policy*, vol. 28, no. 3, pp. 253-275.

Jones, L. (2003). 'Giving and Taking Away: the Difference between Theory and Practice Regarding Property in Rwanda'. In: *Returning Home: Housing and Property Restitution Rights for Refugees and Displaced Persons*, ed. Leckie, S., Transnational Publishers, New York.

Kanyesigye, F., 2012. We Want to See Land Transfer Fees Changed or Reduced – Nkurunziza. *The New Times* (16 July). Online at: http://www.newtimes.co.rw/news/index.php?i=15055&a=55935

Leegwater, M., 2011. 'Sharing Scarcity: Issues of Land Tenure in Southeast Rwanda. *Natural Resources and Local Livelihoods in the Great Lakes Region: A Political Economy Perspective*, eds, Ansoms, A. and Marysse, S., Palgrave Macmillan, Basingstoke (UK), pp. 104-122.

Ministry of Agriculture and Animal Resources (MINAGRI) (2010). *Agriculture Sector Investment Plan 2009-2011*. Republic of Rwanda, Kigali. Online at: http://www.caadp.net/pdf/Rwanda%20Investment%20Plan%2013-05-10.pdf [date of last access: January 2014].

——, (2011). *Strategies for Sustainable Crop Intensification*. Online at: http://www.minagri.gov.rw/index.php?option=com_docman&task=doc_download&gid=86&Itemid=37&lang=en [date of last access: December 2012].

Ministry of Lands, Environment, Forestry, Water and Mines (MINITERE) (2004). *National Land Policy*. Republic of Rwanda, Kigali.

Moyo, S. 2008. *African Land Questions, Agrarian Transitions and the State. Contradiction of Neo-liberal Land Reforms*. CODESRIA, Dakar.

Newbury, C., 2011. 'High Modernism and the Ground Level: The Imidugudu Policy in Rwanda'. *Remaking Rwanda: State Building and*

Human Rights after Mass Violence, eds, Straus, S. and Waldorf, L., Wisconsin University Press, Madison (WI), pp. 223-239.

Ndoli, F. 2012. 'Land Disputes Still Dominate Petitions to the Ombudsman'. *The New Times* (30 April), Kigali.

Ridell, J. 2000. *Contemporary Thinking on Land Reform.* FAO, Rome.

Rwanda Initiative for Sustainable Development (RISD) 2012. *The Impact of Land Lease Fee on Landowners: Rwanda Case Study.* RISD, Kigali.

Sagashya, D. and English, C. 2010. 'Designing and Establishing a Land Administration System for Rwanda: Technical and Economic Analysis'. *Innovations in Land Rights Recognition, Administration, and Governance,* eds, Deininger, K., Augustinus, C. and Enemark, S., World Bank, Washington DC.

Scott, J. 1998. *Seeing Like a State. How Certain Schemes to Improve the Human Condition have Failed.* Yale University Press, New Haven and London.

Sommers, M., 2012. *Stuck: Rwandan Youth and the Struggle for Adulthood.* University of Georgia Press, Athens (GA).

Sommers, M. and Uvin, P. 2011. *Youth in Rwanda and Burundi: Contrasting Visions.* Special report. United States Institute of Peace, Washington, DC. Online at: www.usip.org/publications/youth-in-rwanda-and-burundi [date of last access: 23 January 2012].

Van Hoyweghen, S., 1999. 'The Urgency of Land and Agrarian Reform in Rwanda'. *African Affairs,* vol. 98, no. 392, pp. 353-372.

World Bank, 2007. *Agriculture for Development.* World Bank, Washington DC.

10

'Modernizing Kigali'   The Struggle for Space, in the Rwandan Urban Context

VINCENT MANIRAKIZA
& AN ANSOMS

Introduction

The 2006/7 UN Habitat report estimated that globally from 2007 onwards, more people would live in cities than in rural areas. The same report pointed to the problematic situation for the urban poor, often living in conditions that are worse than those of their rural counterpart (UN-Habitat, 2006). Since then, urbanization has continued at high speed, particularly in developing countries. In Africa, for example, overall population growth in urban areas between 2000 and 2010 (3.38 per cent) was over twice as high as rural population growth (1.67 per cent). Whereas 294 million Africans were living in cities in 2010, this figure will rise to 761 million people by 2030 (UN-Habitat, 2011). As a result of this demographic time-bomb, the already problematic living conditions in African slums have further deteriorated.

Demographic expansion is not the only reason, however, that African slums offer such poor living conditions. In many countries, urbanization policies have failed to take account of the needs of urban dwellers living in those slums. In fact, in many countries, urbanization policies aim for a radical modernization of the urban space – in line with the needs of urban elites – without taking into account the diverse and complex needs of other groups of urban inhabitants (Peemans, 2002, 2008). This often leads to what Dorier-Aprill (2007) frames as 'socio-spatial dualisation' – resulting from a concentration of resources in the modern neighbourhoods and a drastic lack of provision of basic infrastructure in poor neighbourhoods. Moreover, urban policies are often instrumentalized by richer and politically-connected classes to grab urban space at the expense of poorer population groups that are not able to protect their land rights. The land of the urban poor is being grabbed, people are being evacuated, and compensation schemes are often far from sufficient to secure their livelihoods (Zoomers, 2010).

Similar evolution seems to have taken place in the context of Kigali's urbanization[1] and modernization processes. Authorities are committed to

[1] Kigali, the capital city of Rwanda, is one of five administrative subdivisions of the country,

a drastic transformation of the city into a more competitive and attractive environment, capable of capturing the interest of international, regional and national investors (Kigali City Council, 2002). However, these policy ambitions have a drastic impact upon the organization of space and on local living conditions of the majority of urban dwellers. The stringent conditions for urban settlements in line with the city master plan are unrealistic for a large majority of the urban poor. In practice, the implementation of such urbanization policies therefore leads to a geographical dualisation, characterized by a rising gap between the living quality in planned urban quarters and living conditions in spontaneous or peri-urban areas.

The first part of this chapter sketches Kigali's urbanization throughout history, and describes the characteristics of the different types of urban neighbourhoods. We present a classification of Kigali's residential neighbourhoods on the basis of field research conducted in 2011. The second part details how urbanization policies – in line with policy makers' ambition to modernize Kigali – impact upon urban dwellers' housing conditions. The third part looks at Kimironko sector, which was a rural zone located in the periphery of the city until 1990. Today, however, this sector has become one of the important residential areas of Kigali. Between 2009 and 2012, we engaged in field research in the thirty-five villages of all three cells of this sector. We conducted semi-structured interviews with inhabitants and local authorities at the village, cell and sector levels.

The urbanization of Kigali and the configuration of its urban neighbourhoods

The urbanization of Kigali should be framed within the more general context of urbanization in Rwanda. In fact, the first urban centres only appeared in early 1900. Kigali was created in 1907 by the German Richard Kandt. Its location in the centre of the country and its status of capital city since 1962 made Kigali an attractive focus for people all over the country. As a result, the city formed a large part of Rwanda's urban population: about 50 per cent in 1978, 62 per cent in 1991, and 44 per cent in 2002 (MINECOFIN – Ministry of Finance and Economic Planning, 2002). Indeed, since the end of the civil war,[2] the development of other

(contd.) next to the northern, southern, eastern and western provinces. It is composed of three districts and thirty five sectors: the district of Nyarugenge (134 km²) with ten sectors, the district of Kicukiro (166.7 km²) subdivided into ten sectors, and the district of Gasabo (429.3 km²) with fifteen sectors (Republic of Rwanda, Organic law no. 29/2005). Each sector is subdivided into cells composed of several *Imidugudu* (villages).

2 The civil war started in October 1990, sadly culminating in the 1994 genocide perpetrated against the Tutsi during which about one million people were killed, and millions of refugees fled to neighbouring countries.

secondary cities has resulted in a redistribution of urban population growth but Kigali has remained the most important city though its proportion of urban population compared to the previous figures has declined. The spatial occupation of Kigali has been influenced by its hilly topography: the site is covered with multiple marshlands, floodable zones and steep hills. Urbanization occurred hill by hill, with formal settlements concentrating on the tops and less steep hills, while informal settlements developed on the steeper parts of the hills, and in the valleys.

The political changes that Rwanda has gone through have left a profound mark upon Kigali's urbanization process. After the departure of the German colonizers in 1916, Rwanda was occupied by the Belgians. During this colonial period, Kigali's demographic growth remained low because the Belgian authorities tried to limit the number of inhabitants. At the time of independence, Kigali had only about six thousand inhabitants within 2.5 square kilometres. During the post-colonial period Kigali was characterized by considerable demographic growth. People were no longer impeded from living in the city, and moved to Kigali searching for jobs. Indeed, almost all industries present in Rwanda were located in Kigali. But even much more important was the informal urban sector that developed at high speed and absorbed a significant amount of labour. By 1991, Kigali counted about 235,664 inhabitants spread over 112 square kilometres (MINECOFIN, 2002).

During the civil war (1990-1994) and in the immediate aftermath of the 1994 genocide, waves of refugees left the city, significantly reducing Kigali's population to about fifty thousand inhabitants. However, in the years afterwards, old case load refugees[3] returned massively; and many of them installed themselves in the capital city. Indeed, these refugees had often lived for decades in neighbouring countries, and had lost most ties with their 'hills of origin'. In addition, many of them had become wealthy and educated in exile, and had lived in urban centres, such as Kampala, Goma and Nairobi. Therefore, Kigali was often seen as a much more interesting location to resettle. On top of this, many young people confronted with rising land scarcity in the countryside thought that it would be easier to find work in the capital. Together, both trends have entailed a strong demographic growth in Kigali city. According to recent figures from the 2012 population census results, Kigali's population increased by 8.9 per cent per annum between 1991 and 2002 (when it had 603,049 inhabitants), and 6.5 per cent per annum between 2002 and 2012 (with 1,132,686 inhabitants) (MINECOFIN, 2012). The city's population is currently residing on a surface of 730 square kilometres. Throughout history, several urban plans have been designed by policy makers to address urbanization constraints. However, they could not prevent the

---

[3] 'Old case load refugees' refers to Rwandans who were in exile in the neighbouring countries of Congo, Uganda, Burundi and Tanzania between the late 1950s, and their return to Rwanda after 1994.

creation of informal settlements next to planned neighbourhoods and, in fact, more than 70 per cent of the capital city has been constructed outside of official settlement plans.

Planned neighbourhoods, on the one hand, are characterized by clearly separated and demarcated plots and an organized road system. They are equipped with basic infrastructure: accessible asphalted or stone paved roads. They contain buildings constructed with bricks or cement blocks; and with roofing of industrial tiles or metal sheets. Moreover, buildings are constructed according to a certain standard. Their inhabitants are generally from the higher class, members of political and/or economic elites, and from medium classes such as people working in public administration, or successful businessmen. Population density in such planned neighbourhoods lays around two thousand to five thousand people per square kilometre. Planned neighbourhoods are divided into three categories: the 'high standing' sites include modern and well-equipped neighbourhoods and are covered with luxurious houses, generally composed of several floors. Examples are: Estate 2020 Gacuriro and Nyarutarama. The 'medium standing' sites include neighbourhoods composed of villas built with high-quality materials but generally not with multiple floors, such as is the case in Kimironko, Kibagabaga, and Kagarama. The 'low standing' neighbourhoods are constructed on planned sites provided with basic services, but include buildings constructed with less sustainable materials. This is the case in Batsinda, where people removed from the central informal neighbourhood of Kiyovu (also known as *Kiyovu cy'abakene*) are currently resettled. Kigali City's authorities consider Batsinda to be a model habitat for people with low incomes. Houses are built according to a uniform standard with adobe bricks of the hydraform type and with galvanized steel sheet roofing.

Informal neighbourhoods in Kigali, on the other hand, are less precarious than other shanty towns or slums identified in different other developing countries. They can be classified as 'spontaneous neigh-bourhoods' which are, according to Dorier-Apprill (2001), neighbour-hoods full of small individual houses made with bricks (often of the adobe type) or with breeze blocks but without any modern comfort and equipment. Kigali's spontaneous neighbourhoods are – in comparison to the planned ones – less rich and less attractive in terms of urban infra-structure, and are commonly referred to as *Akajagari*. Houses are not built on neatly organized plots in line with an overall development plan. Roads are generally unpaved and mostly only accessible for pedestrians. They are inhabited by people with low incomes, mostly daily wage workers or informal traders. Most of these quarters have been created in zones peripheral to the city centre, and have been integrated in the administrative boundaries of the city throughout time. Population density may be well over ten thousand inhabitants per square kilometre, and sites are characterized by serious land scarcity. This is the case for Nyagatovu, Cyahafi, and Nyabisindu.

Throughout time, many zones have progressively merged and transformed into 'mixed neighbourhoods'. For example, this is the case with Rindiro or Rukurazo in the Kimironko sector. Such mixed neighbourhoods have also appeared when some spontaneous neighbourhoods were upgraded with paved roads. Those who started to construct their houses after this upgrade have introduced housing with more modern architecture in what were previously 'popular quarters'. The upgrading of such quarters is mostly progressing in a gradual way, when plots are bought by new owners who replace the old buildings with houses that respect the official guidelines (construction permit, and use of sustainable materials). This is the case for quarters such as Zindiro, Rubirizi and Samuduha.

To acquire a better view upon the configuration of the 127 residential quarters identified in Kigali,[4] we have made field visits to all of Kigali's thirty-five administrative sectors in order to classify the quarters of each sector in the categories 'planned', 'spontaneous' or 'mixed'. In each quarter, we interviewed key persons on the historical evolution of the quarter and on its location within or outside of the urban perimeter since the first occupation. We combined this with a descriptive study of the quarters on the basis of the type of buildings (with or without floors), the type and sustainability of construction materials (walls and roofing), the size of plots, the status of occupation of the site (formal or informal), the environment of the site (whether or not nuisances were present), and the infrastructure on the site (quality of roads/tracks and presence of water, electricity and other collective equipments). These field data were combined with secondary data drawn from different monographs of Kigali City. On this basis, we identified twenty-three out of one hundred and twenty seven quarters as 'planned', thirty-three as 'mixed' and seventy-one as 'spontaneous'. Only fifty-nine quarters were located within the urban perimeter at the time of their creation, whereas sixty-eight were created in the periphery. However, since the extension of the urban perimeter in 2005, all one hundred and twenty seven sites are actually located within the urban perimeter.

---

[4] The urban perimeter of Kigali is defined by its administrative boundaries. Until independence, the city was limited to the urban area. However, since then, it underwent several territorial expansions in line with the different city plans and administrative reforms that were realized in order to standardize the administration of urbanizing areas and to limit informal settlement. In 1975, for example, the *Commune urbaine de Nyarugenge* was created after a spontaneous expansion of Kigali's borders in post-colonial times. In 1990, the *Commune urbaine de Nyarugenge* was replaced by the *Préfecture de la ville de Kigali* (PVK), created to ensure an efficient way of organizing the capital city (République du Rwanda, law no. 53/90). In 2000, in line with the decentralization policy and to deal with the spread of population over the hills around the original 112 km² of what constituted the *Préfecture de la ville de Kigali*, its boundaries were redefined and its administrative entities restructured. The *Préfecture de la ville de Kigali* became the *Mairie de la ville de Kigali*, across a territory of 314 km² (République du Rwanda, law no. 47/2000). The recent administrative reform of 2005 gave the city its current entities. City of Kigali actually covers a zone of 730 km², including additional urban and rural zones in comparison to the pre-2005 situation (Republic of Rwanda, Organic law no. 29/2005).

Table 1 Configuration of residential quarters in Kigali

Year	Categorization of quarters			Location of the quarters at the time of creation		Total
	Planned	Spon-taneous	Mixed	Within the urban perimeter	In the peri-urban zone	
1907	-	-	-	-	-	-
1962	2	8	5	10	5	15
1990	4	45	23	25	47	72
2012	23	71	33	59	68	127

Source: Field research, 2011/2012

Urbanization policies and the modernization of Kigali

Over the past decades, Rwandan authorities have elaborated multiple urbanization policies that specified their urban planning ambitions. However, fast population growth has impeded the implementation of these schemes, given that in many cases, settlement preceded any possible establishment of infrastructure and road planning. The 1964 plan for example failed because it had not taken into account how fast the population would increase and spread over additional space in peri-urban zones. Also the 1982 plan aiming to correct the failures of the previous plan, and the one of 2001, were never rendered concrete. What they had (and have) in common with the *Kigali Conceptual Master Plan* – in force since 2007 – is that they maintain the idea that vast tracks of land have to be reserved for planned settlements. As a result, its inhabitants are ipso facto submitted to urban regulation to which they cannot conform. They are pushed into illegality and exposed to potential expropriation.

Soon after the end of the civil war and genocide in 1994, the Rwandan government developed a clear ambition to implement strict urbanization policies. In its Vision 2020, the government expressed its determination to better organize and contain non-coordinated urban expansion (Government of Rwanda, 2000). This ambition should be framed in a larger vision to modernize the country. In fact, 'the authorities aim to create a modern and dynamic urban centre that will allow it to improve its image and the touristic and economic attractiveness of the city, which should symbolize the resurrection of the country of a thousand hills' (translation from Michelon, 2008). In the Economic Growth and Poverty Reduction Strategy Paper of 2006, the Rwandan government gives more details of its ambitions to restructure habitat: 'The sites and zones selected will be surveyed, demarcated and sub-divided into building plots. These sites and zones will be provided with relevant infrastructural services. The process will involve the clearance and upgrading of unplanned urban areas. Partnerships between government and the Private Sector will be of essence' (Government of Rwanda, 2007: 59).

In practice, the new urban policy is executed to conform to an urban planning scheme started in 2007 with the publication of the *Kigali Conceptual Master Plan*. In line with this scheme, the City now has detailed plans for all three Districts of Kigali with the completion of the Kicukiro and Gasabo physical detailed plans in 2013, in addition to the existing Nyarugenge detailed plan completed in 2010. The policy implies that certain quarters will have to be renovated, while others have to be drastically redeveloped. This process is already ongoing in the central and pericentral quarters of Kigali, where unplanned settlements have been removed to provide space for business zones (Kiyovu and Kimicanga) and planned quarters (Gisozi, Kinyinya and Rusororo). The population living in the zones to be redeveloped are first expropriated. In line with the current expropriation law, this expropriation is legal as it aligns to overall public interest framed in the urban planning scheme. Real estate developers – in collaboration with the district – proceed with these expropriations to build entire agglomerations of houses that are then resold to individuals. For certain places, the district even proposes a standard detailed plan for all houses.

As well as high and medium standing quarters, the plan foresees the facilitation of planned low standard quarters in which people with low incomes are supposed to live. The houses are constructed with less expensive materials, like hydraform bricks. But also there, certain standards have to be respected (authorities for example provide a standard plan for all houses) to avoid 'the anarchic occupation of space'.[5] The majority of the urban population are not capable of conforming to these standards because of their limited financial means. As a result, they are pushed into building houses which are not considered legally acceptable. As framed by Durant-Lasserve (2006), the norms to construct a legally acceptable house in Kigali are so demanding that between 75 per cent and 80 per cent of all households risk being excluded from their urban space.

The urban planning scheme requires that the improvements of sites are done in phases. For those sites designated for improvement in the near

---

[5] The district determines on which site 'low standing' houses will be constructed (referred to as *Umudugudu w'icyaro*), makes up the development plan and foresees in the division of plots of 15 by 20 metres or 20 by 30 metres. The price of the plot is to be negotiated with the original landowner. However, plots become more and more expensive given the scarcity of land and because of speculation on the land market. As a result, land plots in those low standing quarters can cost one to three million Rwandan Francs (approximately 1666-5000 USD), dependent upon the land size and location. Nevertheless, this price is out of reach for a majority of urban poor. Note that according to World Bank Development Indicators, the official exchange rate in 2011 was 1USD equal to 600,3 Rwandan Francs.

future, the urban planning schemes can place an embargo on all types of construction in the meantime. However, this embargo is circumvented in many ways, often with the complicity of local authorities. Some construct illegally during the night or at weekends. Others request for permission to repair their house, but use the opportunity to make it bigger. Others do not bother asking for permission, but increase the size of their house in a gradual way, by adding a little shed that little by little transforms into an extra room. However, despite the inventiveness of these strategies, in the end, people risk losing their investment when their zone is expropriated in favour of an infrastructural development project, and they struggle again to install themselves elsewhere in the same conditions.

In fact, finding a place to live is an individual affair in Kigali. There is no public administrative service that observes the evolution in housing needs. As a result, the prices of land, houses, and also rent are subject to wild speculation in a market where demand has spectacularly increased over the last couple of years. When spontaneously/informally established urban quarters are 'redeveloped', the existing population of that zone is forced to search for new housing elsewhere. Financial constraints limit their ability to buy houses, and increases demand for rented accommodation. Consequently, this increased demand places additional pressure on an already limited rental market. According to the general census of 2002, it was estimated that 47 per cent of Kigali's population lived in rented accommodation.

Another alternative for evacuated people – and for others not capable of buying a plot of land within the city boundaries – is to move to rural zones surrounding Kigali. This periurbanization currently takes place in different zones such as Runda located in Kamonyi District in the Southern Province, Kajevuba located in Rulindo District in the Northern Province, Karumuna located in Bugesera district in the Eastern Province, and Muyumbu and Nyagasambu located in Rwamagana district in the Eastern Province. The influx of the urban population in these rural zones, already confronted with extreme land scarcity, has further increased the land price and has enhanced speculation.[6] Rural farmers sell their land, often without any prospect to reinvest in an income-generating activity. Others move away to rural sites further from the city, again increasing the competition for land in those areas. Such dynamics profoundly affect the social life of these communities, often at the expense of the poorest groups.

In the following section, we will focus on the case of Kimironko sector to understand the multiple dimensions of Kigali's urbanization process. We focus upon the way in which the urbanization policy has affected people's land rights, and how this has impacted upon the living conditions of poorer population groups.

---

[6] During our research in 2011, the price of a plot of 600 m² was about two million Rwandan Francs in the zone of Muyumbu. In Runda – closer to Kigali - it was about four to five million Rwandan Francs. Three years before, the same plot would not have been sold for more than 500,000 Rwandan Francs in these peripheral zones.

The urbanization of Kimironko: a case study

Kimironko used to be part of Rubungo commune located in Kigali-Ngali prefecture. In 1990, however, it expanded into the perimeter of the *Préfecture de la Ville de Kigali*. Although the sector officially became an urban zone, it initially retained its rural character because of the large percentage of the population that relied on subsistence agriculture. It was not until after 1996 that its development took place. In the first phase, the development plan of the site had to provide the necessary space to resettle and reintegrate refugee returnees. In the second phase, private investors became involved. At this point, Kimironko was already one of fifteen sectors of Gasabo district. It is spread over a surface of 11.43 square kilometres, and composed of three cells and thirty-five villages (Imidugudu): Bibare cell (fourteen villages), Kibagabaga cell (fifteen villages) and Nyagatovu cell (six villages).

The post-conflict situation: the resettlement of ex-refugees in Kimironko
Upon the return of a massive wave of refugees after 1994, their resettlement and reintegration became a major preoccupation for Rwandan authorities. One of the most pressing issues was where to settle them. Nine sites of 303 hectares were designated to that end: Kibagabaga-Nyarutarama, Gisozi, Kagarama, Kimironko, Gikondo, Gacuriro, Kimihurura, Nyandungu and Nyakabanda-Sahara (MINIREISO – 'Ministère de la réhabilitation et de l'intégration sociale', 1994). This project – piloted by the World Bank, and known as TTP (Tent Temporary Permanent) – consisted of developing the sites by dividing them into plots and constructing houses. About 4,210 houses were constructed, but these could only house about 0.2 per cent of all returnees. Paradoxically, at the same time, the project displaced the previous occupants of these sites, estimated at about two thousand families (Pérouse de Montclos, 2000). The other returnees – in addition to rural citizens moving to the city – settled in informal quarters. During this period, many people settled on non-registered land for free, or bought land at a low cost. This greatly contributed to informal urban expansion, mostly in spontaneous quarters, often even located in zones at risk (for example, on steep parts of the hill, or in zones prone to flooding).

Kimironko was one of the nine sites designated for the resettlement of returnees. Between July 1996 and April 2004, about two thousand building plots of 600 square metres each (20 by 30 metres) were demarcated according to the overall plan for the site (MININFRA – Ministry of Infrastructure, 2004). The original inhabitants had the right to stay on their plots, if their houses were not affected by road works, and to acquire other plots for their children by paying 24,000 RwF as a cost for the site development. They had then to start building modern houses within a six month period in line with the standards foreseen in the TTP programme.

A large number of original inhabitants were not capable of respecting these new formal construction rules and were therefore obliged to leave. In line with the 1996 regulations,[7] compensation was only given on the basis of the constructions and crops on the site. The land itself was thus not compensated. Buildings were compensated on the basis of the construction materials.[8] Crops were compensated on the basis of the production and the average price per kilo.[9] Those who were expropriated during this phase consider the procedure as extremely disadvantageous. In total, an expropriated family would receive only about 50,000 RwF.

The new plots were supposed to be distributed among households in need. The recipient paid 102,000 RwF to acquire a plot in the developed site; that is the sum of 78,000 RwF for the land, and 24,000 RwF as a cost for the development of the site. Kigali City – in collaboration with various donors – constructed houses for people who were considered most vulnerable, such as widows, genocide orphans, and the elderly. However, the distribution and occupation of the parcels, managed by the sector authorities, did not happen in a serene way. Certain plots were given twice; others were not attributed to vulnerable categories; certain beneficiaries resold their property, sometimes even selling the same plot to different people; and certain authorities wanted to grab several plots. On top of this, the prices of the developed plots started to increase spectacularly and became the subject of land market speculation.

From resettlement of refugees to involvement of private investors
After the first period during which expropriation was mainly executed to resettle refugees, Kimironko sector started to attract private investors. The modalities for real estate agents to access land are determined by the 2007 expropriation law for public interest (Republic of Rwanda, Law no. 18/2007). In principle, the State remains the only entity that can take the initiative to expropriate land for the public good. The decision to expropriate or not is taken by the district's land commission, and thus takes place at the decentralized level compared to the 1979 law. In most cases, in order to promote investment in a framework of public-private partnerships, real estate investors are often facilitated to expropriate the population and get the land for their projects. When they present

---

[7] The modalities with regards to expropriation for a public cause were fixed by the law no. 21/79 of 23 July 1979. According to this law, only the State can order an expropriation. Compensation could partly be paid in kind, for example by providing an alternative terrain to those who held the customary land rights on the expropriated land or to tenants affected by the expropriation, in case they did not dispose of any other land. Compensation rates for expropriation for a public cause were modified by the ministerial arrest no. 18.08/1185 of 22 April 1996.

[8] For example, a straw roof was valued at about 1,000 RwF per m², whereas a roof from metal sheets was valued at 8,000 RwF per m². A soil of cement was valued at 3,000 RwF per m².

[9] One are of beans was compensated with 525 RwF, while for sweet potatoes, one received 1,800 RwF. An avocado tree of four to five years could be valued at about 8,020 RwF. One are of banana trees was paid at 4,036 RwF.

Table 2 Price evolution of plots in Kimironko (RwF)

Period	Price of developed plot
1994-1995	30,000 – 50,000
1995-2000	102,000 – 200,000
2000-2002	200,000 – 500,000
2002-2005	500,000 – 3,000,000
2005-2007	3,000,000 – 6,000,000
2007-2009	6,000,000 – 10,000,000
2009-2012	10,000,000 – 15,000,000

Source: Real-estate brokers, Field research, 2009 and 2012

a site development plan to the district they often obtain the necessary permissions to engage in expropriation.

In the case of Kimironko, original occupants had the right to stay in their properties if they were capable of exploiting the space in line with the new development schemes. Otherwise, they were expropriated and compensated, this time both for the land and the buildings and crops on the land because the new Rwandan land law adopted in September 2005 gives property rights to the population. However, these compensation rates often did not allow them to secure similar housing conditions in planned quarters. As for tenants, they did not receive any form of indemnity at all.

When real estate agents started to develop the site, the demand for land increased rapidly. Between 1995 and 2000, a plot of 600 square metres or 750 square metres was sold at about 102,000 RwF but by 2009 the price was around 8,000,000 RwF. At that time, an appropriate modern house in these quarters cost about 40,000,000 RwF (Manirakiza, 2009: 58). Currently, plots are sold for prices above 10,000,000 RwF, and an appropriate modern house would now cost around 80,000,000 RwF.

Most of the people who were forced to move from expropriated land were obliged to go to spontaneous quarters or to resettle in peripheral areas in the countryside just outside of the city borders where regulation with regards to housing was less strict. However, some of these spontaneous peripheral quarters have been inserted within the urban perimeter during the 2005 administrative reform, and so again pushed the inhabitants into an illegal housing situation.

Socio-spatial dualization as a result of urban planning
Urban planning in Kimironko sector has led to socio-spatial dualization. In fact, two types of habitat occur in the sector. Most of the villages within Bibare and Kibagabaga cells conform to the formal modern city model,

Table 3 Population and type of settlements in the different cells of Kimironko sector

Cell	Surface (km²)	Total population	Population density (km²)	Number of villages	Types of settlements		
					Planned	Mixed	Spontaneous
Bibare	3.28	20,817	6,344	15	12	3	0
Kibagabaga	6.74	14,606	2,167	14	7	5	2
Nyagatovu	1.41	16,000	11,348	6	0	0	6
Kimironko	11.43	51,423	4,499	35	19	8	8

Source: Field research, 2012

while Nyagatovu and a few other villages within Bibare and Kibagabaga are typical informal spontaneous quarters (see Table 3). These two types of quarters differ profoundly in terms of the type of housing and the availability of infrastructure. Some of the roads in Bibare and Kibagabaga are asphalted and water is well channeled along the roads, which is not the case for Nyagatovu cell. Moreover, there are no schools in Nyagatovu, whereas Bibare has three and Kibagabaga has five elementary schools. The cells also differ in terms of population density: density is much higher in Nyagatovu. This can also be explained by the social category of people living there. In Bibare and Kibagabaga cell, the majority of residents are better-off and live in their own houses. In Nyagatovu cell, however, 80 per cent of its inhabitants are tenants who generally live in less space and in more precarious living conditions. Let us consider the three cells in more detail:

Bibare cell is composed of fifteen villages. In twelve of those villages, settlement is planned and in three others it is mixed. Overall, the cell is well equipped with water and electricity; its road system is well arranged although it is mainly gravel roads. Buildings have generally been built with sustainable materials. The cell started to urbanize in 1991 after the creation of the *Préfecture de la Ville de Kigali* (PVK). After 1994, many returnees installed themselves in this cell. There are also agglomerations created to house vulnerable people and victims of the war and genocide. For example, members of the *Association des veuves du génocide Agahozo* (AVEGA) occupy over one hundred and eighty houses that have been constructed by Kigali City and the Government Assistance Fund for Genocide Survivors (FARG) since 1998; there is an agglomeration named ACCOR for widow refugees who returned in 1994; an agglomeration for genocide orphans living in one hundred and fifty houses constructed by the United Nations Development Programme (UNDP); and an agglomeration of elderly people grouped in the association *Abasheshakanguhe*. However, next to these vulnerable groups, agents of the Commercial Bank of Rwanda received developed land plots from Kigali City in 2000, paying 200,000 RwF per plot for the development of the site.

Kibagabaga cell is considered to be a model of modern urbanization. Its villages are generally well equipped with quite luxurious buildings in sustainable materials, and a standard type of habitation that is part of a modern agglomeration. The road system is of high quality; transport is facilitated by an asphalted road that crosses the cell. Kibagabaga furthermore hosts schools, the district's hospital, administrative offices, religious buildings, leisure centres, hostels, and luxury hotels. Access to water and electricity is almost continuously assured in many of the cell's villages. Most of the cell is planned, as is the case in the zones developed within the framework of the TTP programme, where plots have been distributed among the personnel of different public institutions. In another large part of the cell, four villages became planned zones and were developed by the GOBOKA cooperative.[10]

This cooperative was one of the most important private actors in Kimironko's development. It engaged in the expropriation of the site, its development and division into plots, which were then resold or built upon. By 2009, this cooperative had distributed one thousand and fifty two plots and more than seven hundred houses had been built on a surface of 271 hectares. The compensation paid to the original occupants included a fee for the land and for buildings and crops on the land. In 2006, the cooperative paid 2,000 RwF per m² and resold it at 4,000 RwF. Since 2008, the cooperative has paid 2,500 RwF per m², and resold the plot (after development) at 8,000 RwF per m². Some of the expropriated people were able to use their compensation fees to transform themselves into entrepreneurs. However, for most of the displaced, living conditions deteriorated. One of our interviewees stated: 'the expropriation compensation is too low and calculated by the GOBOKA cooperative itself and we are paid too late'. Those original inhabitants who wanted to stay, had to pay a supplement to obtain their plots once they had been developed, and they had to construct according to modern housing standards. These obligations, out of reach for a large majority of original inhabitants, obliged them to leave the cell and resettle elsewhere.

By 2009, only twenty-five of the original 1,963 households, living there in 1998, had stayed. More than half of the expropriated households

---

[10] GOBOKA has been a cooperative since 18 January 2008, although it has existed since 1995 as a housing association for the homeless. It received authorization from Kigali City to distribute plots after their development in 2000. Since then, GOBOKA has become a private urban developer.

resettled in the popular quarters of Nyagatovu and Nyabisindu, or stayed in locations such as Zindiro, Rukurazo, Masizi – all close to the developed sites – on which they constructed informal settlements when regulation was still relatively flexible. Another batch of households resettled in peripheral rural zones, in places such as Karama, Masoro, Kabuga, Bumbogo, Masaka, Rusororo, Gasogi and Ndera, that were later included in the urban perimeter in 2005. Some of these households were displaced for a second time when the new area where they settled was developed. For example, this is the case in Rusororo which is currently being developed.

In **Nyagatovu cell**, the settlement in all its six villages is spontaneous. The road system is mainly composed of dirt tracks and pedestrian paths. Houses are constructed with adobe bricks and underequipped. Although 'irregular' construction has been prohibited for quite some time, people adopt inventive strategies to circumvent these regulations. However, if people are caught, houses are destroyed by the authorities and the owner does not receive any compensation. In fact, the owner may even be obliged to pay a fine that covers the destruction costs. Between November 2008 and February 2009, for example, sixty eight 'irregular' houses were destroyed in Kimironko sector. The illegality of 'irregular' constructions is extremely problematic for the majority of Nyagatovu's population given that they are not able to build a house according to the required standards. Indeed, most of Nyagatovu's population is of lower and medium classes. Moreover, its population has greatly increased as the cell hosts – next to its original inhabitants – many urban immigrants and people who have been expropriated from other urban zones. In 2004, population density varied between 2,500 and 3,000 inhabitants per square kilometre (MININFRA, 2004), but by 2006 it had increased to 7,005 people per square kilometre, rising to 9,765 inhabitants per square kilometre in 2008 and 11,348 inhabitants per square kilometre in 2012. As a result, over the last couple of years, competition for land and housing has greatly increased, and with it the price of houses and the cost of rent. Indeed, an increasing number of people are not able to buy a property, and are obliged to rent a place to live. The rapid rise in rent in Nyagatovu cell is illustrated in Table 4.

Category 1: This category comprises of a single room in a little house of 3 by 4 square metres, also referred to as *chambrettes*. Most of these are located in Urugwiro and Isangano villages. The housing conditions in these chambrettes are of extremely low quality.

Category 2 and 3: This accommodation mostly takes the form of an annex to a main house. In this way, tenants generally have access to water and electricity. For category 2, accommodation comprises of a small bedroom

Table 4 Evolution of monthly rents for different accommodation categories in Nyagatovu cell (RwF)

Year	Category 1	Category 2	Category 3	Category 4	Category 5
2005	3,000	10,000	15,000	40,000	60,000
2006	5,000	12,000	20,000	45,000	80,000
2007	5,000	15,000	30,000	70,000	100,000
2008	8,000	30,000	45,000	100,000	130,000
2009	10,000	40,000	70,000	120,000	150,000

Source: Field research, February–March 2009

and a little living room. Category 3, accommodation is a small house with three small bedrooms and a living room. Both are generally rented by single people who live on their own (for example, drivers, students and small traders working in Kimironko market).

Category 4 and 5: These two highest categories are generally family houses, with prices varying according to the size of the accommodation, its quality, and fittings. A house with three rooms and sanitary equipment (shower and toilet) outside of the house is generally classified as a category 4 house, whereas those with sanitary equipment inside are a category 5 house.

Renting accommodation has become increasingly challenging for a large number of Kigali's inhabitants. Even public sector employees who earn regular monthly salaries are confronted with this problem. The monthly salary of a public sector employee with a bachelor's degree is about 200,000 RwF. A secondary school teacher earns about 124,000 RwF; and a primary school teacher (A2) only 46,000 RwF. These salaries do not always allow them to find a decent place to stay. As for people without regular employment, their housing situation is even more problematic. Bricklayers for example earn between 3,000-4,000 RwF per day, and many small traders do not earn more than 1,500 RwF per day (all 2013 prices). These people often suffer extreme uncertainty with regards to their housing situation.

Conclusion

Whereas the other chapters in this book generally illustrate the impact of everyday forms of land grabbing in rural settings; this chapter has concentrated on the way in which land acquisitions in the urban space impact upon local living conditions. The mechanisms through which such acquisitions take place, are however very similar. Better-off and better-informed actors are capable of instrumentalizing modernization policies to defend their own interests in the land arena, while poorer actors face extreme difficulties to defend their land rights. Indeed, poorer population categories are confronted with strict planning regulations – in line with 'modern' urban planning – that they cannot conform to, and as a result, they are pushed into de facto quarters which are not considered legally acceptable in terms of urban planning and development.

Real estate investors can be facilitated to expropriate and evict popular quarters under the title of 'public interest': their actions are legitimized by the urban planning schemes that aim for an orderly organization of the city space. Whereas in the initial stage, the 'scaling-up' of popular quarters was mainly occurring in the city centre, popular quarters are now increasingly disappearing in peri-city centre and peri-urban areas. The expropriated land – once developed – is often sold for a figure many times higher than the original compensation fees. As a result, the profits of urban development schemes end up in the hand of the few, while the expropriated are often not capable of securing similar living conditions with the compensation fees offered. The inhabitants of these expropriated quarters are pushed to the remaining popular areas at the borders of the city, or move to surrounding rural settings. This, in turn, has greatly increased competition for land and housing in those areas.

Overall, we might conclude that a transformation of urban space is unavoidable, it is even desirable. However, the urban policies that channel this transformation should not only align to the needs, interests and preferences of urban elites. The city provides a livelihood for an increasing group of urban dwellers. The current demographic explosion is a major challenge for policy makers. It cannot be dealt with by transferring a majority of urban inhabitants into outcasts by declaring their living environments 'illegal' without providing any suitable alternatives. Such alternatives should offer decent and affordable housing located in settings foreseen of basic services and within reasonable reach of the city centre. Kigali does not exist in isolation. As a metropolis, Kigali must be modernized to compete in the global economy (Connell and Lea, 1996). However, different population groups contribute to its dynamism and deserve a place to live there too.

Bibliography

Connell, J. and Lea, J., 1996. 'Distant Places, Other Cities? Urban Life in Contemporary Papua New Guinea. *Postmodern Cities and Spaces,* eds, Watson, S. and Gibson, K., Blackwell Publishers Inc., Cambridge (MA), pp. 165-183.

Dorier-Apprill, E. (ed.), 2001. *Vocabulaire de la ville. Notion et références.* Éditions du temps, Paris.

——, 2007. 'Villes des Suds et développement durable'. *Le développement durable*, ed. Veyret, Y., Éditions sedes, Paris, pp. 320-347.

Durand-Lasserve, A., 2006. 'Market-driven Eviction Processes in Developing Country Cities: The Cases of Kigali in Rwanda and Phnom Penh in Cambodia'. *Informal Settlements: A perpetual challenge?* eds, Huchzermeyer, M. and Karam, A., University of Cape Town Press, Cape Town (South Africa), pp. 207-230.

Government of Rwanda, 2000. *Rwanda Vision 2020, Kigali.* Ministry of Finance and Economic Planning (MINECOFIN), Kigali.

——, 2007. *Economic Development and Poverty Reduction Strategy. 2008-2012.* Ministry of Finance and Economic Planning (MICOFIN), Kigali.

Kigali City Council, 2002. *Kigali Economic Development Strategy.* Kigali.

Manirakiza, V., 2009. *Impacts socio-environnementaux d'une dynamique de modernisation urbaine. Étude de cas du secteur de Kimironko à Kigali (Rwanda).* Mémoire de Master. Université catholique de Louvain, Louvain-la-Neuve (Belgique).

Michelon, B., 2008. Entre Modernisation et Réconciliation. *Urbanisme*, no. 363, pp. 33-38.

Ministry of Finance and Economic Planning (MINECOFIN), 2002. *General Census of Population and Housing.* National Institute of Statistics of Rwanda, Ministry of Finance and Economic Planning (MINECOFIN). Online at: http://www.statistics.gov.rw [date of last access: 20 November 2012].

——, 2012. *2012 Population and Housing Census.* National Institute of Statistics of Rwanda, Ministry of Finance and Economic Planning (MINECOFIN). Online at: http://www.statistics.gov.rw (date of last access: 18 June 2014).

Ministry of Infrastructure (MININFRA), 2004. *Rwanda Urban Infrastructure and City Management Programme.* Ministry of Infrastructure (MININFRA), Kigali.

Ministère de la réhabilitation et de l'intégration sociale (MINIREISO), 1994. *Problème de rapatriement et de la réinstallation des réfugiés rwandais. Proposition de solutions.* 'Ministère de la réhabilitation et de l'intégration sociale' (MINIREISO), Kigali.

Peemans, J.-P., 2002. *Le développement des peuples face à la modernisation du monde. Les théories du développement face aux histoires du développement 'réel' dans la seconde moitié du XXe siècle.* Academia-Bruylant/L'Harmattan, Louvain-la-Neuve (Belgique)/Paris.

——, 2008. 'Territoire et mondialisation: enjeux du développement'. *Territoires, développement et mondialisation. Points de vue du Sud*, ed. Peemans, J-P. Centre Tricontinental, Louvain-la-Neuve (Belgique), pp. 7-35.

Pérouse de Montclos, M.-A., 2000. 'Kigali après la guerre: la question foncière et l'accès au logement'. *Les Dossiers du CEPED*, no 57, Centre français sur la population et le développement, Paris.

Republic of Rwanda, 2005. 'Organic Law no 29/2005 of 31/12/2005 determining the administrative entities of the Republic of Rwanda'. *Official Gazette of the Republic of Rwanda*, Kigali.

——, 2007. 'Law no. 18/2007 of 19/04/2007 relating to expropriation in the public interest, O.G. special no. of 21/5/2007'. *Official Gazette of the Republic of Rwanda*, Kigali.

UN-Habitat, 2006. *State of the World's cities 2006/7*. Earthscan, London. Online at: www.unhabitat.org [date of last access: 17 April 2013].

——, 2011. *Cities and climate change: Global report on human settlements 2011*, Earthscan, London. Online at: www.unhabitat.org [date of last access: 10 Janvier 2013].

Zoomers, A., 2010. 'Globalisation and the Foreignisation of Space: Seven Processes Driving the Current Global Land Grab'. *Journal of Peasant Studies,* vol. 37, no. 2, pp. 429-447.

Conclusion

THEA HILHORST
& AN ANSOMS

The various contributions to this book demonstrate quite clearly how dispossession of land rights and loss of access to, or control over, land are common phenomena affecting large numbers of women and men in the Great Lakes Region. Land alienation is occurring on a daily basis, be it through the denial of rights, by stealth, by means of expropriation or forceful eviction. Moreover, dispossession and land grabbing occur in both urban and rural areas. Each chapter has offered an in-depth perspective on the mechanisms underlying specific examples. The various case studies illustrate how these ongoing dynamics are resulting in greater poverty and disempowerment among already vulnerable populations. Indeed, losing access to land undermines people's ability to produce and hence to generate an income. This is all the more problematic in densely populated settings where small-scale farming is the main livelihood activity. Moreover, loss of land not only equates to loss of assets, it also affects people's sense of belonging and identity. The lack of protection of land rights of smallholders and the urban poor, as well as the perceived impunity of 'land grabbers', commonly undermine people's trust in institutions and the State. Moreover, land concentration in the hands of a privileged elite enhance competition over whatever land and natural resources remain to be claimed. Conflicts over land, and instances of land grabbing and eviction, tend to fuel existing grievances and frustrations. This may contribute to structural instability and might constitute a trigger for further violence in the Great Lakes region.

The many faces of dispossession and loss of rights

Proactive responses to denial of rights, dispossession and land grabbing require an understanding of the various processes and mechanisms at play. As the chapters of this book illustrate, denial and dispossession of land rights come in many forms: between families, within and amongst communities, in consequence of violent conflict, elite manipulation or government intervention, or due to a lack of enforcement when it comes to individuals' rights. Discourses in defence of sustainable land use planning and protection of the public good are often instrumentalized and abused to justify land alienation among less powerful actors. Land grabbing may be encouraged through either action or inaction on the part of government officials, courts of law, traditional authorities, local elites, land speculators, war lords, rival communities and groups, neighbours, family members and so on.

Many of these important dimensions of land alienation and dispossession have been discussed in great length and depth in this book in the context of the Great Lakes Region. All chapters have highlighted local instances of land grabbing. While such examples are not prominent in the current wave of literature on the global land grab, they are obviously crucially important in the context of local livelihoods. In the chapters, much attention has been paid to the roles of local elites in processes of land alienation and dispossession. Within communities, attempts to grab land tend to occur and to succeed when local institutions, both formal and informal, fail to act. Small landowners lacking the necessary resources to defend themselves in the formal and informal land arenas (i.e. the elderly and ill people, widows with small children, orphans...) are of course particularly vulnerable. So while many of the cases of land grabbing discussed in this book are quite localized examples, generally centred around no more than a few hectares of land, the incidence is such that it demoralizes population groups and undermines their trust in both the prevailing formal and informal institutions.

A history of violent conflict adds further to the complexity of land competition in the Great Lakes Region, another aspect that has been extensively touched upon by the chapters of this book. Consecutive struggles and wars have resulted in waves of displacement and eviction, be it of individuals or entire communities. Indeed, the occupation of land vacated by refugees and internally displaced persons is a common occurrence in this densely populated region. Those moving in, may be relatives, neighbours or rival groups. The longer it takes before the refugees return, the more complex such situations are likely to become. Moreover, matters may be further exacerbated by government having sanctioned others to move into land that has been (temporarily) abandoned by refugees. Peace agreements generally contain provisions dealing with such land conflicts, yet this remains a sensitive and easily politicized issue in a context of land scarcity. Land sharing with, or the allocation of land and homes to, refugees may be perceived as dispossession by whoever currently owns the land, be it after previous government-driven allocations or resettlements, or after having inherited or purchased the land without having previously been involved in the original land transfer.

A third crucial point, emphasized extensively in the book, is that these many faces of dispossession and loss of rights are often rooted in history and intensified due to growing competition for land. Indeed, the chapters illustrate that contested land right transfers and outright land grabbing are by no means new phenomena in the Great Lakes region. Land conflicts often have a long lifespan. There are also striking parallels to be drawn between the recent wave of land grabbing and the historical processes of land alienation and dispossession. Nevertheless, what is new about the recent wave of land grabbing is the increasing commodification of land. The value of land appears to be rising in rural, peri-urban and urban areas, fuelling land speculation. In fact, the very prospect of windfall profits from land transactions has further accelerated the process of commodification, stimulating the conversion of agricultural land into residential areas. The prospect of formal registration of such claims may further fuel this process in an already conflict-prone environment.

Certain dimensions of the land issue have remained relatively out of focus in the course of this book, even though they are crucially important and clearly deserve closer attention in future research. Within households and families, for example, women in particular face a greater risk of denial and dispossession of land rights, often blamed on land scarcity, tradition or customary norms, and facilitated by a lack of legal provisions. In many cases, daughters are unable to inherit land or to claim their rightful share; widows may likewise be unable to take possession of the land owned by their late husbands. Providing legal measures to counter gender discrimination in land access – as has happened in Rwanda – is a first step. Legal provisions foresee the possibility of registering land rights in the name of women or establishing a joint title (husband and wife) in the land registration programme that covers all farmland in the country. However, the implementation of a legal land registration process poses many challenges, particularly for women, who often lack the means to claim their titles. Moreover, formal law should also take into account the vulnerability of women in non-official or polygamous marriages, as well as that of their 'illegitimate' children. Furthermore, land scarcity can create tension or even violence between parents and their children as they compete for a plot to farm and to live on. Struggles between siblings are frequent, and may result in sisters or other siblings being forced to relinquish their rights to a more powerful or better-connected brother. Dispossession of land rights within families is an increasingly common occurrence, causing frequent ruptures in the social tissue and networks that are crucial to people's wellbeing.

Another population group that has felt the full impact of continuing competition in the land arena, yet has remained relatively invisible in current research, is the Batwa community. This minority ethnic group with forest-based livelihoods and limited tradition in farming has inevitably been affected by centuries of competition over land: with the clearance of forests to create farmland, they have lost and continue to lose their land rights. Today, almost all forest in Burundi and Rwanda has vanished, while the remaining forested areas in Eastern DRC are under severe strain from illegal logging and encroachment. The displacement of the Batwa is a known problem, and governments have on occasion allocated public land to some groups. On the whole, however, the Batwa's relatively limited weight in the overall population means that their plight is often overlooked.

A third group that remains largely ignored in research into land competition are the pastoralists, who move with their herds between (primarily public) grazing lands and water sources. Pastoralist movements are discouraged in Rwanda and Burundi, but still occur locally. It remains an important livelihood activity in Eastern DRC, though, and people dependent upon it must often compete with other land claimants on grazing areas. Land conflicts in relation to transhumance are frequent, as customary agreements between pastoralists and farmers have become strained and eroded. Confrontations between the two opposing groups again have the potential to trigger local-level violence.

Overall it is clear that land dispossession occurs in many different ways, and that it takes many different forms that each deserve the attention of in-depth research. Understanding the diversity in the underlying dynamics and mechanisms is crucial for a more complex understanding of dispossession and land grabbing in the Great Lakes Region.

The influence of state actions and inactions

As the contributing authors to this book demonstrate, government institutions and the policies they elaborate in relation to land rights have a profound impact on the struggle unfolding in the land arena. There are many caveats in the legal and institutional frameworks. First of all, not all rights are recognized and protected. The provisions in the regional land laws on 'unused land' and 'vacant land' have resulted in massive denial of the rights of rural land holders, and they continue to undermine customary rights. Land administration systems that fail to recognize existing rights and cannot prevent the registration of contested claims solidify land dispossession and offer impunity to some of the more powerful actors involved. In addition, developmental narratives on modernization have provided a justification for weakening smallholders' land rights, and have facilitated land dispossession and land grabbing. Government regulations with regards to land claims in favour of the national interest (for protection of natural parks, city expansion, etc.), are often instrumentalized by political and economic elites. Regulations that impose restrictions on land use and on the registration of small plots, create even more insecurity for the poorest and tend to turn the odds in the land arena in favour of the more powerful and the better informed. The instalment of complex and costly procedures for dealing with land conflicts favours those with sufficient means. Legislation for other sectors, such as mining, forestry, biodiversity or urbanization, also impacts on land rights.

The analyses of diverse land conflicts in the preceding chapters suggest that the 'rule of law' is a relative concept. The region has experienced periods of destructive governance, producing state-supported social divisions that have tended to degenerate into violent conflict. This has resulted in dispossession of land, displacement, attacks and counter-attacks. As the examples in this book illustrate, laws are sometimes put in place in order to dispossess opponents. Profound changes in power constellations are common and with every instance of political upheaval, the dynamics of land struggles are altered. As a result, seemingly 'resolved' land conflicts are never definitively settled: those who have lost land rights may initially seem to have opted for a non-confrontational approach, while in fact they are waiting for the 'coins of power to turn'.

Yet the State's legislative, executive and judiciary branches, its legal framework and institutions, have the potential to play a role in the protection of the land rights of poorer and less powerful groups. Legal rights are no guarantee against dispossession and land grabbing, but they do constitute an important step towards the reinforcement of weaker groups' agency in the land arena.

Moreover, land governance depends on an even broader context. Ultimately, people's trust in government and its actions determine that government's legitimacy within the land arena, and its capacity to contribute to tenure security and to combat dispossession and land grabbing. In the course of this book, it has become clear that regional security and violent conflict impact significantly on land issues. Therefore, peace and stability should be prioritized, including with a view to improving land governance.

In addition, land governance is embedded in a broader policy framework of pro-poor development. We have illustrated in this book how policies and strategies in favour of increasing agricultural production, stimulating mineral resource extraction, establishing special economic zones and attracting foreign direct investment can be counter-productive if they fail to take into account the interests and vulnerabilities of poorer population groups. The various chapters show that relying merely on formal procedures will not prevent dispossession and conflict; in fact they suggest that the opposite may be true. Due diligence and careful local consultation must be part of any strategy in respect of land rights.

What next?

So where to go from here? Which lessons may be drawn in relation to future land dynamics in the Great Lakes Region? Unfortunately, there are no easy answers. As the chapters illustrate quite clearly, there are no ready-made solutions for improving land governance, preventing future land grabbing and redressing dispossession. Transformative change can come only from within, by more vulnerable actors getting organized in order to make themselves heard in the local, national and international policy arenas. This represents a huge challenge in a context where peace is fragile and where freedom of speech is not a given. Moreover, land struggles commonly involve groups with extremely fragile livelihoods, which makes joint action against exploitation by more powerful actors an even greater challenge. Powerful actors often instrumentalize disagreement between weaker groups through an opportunistic 'divide-and-rule' approach. Therefore, overcoming internal divisions at the local level is crucial to being able to make a firm stand in the national land arena.

However, although transformative change will have to come from within, there is also a role to be played by external actors. International bodies, donor organizations, NGOs and private concerns – including firms involved in the extractive industry and mining – are prominent in the region. Moreover, their actions and inactions can change the stakes in the land arena. Support may be proactive and substantive when it aims to strengthen the voice and agency of those people and communities most in need of having their rights protected. These vulnerable groups tend to include women, smallholders, urban poor and minorities. The implication of international donors and local-level civil society – in collaboration with state actors at all levels within the administration – is crucial in the process of developing a framework for pro-active land governance. This should be done in dialogue with local-level stakeholders in the land arena, including customary authorities.

Land reform processes are ongoing in all four countries discussed in this book, but at very different paces. Such processes require a comprehensive outlook on land governance, covering urban and rural rights recognition, formal and informal land institutions at the national and local levels, public and private land management, and – most importantly – various mechanisms of dispute resolution and mediation. Land reform processes should be based on identifying the opportunities to provide leverage to vulnerable groups' land claims. Formal policies and institutions should be better connected with the realities on the ground, and address the most salient demands for land governance, rights protection and conflict management locally. Providing systems for land administration that are accessible and affordable to smallholders may provide a way to better protect the assets of the poor and reduce conflict, but safeguards are needed to prevent land administration from becoming an additional tool in the hands of the more influential and affluent to legitimize fraudulent claims or instances of land grabbing.

The most fundamental argument put forward in this book is, perhaps, that we should learn from the past in order to do better in the future. By adopting a historical perspective on competition in the land arena, and on the broader political economy of the Great Lakes region, one can gain an understanding of how governance failures and elite manipulation can induce land dispossession, rights alienation and grabbing. Therefore, careful and regular monitoring of the dynamics unfolding in the land arena in interaction with policy processes is crucial to tracking any progress made and to identifying failures. Future in-depth research – including on seemingly trivial and localized instances of land grabbing – may shed further light on what works and what does not. And this is all the more relevant in a volatile environment such as the Great Lakes Region, where peaceful settlement of outstanding land conflicts is likely to be crucial to the chances of long-term stability.

Lightning Source UK Ltd.
Milton Keynes UK
UKHW021333040121
376391UK00007B/531